To Thad –

Welcome home!
Proud to be your fellow Veteran
Thank you for your service to
our nation –

May God continue to Bless,
guide & protect you & yours

12 Nov 2010

Captain Roger H. C. Donlon

Beyond

Ashes of Camp Nam Dong, July 6, 1964

**Foreword by
General William C. Westmoreland**
U. S. Army (Retired)

Nam Dong

Reconciliation, Nam Dong Cemetery, March 1993

Colonel Roger H. C. Donlon
U. S. Army (Retired)

Copyright © 1998 by R ∞ N Publishers, 2101 Wilson Avenue,
Leavenworth, Kansas 66048
913-682-5480 Email: Rogerdonlon@aol.com

First Edition December 1998
Second Printing July 1999
Third Printing December 1999
Fourth Printing March 2000
Fifth Printing September 2000
Sixth Printing June 2001
Seventh Printing April 2002
Eighth Printing July 2002
Ninth Printing November 2002
Tenth Printing August 2003
Eleventh Printing September 2004
Twelfth Printing Febuary 2008
Thirteenth Printing September 2009

International Standard Book Number 0-9621374-8-0

Library of Congress Catalog Card Number 98-68197

All rights reserved. No part of this book may be reproduced in any form or by
any means, electronic, photocopying, recording, or otherwise, without the
written permission of the publisher, except in the case of reprints in the context
of reviews.

Jacket design adapted from a painting of Captain Donlon from the cover of the
Saturday Evening Post for October 23, 1965, © The Curtis Publishing Company,
used with permission.

Beyond Nam Dong

To Vietnam Veterans everywhere . . .

Some gave all . . .

All gave much . . .

WELCOME HOME!

Contents

The White House 1

The Family Team 15

Growing Up In Saugerties 29

Those Syracuse Girls 41

The Uniform Beckons 47

A Civilian Life? 57

The Uniform Beckons Again 61

North To Alaska 67

The Quiet Professionals 71

Team A-726 81

Teamwork! The 100-Mile Hike 89

The Devil's Wedge 95

Vietnam 105

Before The Battle 123

The Battle For Nam Dong 133

Victory At Nam Dong 153

Healing The Wounds Of War 169

Norma 179

Our Family Team 193

Beyond Nam Dong 205

Epilogue 221

Foreword

The Green Beret . . . proudly worn by the United States Army Special Forces . . . and acclaimed by our late President, John F. Kennedy, as "a symbol of excellence, a badge of courage, a mark of distinction in the fight for freedom . . . " In Vietnam the men of Special Forces were the first to go. They frequently fought, not in great battles with front-page attention, but in places with foreign sounding, unknown names; and often times no names at all.

One such place was Nam Dong. In July of 1964 this Special Forces Camp, in the jungle-clad mountains near the Laotian border, came under a fierce attack. It was the first time that regular North Vietnamese Army forces joined the Viet Cong in an attempt to overrun an American outpost. The North Vietnamese reinforced battalion of eight hundred men was determined to eliminate this camp—an impediment to their further infiltration down the Ho Chi Minh trail from Laos to the south of Vietnam.

Roger H. C. Donlon, then a captain and, commander of the Special Forces Detachment A-726 at Camp Nam Dong along with his brave twelve-man team, 60 Nungs and 100 loyal Vietnamese successfully defended the camp. For their valor two of his sergeants were posthumously awarded the Distinguished Service Cross. Four other team members were awarded Silver Stars, and five more Bronze Stars with V for valor.

Roger Donlon was the first soldier I recommended to receive the Medal of Honor for heroism which was later presented to him by President Lyndon Johnson. He was the first soldier of the Vietnam War to receive this award. *"Beyond Nam Dong"* is his personal story . . . from his scouting days as a boy in upstate New York, through the Vietnam conflict, to his present efforts at reconciliation. It is the inspiring story of a courageous soldier and patriot.

General William C. Westmoreland
United States Army (Retired)

President Johnson awards the Medal of Honor to Captain Roger H. C. Donlon, The White House, December 5, 1964.

The White House

December 5, 1964 . . .

"The President of the United States of America, authorized by Act of Congress, March 3, 1863, has awarded in the name of the Congress the Medal of Honor to Captain Roger H. C. Donlon, United States Army, for conspicuous gallantry and intrepidity in action at the risk of his life above and beyond the call of duty."

I was standing at attention—friends said afterward it was at *ramrod* attention—never batting an eye, as Secretary of Defense Robert S. McNamara began to read the citation in the East Room of the White House. For the first time I was hearing the words which described my actions on July 6, 1964, near Nam Dong, Republic of Vietnam, when my Special Forces Detachment A-726 fought off a withering assault by a reinforced battalion of Viet Cong.

Nine servicemen—three soldiers, three Marines, and one each from the Air Force, Navy and Coast Guard, formed the color guard with the American flag, Presidential banner and service flags heavy with their battle streamers.

Crystal chandeliers and two immense electrified candelabra bathed the East Room in light. Windows at the end of the room were framed in gold silk, and gigantic mirrors on the walls reflected the brilliance of the setting.

Calm and serene, my mother looked radiant sitting in the front row. I could tell that inside she was bursting with pride. She smiled her approval as Secretary McNamara continued.

"Captain Roger H. C. Donlon, Infantry, distinguished himself by conspicuous gallantry and intrepidity at the risk of his own life above and beyond the call of duty while defending a United States military installation against a fierce attack by hostile forces on 6 July 1964, near Nam Dong, Republic of Vietnam. Captain Donlon was serving as the commanding officer of the United States Army Special Forces Detachment A-726 at Camp Nam Dong when a

The White House • 1

reinforced Viet Cong battalion suddenly launched a full-scale predawn attack on the camp. During the violent battle that ensued, lasting five hours and resulting in heavy casualties on both sides, Captain Donlon directed the defense operations in the midst of an enemy barrage of mortar shells, falling grenades, and extremely heavy gunfire. Upon the initial onslaught, he swiftly marshaled his forces and ordered the removal of the needed ammunition from a blazing building. He then dashed through a hail of small arms and exploding hand grenades to abort a breach of the main gate. En route to this position he detected an enemy demolition team of three in the proximity of the main gate and quickly annihilated them. Although exposed to the intense grenade attack, he then succeeded in reaching a 60-millimeter mortar position despite sustaining a severe stomach wound as he was within five yards of the gun pit."

I was reliving each agonizing moment of the five-hour siege as the Secretary of Defense continued.

"When he discovered that most of the men in this gun pit were also wounded, he completely disregarded his own injury, directed their withdrawal to a location thirty meters away, and again risked his own life by remaining behind and covering the movement with the utmost effectiveness. Noting that his team sergeant was unable to evacuate the gun pit, he crawled toward him and, while dragging the fallen soldier out of the gun pit, an enemy mortar exploded and inflicted a wound in Captain Donlon's left shoulder. Although suffering from multiple wounds, he carried the abandoned 60-millimeter mortar weapon to a new location thirty meters away where he found three wounded defenders. After administering first aid and encouragement to these men, he left the weapon with them, headed toward another position, and retrieved a 57-millimeter recoilless rifle. Then, with great courage and coolness under fire, he returned to the abandoned gun pit, evacuated ammunition for the two weapons and, while crawling and dragging the urgently needed ammunition, received a third wound on his leg by an enemy hand grenade. Despite his critical physical condition, he again crawled one hundred and seventy-five meters to an 81-millimeter mortar position, and directed firing operations, which protected the seriously threatened east sector of the camp. He then moved to an eastern 60-millimeter mortar position and upon determining that the vicious enemy assault had weakened, crawled back to the gun pit with the 60-millimeter mortar, set it up for defensive operations, and turned it over to two defenders with minor wounds. Without hesitation, he left this sheltered position and moved from position to position around the beleaguered perimeter while hurling hand grenades at the enemy and inspiring his men to superhuman effort. As he bravely continued to move around the perimeter, a mortar shell exploded, wounding him in the face and body. As the long awaited daylight brought defeat to the enemy forces and their retreat back to the jungle, leaving behind fifty-four of their dead, many weapons and grenades, Captain Donlon immediately reorganized his defenses and administered first aid to the wounded. His dynamic leadership, fortitude, and valiant efforts inspired not only the American personnel but the friendly Vietnamese defenders as well, and resulted in the successful defense of the camp. Captain Donlon's conspicuous gallantry, extraordinary heroism, and intrepidity at the risk of his own life above and beyond the call of duty are in the highest traditions of the United States Army and reflect great credit upon himself and the Armed Forces of his country."

While Secretary McNamara was reading the citation my thoughts raced back to my youth, to my years wearing uniforms . . . Air Force Blue, Cadet Grey, Army Green . . . to that bloody night at Nam Dong—and the members of A-726 who died that night.

I was wishing that Pop and John, and Kevin Conway and Doc Hickey could be with the rest of us in the East Room. Not so. Not so.

Master Sergeant Gabriel Ralph Alamo—Pop—burned and mortally wounded, died in a mortar pit, firing a 57-millimeter recoilless rifle. Sergeant John Lucius Houston was cut down as he darted from place to place, returning the fire of the 800 to 900 Viet Cong attackers.

Pop and John were the only men of A-726 whose wives were

The White House • 3

pregnant. When Pop's wife in Newark, New Jersey, received word of his death she tragically lost their baby. Upon hearing that John was dead, his wife gave birth prematurely, delivering twins. Again, tragically, only one lived . . . the casualties of war go far beyond the battlefield.

Pop and John were awarded our country's second highest decoration, the Distinguished Service Cross, posthumously—in the words of their citations—for "extraordinary heroism, fortitude, courage, determination and conspicuous gallantry . . . in the highest traditions of the United States Army . . ."

I was present at Orlando, Florida, to witness Mrs. Houston's acceptance of John's Distinguished Service Cross. Asked how she would respond if her son grew up and wanted to enlist in the Army, I will never forget her reply. "I would say to him the same as I said to his father. My son would have to make the decision himself. If he wants to go into the military, I would be as proud of him as I was of his father."

Kevin Conway had been the most experienced guerrilla fighter at Nam Dong. An Australian warrant officer, who had gone up against guerrillas in Borneo and Malaysia, he had only recently joined A-726—a welcome addition to our team. That night he seemed to be smiling as he descended the concrete steps of the mortar pit where Pop later died. He was actually walking, not running. His smile seemed to say, "Not to worry, chaps! It'll be over soon and we'll be okay!" Kevin died on the bunker steps, hit by a bullet between the eyes.

Dr. Gerald C. "Doc" Hickey, like Kevin, joined A-726 shortly before the assault on Nam Dong. Doc came through the long ordeal unscathed, and had remained in Vietnam. He was a Rand Corporation anthropologist, an expert on the language and culture of the *montagnard* tribesmen of the Vietnam highlands. We made the wise and witty Doc an honorary team member.

The remaining nine men of A-726 were present in the East Room, along with General Earle G. Wheeler, Chairman of the Joint Chiefs of Staff, and Senator-elect Robert F. Kennedy of New York. The team members sat proudly as the ceremony unfolded, looking sharp in their dress green uniforms, shiny boots and carrying the Green Beret. President John F. Kennedy had called the Special Forces beret "a symbol of excellence, a badge of courage, a mark of distinction in the fight for freedom."

How right our President was. The Green Beret was all of that and more. The men who wore it were ready to die for it, just as Pop and John had done at Nam Dong, a bloody piece of ground that Army Chief of Staff General Harold K. Johnson described as "an outpost of freedom over 5,000 miles from our shores defended by American lives."

You could call the Green Beret a symbol of a symbol. Soldiers fight so that freedom will prevail. The beret was the badge of men selected for special training from within a proud, professional Army.

Men and women of all branches of the Army have special skills— the same skills embodied in Special Forces. But Special Forces is the Army's premiere cadre of skilled individuals. They are trained in guerrilla warfare, psychological warfare, and counter-insurgency. Enlisted soldiers are triple volunteers—for the Regular Army, the Paratroopers, and Special Forces. They are trained and cross-trained until they can handle virtually anything, from stopping an epidemic of sleeping sickness to fighting off two enemy battalions. They did both and so much more in Vietnam.

I remember, as I stood at attention, giving thanks to God for the honor of having commanded the men of A-726. I gave thanks for those who had lived, and I asked God to bless those who had died.

Standing beside President Johnson and Secretary McNamara, I looked at the men of my team—our team.

Lieutenant Julian M. Olejniczak, twenty-five, hailed from Chicago. At Nam Dong we called him "Lieutenant O" because Olejniczak was too difficult to pronounce. He was a 1961 graduate of the United States Military Academy, an exemplary officer and leader—one of the best of the best.

Sergeant First Class Thurman R. Brown, thirty-five, was from Lewisburg, Kentucky. Brownie was the most qualified all-around soldier. When the need arises in the Army we call upon the best tacticians, the best marksmen, and they deliver—the first time. Brownie had a long list of skills, and whatever the assignment, he accomplished it with zero defects in combat in both Korea and Vietnam.

Sergeant First Class Vernon Lee Beeson, thirty-four, came from High Point, North Carolina. Bee was iron-nerved in combat, a savvy soldier who came through Korea and Vietnam unscathed. He was skilled in artillery, airborne and infantry tactics, and performed magnificently with an 81-millimeter mortar.

Staff Sergeant Keith E. Daniels, twenty-seven, was from Battle Creek, Michigan. I came to know him as a perfectionist—quiet, tough, a consummate communicator who got the message across. He understood the success of the operation depended upon communications, a point he drove home to us again and again.

Staff Sergeant Raymond B. Whitsell, twenty-six, called Madisonville, Kentucky, home. Whit was a former Marine, always in top physical condition. Never a complainer, he was a skilled engineer and demolitions specialist. The night of the siege on Nam Dong he fought so quietly I wondered if he were dead or alive. Finally, daylight revealed all that he had done.

Staff Sergeant Merwin D. Woods, thirty-seven, was from Canton, Illinois. As the biggest man on the team and for that reason, at times the target of our humor, Woody could make us laugh when we needed one. He fought the battle of his life wearing only his GI drawers.

Sergeant Michael Disser, twenty-one, called Shelbyville, Indiana, home, but he had lived in a lot of other places where his father, a career Army officer, was stationed. Like Whit Whitsell, he worked at staying physically fit. The youngest member of our team, he shared my fondness for peanut butter.

Sergeant Thomas L. Gregg, twenty-six, came from Rising Star, Texas. He was equally skilled as a medic and with a shotgun. Every team has one man who is always talking pridefully of his wife and family. That was Gregg.

Sergeant Terrance D. Terrin, twenty-two, of Flagstaff, Arizona, was our other medic. Determined to be the very best medic, he drove himself to be the best soldier as well.

The months of training we had undergone before arriving in Vietnam had paid off for the men of A-726. As I thought about each of them present at the White House, I had the feeling that we would somehow remain in touch during the rest of our lives. Whatever good came my way with the Medal of Honor, belonged also to these men. I would always wear the medal on behalf of our team.

This medal, the 3,170th awarded since created by Congress in 1863, the first since the Korean War and first ever in a "cold war" situation, was every bit as much their Medal of Honor as mine. It was *Team A-726*. I was privileged to be their leader. These men were now members of my extended family, almost as precious as my own family, assembled in the East Room to share in this great moment.

President Kennedy said the Green Beret was "a symbol of excellence, a badge of courage, a mark of distinction in the fight for freedom." He said Special Forces fight "another kind of war—new in its intensity, ancient in its origin—war by guerrillas, subversives, insurgents, assassins, war by ambush instead of by combat; by infiltration instead of aggression, seeking victory by eroding and exhausting the enemy instead of engaging him . . ."

My mother and family were seated in the first row. Her husband and five sons had served in uniform, and she was proud of each of us.

"Roger has always worn *my* Medal of Honor," she informed the reporters who had called.

My thoughts went back to the ups and the downs in the lives of the Donlons. I thanked God that mother was able to share this moment, and wished that daddy were alive to share the honor. Paul A. Donlon died in 1947, the year I turned thirteen.

With mother were the rest of our family: Mary Bernadette; Paul; Michael, Jack, and Gerard with their wives; Adrienne; and Barbara with her husband, Army Captain Jerry H. Huff, a West Point graduate and assistant professor with the Department of Ordnance.

We were children blessed with parents who taught us to keep getting up whenever there was a setback, and it had seemed like it was continually up and down for the Donlon family. We were taught to try, try again. And though we were headed in different directions, we remembered what we had been told at home.

Or, you die trying, I mused, like Pop and John and Conway, and daddy, who had fought a long, final battle with cancer. As President Johnson began to speak, I was jolted out of my reverie. I was standing in the White House. I was not dreaming. This was really happening, and it was happening to me.

"Mrs. Donlon, Senator Hayden, Senator Keating, Senator-elect Kennedy, Secretary McNamara, ladies and gentlemen.

"This is a proud moment for all Americans. We are here today to present this nation's highest honor to Captain Roger H. C. Donlon, United States Army.

"On July 6 of this year, Captain Donlon was the commanding officer of the United States Army Special Forces Team A-726 at Camp Nam Dong in the Republic of Vietnam. Under cover of night, a reinforced Viet Cong battalion launched a full-scale attack on the camp. A violent battle took place lasting five hours. The Viet Cong enemy used mortars, grenades and very heavy gunfire . . ."

Mortars, grenades, withering gunfire. Yes, Mr. President, I remember. I remember the burning buildings, the intensity of a protracted night battle. I remember the dead and wounded—Pop, John, Conway, Mike, Woody, Jay, Whit, Terry, Brown, the Vietnamese and Nung tribesmen . . . mortars, grenades, withering gunfire . . .

"Captain Donlon was wounded four times—in the stomach, in the leg, in the shoulder, and in the face," continued the President. "Wounded though he was, Captain Donlon directed a successful defense of the camp. He moved from post to post and from man to man within the camp perimeter. Despite his multiple wounds, Captain Donlon, with great courage and coolness, inspired the American personnel and the friendly Vietnamese troops to a successful defense

8 • *The White House*

of their camp."

The defense of our camp was my responsibility. I was the senior American. It fell to me to see how my men were doing, to urge them on, and to communicate. And there was no other way to communicate except to move among the defense positions, checking, asking, telling, helping. These are a commander's responsibilities.

"No one who has seen military service will fail to appreciate and understand the magnitude of Captain Donlon's heroic performance under enemy fire in the darkness."

Yes, Mr. President, the darkness was the worst part, and for five hours which seemed to last almost forever, the darkness of not knowing how it would end.

"This Medal of Honor awarded in the name of the Congress is the first such honor to be bestowed upon an American military man for conspicuous gallantry above and beyond the call of duty in our present efforts in the Republic of Vietnam. Individual bravery among the members of our forces there is much more the rule than the exception. I think it detracts nothing from the honor that a grateful nation pays today to Captain Donlon to say, as I am sure he would say, that we proudly salute all the men of all the services who are participating so valiantly in that effort.

"I had a full and complete report from General Taylor (Maxwell D. Taylor, U.S. Ambassador in Saigon) which gave me great pride in all the men in that area. And it is not given to all of us here at home to be called upon to make the choice of sacrifice and risk that Captain Donlon made at Nam Dong this summer. But it is given to us to draw new strength and inspiration from the gallantry and unhesitating bravery of this man's action under hostile fire. The Vietnamese are seeking to triumph over communism manifested by insurgency, terrorism and aggression."

My thoughts went back to the terrorism of two village chiefs executed, one on his front doorstep. Terry returning from his three-day patrol found them the day before we were hit at Nam Dong.

"Because we recognize the justice of their cause and its importance to all free men, we are there to provide them with support and assistance.

"Now let any who suggest that we cannot honor our commitment in Vietnam find new strength and new resolution in the actions of this brave man and his comrades in arms far away from us today.

"To you, Captain Donlon, may I personally express the gratitude and respect of all your fellow countrymen. The example that you have set shall not be lost.

"In the early hours of this morning, I awoke and I read again the account by my bedside of Captain Donlon's heroic feat. I wondered how many of us could stand in his presence today and say confidently that we, too, have done all that we could to support and to serve the cause of our country and mankind.

"There are some men in Washington and some men throughout the nation, and women, too, who resist the glamour of gold and come here at great sacrifice to do for freedom in the capital of the free world what Captain Donlon did for freedom in Vietnam. So very often nine-to-five hours, Saturday at the country club, profit sharing and pension trusts all mean so much that the call of country is sometimes answered with a 'no.'

"But I was thinking this morning about that old World War i recruiting poster, with Uncle Sam pointing his finger and saying, 'Your country needs you.'

"Well, your country does need you today, in these times. And the finger points at every American, of every age and of every station. We need women and we need men for service in the cause of freedom, in the cause of this great government, this noble cause— men and women from industry, from business, from labor, from banks, from campuses, and from farms. America needs from civilian life, as we have, I am proud to say, in our military forces, the very best talents and minds of these times.

"And standing to my right as a civilian is one of the great examples of which I speak, the Secretary of Defense, Mr. McNamara. He represents to me in our civilian life what Captain Donlon represents in the military life, the very best of America. And this government must have the very best.

10 • *The White House*

"So, I hope your example, Captain Donlon, will help to inspire others to step forward and to answer 'yes' when their country calls.

"Captain Donlon, as President of the United States, it is now my very high privilege to decorate you with the Medal of Honor, awarded to you in the name of the Congress of the United States."

Major General Chester V. "Ted" Clifton, the President's military aide, handed the medal to Mr. Johnson. The President said something to me, but I do not recall what it was. All of what had just transpired had left me numb. I had relived the battle and now I was experiencing the honor of this medal ceremony. I did have the presence of mind to not give the President a strong handshake, as I would have liked to do. He was still wearing a bandage on his right hand following a recent skin operation.

I could feel the sweat on my body. I saw that the President was also perspiring.

"Would you want to say a few words?" he asked. "No sir, no thank you, sir," I replied.

At this point the President was to be introduced to my mother. I started to move toward her, but the President touched my arm.

"They'll get her," he said, and General Clifton escorted mother to the President.

"Our country certainly has a right to be proud when it has men such as you running the country," mother told the President.

"Thank you, Mrs. Donlon," he responded. "And you have every right to be proud of your boy."

"Thank you, Mr. President," mother said. "I am proud. And his father would be proud, too, if he were here today. May God bless you."

The President walked to the middle of the room. People were all around us and flashbulbs were popping. Congressional and Pentagon dignitaries were extending congratulations. Other family members were introduced to the President, including my Aunt Ruth Howard, who was Sister Mary Florence, and her "commanding officer," Mother Mary Regina Cunningham, Mother General of the Sisters of Mercy of the Union.

Extending congratulations were Senator-elect Robert F. Kennedy, Senator Kenneth B. Keating of New York and Senator Carl Hayden of Arizona, the president pro tempore of the Senate, and Joseph Y. Reznick, Representative-elect from my district in New York.

Present representing the Department of Defense were Deputy Secretary Cyrus R. Vance, Assistant Secretary Arthur Sylvester, and General Earle G. Wheeler, Chairman of the Joint Chiefs.

Also present were Secretary of the Army Stephen T. Ailes; Major General William P. Yarborough, commander of Special Forces; Colonel Edward E. Mayer, commander of the 7th Special Forces Group; and Brigadier General Lester L. Wheeler, my former commanding officer in Alaska and his wife Dottie.

President Johnson graciously posed for pictures with members of my family, Brigadier General and Mrs. Lester Wheeler, and with General Earle G. Wheeler, mother and myself.

Before the ceremony began I had the opportunity to meet and chat with the President and Secretary McNamara in the Red Room. They put me at ease instantly. It was a good feeling to know that these men of power were, after all, human. Perhaps recalling our conversation of the Donlon family having their first reunion since the death of my father in 1947, the President turned to me and said, "Bring your mother and we'll go upstairs." Surprised at the invitation, I turned and gave an apologetic look to the rest of the family. Mr. Johnson smiled and said to one of the Secret Service agents, "Bring them all!"

Upstairs in the private living quarters, the President ushered us into his bedroom. I noticed that the bed was unmade, suggesting he was in the habit of grabbing a quick "power nap" now and then. He opened his closet and took out some souvenirs. Autographing a copy of his book, *My Hope for America*, he gave one to mother and one to me.

Mr. Johnson pointed to a painting over his bed. "That's the house I was born in," he explained. It reminded me of the house in Saugerties, New York, where I was born. Now I was standing in the President's bedroom in the White House and he was showing us a picture of the humble home where he was born. Now this man was carrying the responsibilities of our entire nation.

"Come on, I'll show you around," the President said.

As we walked down the hall he showed us where his daughters Lynda and Luci lived, the Lincoln Bedroom, the Treaty Room, and Mrs. Johnson's living quarters.

"Let's go back to the Treaty Room and have a picture taken," he said.

Barbara approached the President with her program from the medal ceremony. "Mr. President, would you, please?" she asked, extending the program. He signed hers and then autographed everyone else's program.

As a photographer took pictures, the President told us the history of the Treaty Room. Abraham Lincoln's appointment book rested on a table where our country's treaties had been signed.

Next he showed us the Queen's Room across the hall, explaining that five queens had been guests there—Elizabeth II of England and the Queen Mother; Fredericka of Greece and Juliana of the Netherlands and her mother.

Then the President introduced Rufus Youngblood, his personal bodyguard, who had been constantly at Mr. Johnson's side. A man of steady eye and determined bearing, it was easy to visualize him throwing his body across Mr. Johnson's as he had done on that awful day in Dallas, Texas, when President Kennedy was assassinated.

"Well, folks, I'd better make my next meeting now," the President said, bidding us farewell. Two police motorcycles escorted the car that took us to our hotel, the Madison.

Secretary Ailes hosted a luncheon at the hotel. It was quite a gathering, with top Pentagon officials, my family, and members of my team and others from Fort Bragg, North Carolina, in attendance.

July 6, 1964, was the longest day of my life. December 5, 1964, had been the greatest day of my life. And what pleased me most was that I had done something to make my family as proud of me as I was of each one of them.

Following the luncheon the team and I went to Arlington National Cemetery. We visited President Kennedy's grave and the Tomb of the Unknown Soldier. We were filled with emotion as we paid our respects to Sergeant John Houston. His simple granite marker reads, "John L. Houston, Sgt., U.S. Army, Vietnam, Nov 6, 1941, Jul 6, 1964 DSC PH." On the back is "John L. Jr His Son, Jul 7, 1964 - Jul 8, 1964." Placing some flowers, we each said a silent prayer, then left him a piece of our hearts.

Headstone of John L. Houston and his son, Arlington National Cemetery.

The Family Team

January 30, 1934 . . .

Our governor, Franklin Delano Roosevelt, had only recently been chosen to lead the nation. I didn't know it at the time, but FDR and I had something in common—the same birthday. The President turned fifty-two the day I weighed in at the Donlon house on the corner of Main and Mynderse in Saugerties, New York.

I was the eighth child for Paul and Marion Donlon. Two more would be born. God must have had a plan for me from the beginning as the child born just before me, Marion, and another son, Joseph, who was born after me, both died in infancy.

Mother's doctor, Hugh Chidister, a wonderfully kind man, had been involved in an automobile accident just the day before. Not knowing if Dr. Chidister would live or die my parents decided to give me his name. No one ever told me where the "Roger" came from, but I find it ironic that it means "famous warrior." I took Charles as my confirmation name from my Godfather, Uncle Charlie Dale.

In the absence of the doctor, my mother was attended by one of my aunts. After the birth she wrapped me in a clean blanket and deposited me on the couch in the living room. Hurrying back upstairs to see to my mother, she felt that I would be safe since I was surrounded by all of the day's clean laundry and no one would sit on the couch.

As luck would have it, my oldest sister, Mary Bernadette, came in from school and dutifully began putting away the clean linen. When she tried to put the new white blanket into the closet I let out a wail! Startled, she almost dropped me. She peeked inside and said, "Oh my gosh, another one!"

Years later whenever I would give the family some grief with one of my mischievous incidents, Mary Bernadette would shake her finger at me and say, "Roger, I wish I had put you in the linen closet the day you were born!" I'm afraid that at times, she was only half joking.

I shared something in common with all but one of my siblings. We were born at home, in the house that my father had helped to build as a young man. My father, Paul A. Donlon, Sr., stood six feet tall. He was slender and tough. Always at home in the outdoors, he loved the rolling verdant countryside of the Hudson River Valley. He liked nothing more than striding across the land, moving as a frontiersman might have walked—quietly, boldly, assuredly. Like his parents before him, and all of his children, he was born in Saugerties. Daddy followed in his father's occupation, managing the M. E. Donlon Coal and Lumber Company.

He was a quiet, gentle, soft-spoken man who put more weight in deeds than in words. When he did speak it was with authority, and we all knew we had better "listen up." Daddy placed his faith and trust in the Creator, in our mother, in our country, family and friends. It was steadfast and unshakable.

When he met and married Marion Howard they became an unbeatable team of strength and unity. Mother was a petite five feet tall. Her size belied the amount of hard work she could accomplish. Up before dawn and working late into the night, she was the consummate homemaker, baking bread almost daily. I can still smell the wonderful aroma of fresh bread and rolls coming from her oven.

Mother was the most genuinely religious person I have ever known and my earliest memories are of her voice awakening me each morning and tucking me in at night. Gently making the sign of the cross on my forehead, she would say, *"Good morning, sweet Jesus; good morning, sweet Mary, I give you my heart and my soul. Keep me from sin this day and forever."* These words are still my first and last conscious thoughts as I begin and end each day.

Probably because of daddy's love for the outdoors, each time another Donlon entered the world he gave thanks by planting a tree in our yard. Each of us knew which tree was "ours." My pear tree is still bearing fruit. One of my earliest memories is of gazing at my pear tree, circling it again and again, admiring the beauty of its springtime blossoms and the bounty of its fall munificence. Family members told me I would clasp my hands behind me, looking intently, the way I remember my father walked and looked when he was at peace in the outdoors.

Daddy saw that we had variety in our little arbor. Pear, cherry, ash, maple, and an enormous apple tree from which we suspended the obligatory swing. Daddy planted grapevines by the garage. I modified the garage into a chicken coop for about fifty chicks, and later, Jack modified the chicken coop into a gymnasium. He would invite me to join him in workouts—my first physical training. Afterward we would share a cold bottle of milk.

We need only cross Mynderse Street to disappear into big woods, which we boys in particular were fond of exploring. Next to our house there was a big empty lot that became the designated Donlon playground, and behind it a rolling meadow that reached to St. Mary's hill, over a half-mile from our house.

When the slopes were snow-packed and our older siblings were skiing and sledding, Barbara would join me in games of hide-and-seek, or cowboys and Indians. I remember a living room sofa that was one of our hiding places where we would crouch, trying not to make a sound, as daddy thumbed the pages of his newspaper.

Being a veteran of World War I, he was always interested in the current event of the day, paying special attention to the progress of the U.S. involvement in the war in Europe. One day we heard him shout, "Hitler! Hitler! He's one big threat. When he's dead and gone we'll still have to fight communism!"

Neither my sister nor I had any idea what had upset our father. From the kitchen came mother's reply. They understood one another and shared a deep, abiding love.

Daddy had his own little library of possibly five hundred books. He enjoyed reading—the classics, nonfiction, encyclopedias. He would pore over encyclopedias with his children, or suggest where they should look for answers and information. I envied this attention given to my older brothers and sisters, and was anxious for the day when I could take a place at the dining room table and draw from the wisdom of my father.

Of course the older children helped the younger Donlons, with mother always close by. All of us were schooled at St. Mary of the Snows, a short walk from our house. Mary Bernadette, Paul, Mike, Jack, Adrienne and Gerard gave ample, if not wise coaching on how to outsmart Sister Mary Aloysius, the Mother Superior, and Sisters Mary Rose Regina, Mary Miriam and Mary Anne, and the other Sisters of Charity who challenged us, encouraged us and loved us all. Eventually we came to the realization there was no outsmarting these holy women. They were masters of discipline and if there was any smarting, it was ours, at the end of a yardstick.

Daddy had an assortment of hand tools, and would show us how to use them for fix-it jobs in the house or outside. I always looked forward to his next how-to-do-it lesson. It was good training for the day when I would be responsible for keeping my weapons in perfect condition.

Some of our best times together would come when daddy said "Come on, Roger, let's chop some wood!"

I would fall into step behind him, a little shadow following a towering man. Usually he would give me a hatchet, and while he split the bigger logs I flailed away at the smaller ones. No conversation. Just chop, chop, chop. When daddy said we had sufficient firewood we carried the sticks inside to feed the stove, or piled it outside for the furnace. I awaited the day when it would be my turn with the ax, but my apprenticeship was limited to the sledge and learning how to properly stack three or more cords of wood.

All of us had our assigned chores. The garbage pails were cleaned out on Saturdays. This detail was hands-down my least favorite. From emptying garbage pails you advanced to packing wood for the kitchen stove. When you were strong enough, you helped haul away furnace ashes. Wood chopping was the work of the oldest boys. The woodchoppers waited for the day when they could hire out for a paying job after school or on weekends.

We Donlon children understood respect. Daddy demanded it,

18 • The Family Team

especially toward mother. It wasn't a wise move to even so much as raise your voice to our mother. If any of us did, we had to deal with daddy.

"The Fourth Commandment, Roger," he reminded, delivering a smack across the seat of my pants. "Honor thy father and thy mother!"

When cancer finally weakened daddy, the spankings were no more. But he was still very much in charge of the house, albeit from his sickbed. If any of us got too boisterous mother placed a finger to her lips. "Be quiet," she would say. "Have respect for your father." This almost always worked. But if it didn't, or if we misbehaved in some other way, daddy was waiting upstairs with his Fourth Commandment speech. And stern words, no matter how well meant, always seemed to hurt more than a spanking, and watching him battle the pain while delivering the lecture.

Once he hand-printed small signs with the words

"Silence is a virtue. So shut up and help your mother."

He instructed mother to paste them on the kitchen wall over the sink, on the bathroom mirror, and at other places where we couldn't miss the message. For several days I thought about these early "Post-It" notes. Succumbing to temptation, I shortened the message. I changed them all to read

"Silence is a virtue. So shut up, mother!"

I can't recall when there was more giggling in the house. It lasted almost a full day. Mother didn't see my editing efforts immediately, but she knew something was afoot. When her gaze finally rested on one of the mis-messages she immediately took hold of me and before I could pull away I had another spanking for my efforts.

None of us could ever fathom how our parents seemed always to know which one of us had stepped out of line. We wondered if

The Family Team • 19

they could read minds. Occasionally at mealtime, if mother's back was turned away, one of us kids might poke the one closest to us. Then the pokee became the poker, returning the jab. Mother would see this response and punish the one who had returned the favor. But like as not we would get both barrels—the retaliatory jab and mother's on top if it. I couldn't figure out how she could see without eyes in the back of her head. Finally I discovered her secret. All of us at the table were in full sight—reflected in the window over the kitchen sink and the glass door on the china cabinet.

My early years had their frustrations. As next to the youngest Donlon I was either not old enough or not big enough for anything that the others were doing. But I managed to turn disadvantage into advantage. It made me more determined and more of a competitor. It also got me a bloody nose now and again at the hands of brother Gerard, closest to me in years. My brothers were all good athletes. All of my brothers and sisters got good grades in school. As a consequence, Barbara, the youngest, and I were continuously under pressure, having to push harder it seemed, just to keep up.

When I finally started school, the older Donlons were starting to go their separate ways. Mary Bernadette, the eldest, contracted tuberculosis when she was a teenager and was sent to a sanatorium. We came close to losing her at least three times, the doctors practically declaring her dead. As always, mother's prayers were answered and after nine years she came back to Saugerties, looking as young and pretty as ever. Her friends, meanwhile, had gone on to other lives. Most everyone she had known while growing up had left Saugerties. Living a quiet life, and taking care of mother in her later years, made her the closest thing to a saint in my eyes. Mary Bernadette died in April of 1986 and is buried in the family plot near St. Mary of the Snows.

Paul, named after daddy, saw action as a machine gunner in World War II. He served with M Company, 30th Regiment, Third Infantry Division, fighting his way from Anzio through Rome and France. He was wounded at Saint Die in the Vosges Mountains. He earned the Combat Infantry Badge, the European-African-Middle

Eastern Service Medal with three clusters for the Rome-Arno, Southern France and Rhineland campaigns; the Fourragere in Colors of Croix de Guerre; the World War II Victory Medal; the American Campaign Medal, and the Purple Heart. After the war he graduated from Manhattan College in New York City, where he settled and went to work for the *New York Times* and later the Dow Jones Company. After daddy died Paul became the mainstay of the family. Today he is retired and lives in the family home on Main and Mynderse.

Michael was with the Army of Occupation in Germany. He was discharged just before the 1948 Berlin Blockade. The Berlin Blockade was a reminder of our father's prophetic statement on communism. Michael graduated from Loyola of the South in New Orleans with a degree in economics. He pitched for the Loyola baseball team and spent his summers working in the Texas oil fields. His life's work was with computers, and he held many responsible positions with companies like General Electric. Following in the tradition of our parents, Michael and his late wife, Frances, raised four sons and five daughters. Today Michael is retired in Basking Ridge, New Jersey.

Jack was the "jock" of the family. He did press-ups daily with weights. It was Jack who always excelled at basketball and soccer. He enlisted in the Air Force and had a distinguished twenty-six year career as a dental technician, retiring as a master sergeant. One of the highlights was working on the returning Vietnam POWs while he was stationed at Clark AFB in the Philippines in the early 1970's. Jack and his wife, Fran, a sweet lady from Georgia, raised two sons. They are retired in Panama City, Florida.

Loving big city life, my sister Adrienne moved to Chicago. There she began a career with the *Chicago Daily News*, working for Mike Royko, the columnist with the caustic wit. She still loves the windy city and is now retired.

Gerard, always my nemesis, was the only one I could take on in a test of strength and have a chance of coming out on top. It didn't happen very often. I'll never forget the time he agreed to let me accompany him on his paper deliveries. He said I could deliver to his special customers. Invariably the dog of one of these "special" customers would chase me. I finally figured out that I had been "had" when I saw Gerard, behind a tree, laughing uncontrollably. At seventeen Gerard joined the Air Force and on his first overseas assignment was sent to the Philippines. It was there that he would make his home as an expatriate. He spent many years in the import-export business in Manila and raised three girls and a boy with his former wife, Nita. Gerard continues to enjoy the tropics in his retirement years.

Barbara married and raised two daughters with her former husband, a West Point graduate and career Army officer. As the "baby" of the family, none of us expected to attend her funeral, but in June of 1998 she passed away. Her burial service, in the family plot in Saugerties, brought four of the Donlon brothers (only Gerard was not in attendance) together again for the first time since the ceremony at the White House. Barbara would be pleased to know that we plan to meet annually from now on.

As the years passed I came to appreciate the many good qualities of my brothers and sisters—character, training, discipline—and I know it was all due to our parents who taught us to be true to ourselves, to look out for one another, to be loving and caring.

And the lessons learned under the watchful eyes of the Sisters stayed with us as well. Back then only boys were permitted to serve at mass. Today in some areas girls share this privilege. Back then we were obliged to memorize the Latin responses. Today in almost all Catholic churches these prayers are in English.

You had to be eight years old to be a mass server. Again, as the youngest boy in the Donlon family, I was the last to become an acolyte, and I recall my impatience as I counted the days to my eighth birthday. We devised devilish initiation rites for the new acolytes. We blindfolded one kid, making a shroud out of his cassock, and lowered him into a newly dug grave in the St. Mary's Cemetery. Then someone dropped some dirt on top of him and he was out of the hole faster than you could say *Requiescat in pace*.

Mother knew nothing of our server shenanigans. She could always be counted upon to walk with us to St. Mary's when we served at early weekday mass.

As altar boys we came to a better understanding of our religion and our obligations. And we came to know a lot of priests.

I remember Father Vogel in particular. He had been a missionary in China for a score of years, captured and tortured by heathens. His bishop saw St. Mary's as an assignment where Father Vogel could take things more at ease. He wore a black cape with a hood, whether it was in the parish or in the movie theater for the Saturday matinees. There he would join us to thrill at the excitement of the latest Tom Mix serial adventures. Like the Sisters, Father Vogel was all business when it came to acolyte decorum. He did not hesitate to rap someone's knuckles if it became necessary.

We paid Father Edmund Harty the supreme honor of naming our drum and bugle corps after him. And we managed to raise $2,000 so he could revisit his native Ireland. Father Augustine Donahue kept a horse and rode it around Saugerties. He would go on hikes in the woods or along the river; leading bunches of us kids like a pipeless Pied Piper.

I was in the first grade at St. Mary's when I experienced one of my early setbacks. I was *not* musically gifted. Sister Miriam organized a rhythm band, complete with drums, triangles and cymbals. She let me try my hand at each. When I couldn't manage even the cymbals I became a rhythm band dropout. I simply could not keep time. To this day I dance as well as I played the cymbals. The miracle is that I was ever able to march in formation.

It was great fun going to school. I have fond memories of the hot soup, chocolate milk and homemade cookies. The chocolate milk was courtesy of Schroeder's farm and those wonderful cookies were from Mrs. Bitterman's kitchen. As I recall there were eight Bitterman children in St. Mary's, and being in the same class with a Bitterman meant you could look forward to one of her prize-winning cookies once a week. The Bittermans came to school on cookie day, each carrying a bag of cookies, which we devoured

The Family Team • 23

during recess.

"Hey, Roger, you want in on some fun?" A new classmate who presumably knew his way around dangled the bait.

"Sure," I replied.

"Okay, then, follow us."

Follow I did. We climbed the steps to the attic of St. Mary's, where supplies were stored. Then we found the opening behind inner walls of the old schoolhouse. The walls were lined with wood panels. The secret space between them was wide enough to allow us to squeeze in. Once inside, we could move along this hidden hallway. It was easy enough to know when we were opposite a classroom, because we could hear what was happening on the other side of the panels. There were even occasional cracks in the panels so we could get a tiny glimpse of what was going on in the room.

My "friends" on this adventure started pushing against the panels. Whatever was hanging on the other side of the wall, a crucifix, pictures of the Sacred Heart or of Washington and Lincoln, began to bump against the gently swaying wood partition. Above this sound could be heard the giggles of the kids in the room. At this point the designated lookout among us warned, "There she goes!"

That meant Sister was on a dead run, intent upon catching us in the act. Someone gave the wall panels a couple of good-bye bumps and we were out of there as fast as our feet would carry us. Apparently the hidden hallway gang knew the maze of passageways better than the nuns did, because we escaped through an uncharted exit. I saw no harm in all of this and occasionally I would return for another game of bump-and-run. I discovered it wasn't always necessary to hot tail it out of the passageway. If you didn't make any giveaway sounds you could simply wait in the dark until the prankster patrol abandoned the search.

Occasionally the Sisters won a round. That meant a crack across the knuckles. It would have been poetic justice if the yardstick had come from the Donlon lumberyard.

The toughest times of all were when it became our fate to go before Sister Aloysius, the mother superior. She specialized in

24 • *The Family Team*

surprise inspections. Maybe we were just standing in line waiting for a drink of water. Sister Aloysius was death on shirttails hanging out, shoestrings that weren't tied, or tousled hair. We were always to be neat, and anything less than neat meant you probably would be pulled out of line and dressed down. Sister Aloysius could have taught first sergeant school.

I don't know why we did some of the vexing things we did at St. Mary's. Sometimes when one of the Sisters was administering three whacks to the hand with a ruler, after the second whack we would draw back our hand. The third whack would fall on Sister's knee instead of our knuckles. The dear nun never did seem to catch on, we thought. Eventually I realized that that kind and saintly lady was probably chuckling at us and how *we* never caught on.

As the years passed, it was becoming evident that the cancer was taking its toll on daddy. He could no longer work and much to Barbara's and my delight as the "tail end Charleys," he spent more and more time with us.

On my ninth birthday daddy launched me head first into the broiler business. Fifty chicks were a surprise gift. He had raised chickens many years ago. Now it was my turn. There was one problem. The chicks didn't come with an instruction manual.

"Well, Roger," daddy quizzed, "now that you're in the chicken business do you know what to do?"

"No, sir," was the whole truth and nothing but the truth.

Daddy explained that my brood needed to be kept behind the kitchen stove for a time, until they got bigger. So the first thing every morning, and again after school, I checked my chicks. I held them and fed them and as instructed by daddy, looked for any sign of rickets.

I found a shoe box into which I would place some of the chicks. Since daddy was now confined to bed I had to carry them upstairs for his critique. Mother didn't appreciate me carrying the chicks through the house, but it pleased daddy and so it was permitted.

"What happens when they get bigger?" daddy asked.

"Don't know," I replied. "Build a chicken coop?"

The Family Team • 25

"Yes," he said. You will have a coop, and you will have to keep it clean or it will draw mice. The feed will attract them anyway. You'll need mouse traps."

My adventure in poultry farming was beginning to look like work. And one of the chicks didn't look as frisky as the rest.

Daddy suggested the garage would make a proper chicken coop, so I cleaned it and set up pens, a feeder, feed bin and plenty of mousetraps.

When my one lethargic chick got worse, I took it to daddy for a professional opinion.

"Rickets," he declared. "You will have to kill it, Roger."

As I walked downstairs with my sick chick I contemplated what was coming next. *I* didn't know how to kill a chick, and I had too much pride to ask daddy for guidance. By this time I was old enough to wield a hatchet, so hatchet and condemned chick in hand, I headed for the chopping block behind our house.

The chick wasn't well, but it wouldn't hold its head still on the chopping block either. I thought about dispatching the poor bird with a single-edge razor blade, but decided against that approach as well.

So I took hold of its head with one hand and its body with the other hand. I closed my eyes and twisted. I almost became sick to my stomach. But daddy had spoken. He explained it would have always been sickly and as a consequence, of no use to anyone and that it was best that it be killed. It was a dark day in my young life that I would never forget.

Fortunately for me the other forty-nine grew into fine White Leghorns. I sold eggs door-to-door, and with this working capital I invested in some Rhode Island Reds and Plymouth Rocks. I learned a lot working with my chickens and grew to like the experience, even if I did get off to a pretty shaky start.

Daddy and I talked about how I might get my chickens to lay more eggs. We dined on eggs for breakfast. I had my regular customer delivery route in the neighborhood. Sometimes I delivered on the way to school, but I also accumulated eggs so there would be enough to meet the demand on Saturdays, my big egg-selling day. I opened a bank savings account, taking out of the account only what was needed to purchase feed or other necessities for my chickens. When I left home to attend Syracuse University I closed my savings account. There was almost ninety dollars, which I spent on books.

My coop could always be tapped for three or four chickens for the main fare at Sunday dinner in our house. It was up to me to dress these birds.

Once when a cousin, Joseph Dunleavy, was visiting from Brooklyn and I was cleaning chickens, a headless bird got free and dashed across the street and into the woods, never to be found. Whenever Joe returned for a visit he would tweak me, saying "Hey, Rog, let's go look for the headless chicken in the woods."

On another occasion I took a couple of city cousins with me to milk some cows. They knew nothing of farm life.

"We don't drink cow's milk," they declared. "We drink Otto's milk!" Otto was the proprietor of a neighborhood deli.

I owe a lot to my chickens. They were my first opportunity to contribute to our household. I kept them for several years, until I entered high school. By then I was able to manage an after-school job carrying packages for Doc White's drugstore. Later I worked at Lachmann's bakery as a helper, and then at the Saugerties Sweet Shop as a soda jerk. Soda fountain work was the best of all because you controlled the size of the servings and no one counted how many sodas or sundaes you served yourself.

Mrs. Rodney Ball, a neighbor and friend who was a registered nurse, was spending more and more time at our house. Always a slender man, daddy was now thin and gaunt. Despite Mrs. Ball's efforts to keep him comfortable and all of mother's prayers, his pain got increasingly worse.

Finally on July 21, 1947, daddy died. As we gathered together that evening for our usual family rosary, his death really hit home with me when I heard my mother's soft voice praying for the repose of the soul of our daddy. I desperately wish that I could have known him better.

**Daddy,
Paul Augustine Donlon**

**Mother,
Marion Howard Donlon**

My Sisters

Adrienne

Mary Bernadette

Barbara

Growing Up In Saugerties

1947-1952 . . .

My father's death in the summer of 1947 left me a confused, hurt, and angry thirteen-year-old. Outwardly I seemed to be the same old Roger, full of pranks and jokes. Inside I ached every time I saw my friends with their fathers, especially when it came to things like fishing, boating, and playing ball.

One of the last things daddy did before he died was to sign off on my Boy Scout Tenderfoot test record certificate. It is the only piece of paper I own today with his signature. My involvement in Scouting was yet another "team" effort, and though I didn't realize it at the time, all my Scoutmasters were to become my surrogate fathers.

George Thornton, owner of the local Orpheum Movie Theater, saw that he could help our community by spearheading an effort to start a Boy Scout program. He successfully recruited the Catholic parish of St. Mary of the Snows to be the sponsor, and enlisted Tommy Thornton and Freddie Hull, two of our returning World War II veterans, to help him. Rounding out the leadership team were Henry Schroeder, Lawrence "Coach" Cahill, and Edward M. "Flywheel" Flanagan. These generous men spent countless hours shaping our future and helping us set goals.

"George," as we respectfully called him, was cut from the same bolt of cloth as my mother when it came to living one's religion. He continually drew the parallel between Scouting and Church teachings, reminding us that God is all loving and forgiving. This was especially important, as it seemed someone was always in need of forgiveness for one prank or another.

I used to think that both George and mother had a sixth sense. They always seemed to know when I had not followed the Ten Commandments or lived up to the Scout Oath. Come Saturday, it was suggested that I might want to go along with them to confession in order to fully prepare myself for Sunday's Holy Communion. George always seemed to be a couple of inches taller than his normal six feet, six inches, as he led his Scouts to receive Communion at Sunday mass.

At the very first Scout meeting I attended, Edward Flanagan, one of our Scoutmasters, brought his son. Home on leave, Ed Jr., was the epitome of an officer and a gentleman. Tall, with ramrod posture, he proudly wore his U.S. Army uniform. His chest was heavy with medals. He wore an overseas cap with the Airborne patch of the time. His boots were polished to a blinding gloss.

The room quieted until you could hear a pin drop as Captain Flanagan spoke of his men, especially the ones who did not return from the war. He shared with us the importance of respecting our flag . . . Old Glory. And on behalf of all his fellow soldiers, he led us in the Pledge of Allegiance and National Anthem. As we sang, " . . . and the home of the brave" we could feel him recalling the names and faces of the men that he had lost.

This visit by Captain Flanagan left a lasting impression on me. It was not just the picture of the "perfect soldier," but something in the way he spoke that stayed with me. The true emotion and passion that only those who have served can share, came through in his remarks.

As I lay in my bed that night my mind flashed back to all the times I had watched my father hang our flag on the front porch post. It was a daily ritual, but on special days he would always pause a little longer. It was a moment of reflection known only to him, but I recalled one day that I felt I knew what he was thinking and feeling.

It was the day after we received word that my oldest brother, Paul, had been wounded in action. The next morning as we reverently unfurled the flag I could feel daddy's heart saying, "Please, dear Lord, bring our Paul home safely." These were the exact words that daddy added to our prayer of grace that evening as we began and ended our meal.

30 • Growing Up In Saugerties

Today, our flag hangs proudly from my front porch post. I thank my parents for instilling in me this love and pride in our national symbol. If they were still living, I'm sure they would disagree that we should have a "law" to respect the flag. They felt it was the responsibility of each and every parent to teach their children love of country and respect for the flag. Thank God they were never witnesses to the desecration of this sacred and revered symbol.

Work was also becoming a big part of my life now, and I was always proud to bring home my paycheck. It was a good feeling to be able to help mother "pay the bills" as I had seen my brothers and sisters doing for years.

As the summer wore on, I tried hard to shake off my feelings of loss, and even began to enjoy hanging out with my friends. At thirteen there seemed to be no limit to the opportunities for summertime adventure.

Buzz Burhans, Joe Lahoud, Jerry Brice and I were four young explorers from Saugerties looking for excitement. Our village was nestled on the west bank of the Hudson River, and we would hike up and down the river constantly. Looking across to the other side, we imagined all kinds of wonderful discoveries just waiting to be found.

One day we hiked upriver to the land of the mushroom moguls. There was quite a business growing mushrooms in the dark caves. When we were older we would all have summer jobs picking the mushrooms.

The men who owned the mushroom company had a yacht. It was elegant, and it was a thrill just to watch it gliding in and out of the boathouse, its brass fittings reflecting the sun's rays off its polished mahogany decks and its pennants fluttering in the breeze. Oh, what we would have given for a ride on that yacht.

On the day of our (mis) adventure, we discovered that the boathouse was empty. There didn't seem to be anyone in or around it. One of my companions spied a green canoe. To us it was the biggest and most beautiful canoe ever built, all of twenty feet from bow to stern. It had built-in air pockets, intended to make it

Growing Up In Saugerties • 31

unsinkable. It was gently rocking in the water by the boathouse, and immediately we knew it was a canoe just waiting to be paddled down the river.

Our first mistake was in paddling too far downstream to have time to return it to its mooring spot before dark. So we did the next best thing and hid it in some bushes along the bank, intending to return it the following day. But adventure canoeing was so much fun that we returned to its hiding place again and again, enjoying long days of river adventure before returning it to its hiding place instead of its intended mooring place.

One of our group realized that the canoe was our ticket to see the train on the opposite side of the river. We had wondered about the train that ran between Albany and New York City, because it did something mysterious as it raced past Saugerties. When it reached a certain place, and for some distance, the engine emitted an enormous spray of water. None of us could ever figure out why. Now we saw the canoe as the key to unlocking this mystery. We discovered that between the rails, for a distance of a hundred or more yards, there was a water trough. When the train slowed to snag mailbags it would also drop a scoop into this trough to take on water. When that happened a gigantic spray resulted. Mystery solved!

Moving on to higher adventure, we paddled off to a nearby island where, as legend had it, Indians had once roamed and there were arrowheads just waiting to be found. Well, we never did make it to the island. We didn't know it but there was an elderly lady who passed her days on her front porch of the historic Mynderse House. Equipped with binoculars, she was a self-appointed water patrol person. When she saw us in our borrowed canoe, she called the Coast Guard. The next thing we knew there was a big Coast Guard boat racing towards us. The crew took the canoe in tow and proceeded to question the four of us.

"Your name, young man?"

"Pete O'Connor," I said.

"Your address?"

"Oh, we're not from around here," I lied again. "We're from

32 • Growing Up In Saugerties

the city, from the Bronx. We just got here. We're visiting relatives and we were out scouting around, and now we have to get back to our folks. We're going back to the city."

My companions joined in more misinformation, giving basically the same story and fictitious names.

We might have fooled the Coast Guard but there was no fooling Deputy Sheriff Sammy Fluckiger, who was waiting on the dock. He was also the truant officer and owner of the farm from which we purchased all of our dairy products—milk, cheese and butter.

"Hello, Roger," he called out, and we knew that we had been "had." The Coast Guard readily released us to the deputy, who took us forthwith to the home of Mr. Thornton, the leader of our Boy Scout Troop 36. George proceeded to refresh our memories about such things as being truthful and respecting the property rights of others. Upon reaching home, mother covered all of the same ground—with gestures for added emphasis. Needless to say we finished out that summer as landlubbers—and with our real names.

Between owning the movie theater and dealing with a cinema filled with noisy children, and his service as Scoutmaster, George was an expert child psychologist. We didn't realize it at the time, but he gradually increased our Scout responsibilities, picking up junk, collecting old newspapers, and assorted good deeds. His keep-them-busy-and-they-won't-have-time-for-mischief strategy worked. Because of George, in six years I attained the rank of Life Scout.

George was a great user of the compass that was given to each new Scout. It was a World War II "issue" Lensatic compass made by the Witthauer Company. Many times the compass was taken out of our pockets to find our way around the Catskill Mountains. George never missed an opportunity to compare it to our "moral compass" and how we should remember to shoot a back azimuth from time to time.

The deputy kept tabs on us as well. I lost count of the times he picked me up in his old car and delivered me home. When she saw the deputy's car and me climbing out of it, mother didn't know if I had been caught again by the long arm of the law or just lucky to get another ride home.

The deputy was a kindly man, and didn't deserve the treatment he received from our "gang of four." His cows supplied our milk, and on occasion we would treat his small herd to a bunch of wild onions so that their milk tasted like onions. At other times we gave these poor animals rotten apples to make them "drunk." Then we would chase them down the hill. Cows don't run well downhill, and it was great fun watching them go end over end down the hill. Once in a while we would climb a tree and drop onto a cow's back a la bronco-busting cowboys. That was our final bovine bashing insult. It was great fun unless you were a cow.

By the time we reached the eighth grade at St. Mary's we considered ourselves to be pretty savvy Saugerties teenagers. I was now almost six feet tall. Others in the class were even taller. On day one in the eighth grade Sister Mary Anne Delores, our teacher, announced in a kindly voice:

"Okay, I understand some of you boys like to give us a hard time. Well, let me tell you. My last teaching assignment was on the Lower East Side of New York City. I've handled the roughest. Don't try anything on me because I know all the tricks. Be cool and everything will be okay. Understand?"

That slender, attractive nun was as good as her word. One day she discovered some of us at horseplay in the cloakroom. One boy was six feet and weighed almost 200 pounds. Sister Mary Ann Delores went on the offensive. She gave him a slap across the back of his head with such force it knocked him through the nearby wall. He was a sight to behold with his head sticking out on one side of the wall and his body on the other. The way his head projected into the classroom gave him the look of a wall-mounted taxidermist's creation, except that his head was moving.

When we were younger we passed time on Saturdays with neighborhood "war games." It was a natural thing to do during the World War II years. Bill Brinnier was the organizer and our field commander. He was several years older than the rest of us, but too young to enlist for service. We addressed him as "General Brinnier" and we pretty much followed his directives. We had plenty of role models in the movies and adventure comics of the '40s. We were also pretty inventive and some of our "dirty tricks" maneuvers were classics.

All of us in Bill's Battalion were organized into squads and platoons. Mostly we went into battle under the Main Street banner, but now and again we traded some of our regulars for replacements from other platoons.

We weren't very selective about picking the battleground. It might be an empty lot or a much larger acreage, or even the nearby woods. When General Brinnier tooted his whistle, it started. It ended when we had gained our objective, or until there was a casualty. Fortunately we always escaped serious injury.

We were resourceful when it came to weaponry. Eggs from my coops—the older the better—were our hand grenades. So were ashes wrapped in tissue paper. They would "puff" on impact, which was more exciting than a direct hit with an egg grenade. Armament didn't have to be fancy. Slingshots, spears, rocks, horse chestnuts— all were standard issue. Air rifles were the ultimate assault weapon. Mostly we aimed low, but once in a while there would be a real cry of pain and you knew it was for real.

We had our own secret weapon. One day it saved us from being overwhelmed. We had assumed a defensive position but a superior force was rapidly advancing. We waited until we could "see the whites of their eyes." At the last moment we put a match to about a dozen brooms that had been soaked in gasoline. The oncoming assault was instantly turned away.

We had the benefit of adult supervision in high school and thus our energies were directed in productive pursuits. I lettered in track, throwing the discus, and in six-man football. They had dropped 11-man football at Saugerties High School because of some earlier fatalities, but have since restored it. The Sawyer Yearbook for my senior year, 1952, included a picture of me on the gridiron. The caption read "Roger Donlon Missing a Tackle." In reality I was on the field for almost every minute of every game. Mother wasn't big

Growing Up In Saugerties • 35

on football, but she did travel to one "away" game without telling me she would be in the stands. That was the game in which I was knocked cold in the first quarter.

In another section of the yearbook I also made headlines. In the "We'll Always Remember" column was a reference to " . . . Roger Donlon's cute (?) jokes and pranks." They seemed cute to me then, but upon reflection I would have to agree with the parenthetical question mark inserted by the yearbook staff.

The stuffed weasel that Bob Lezette brought to school was a case in point. He let me borrow it and I took it over to some girls who were talking in a hallway, to see if they would react. They did, and it brought a teacher on the run, fearing goodness knows what.

Occasionally seniors would get into the school during the night for a game of basketball or a workout on the trampoline. Entry to the school after hours was by climbing a tree next to the gymnasium. After reaching a certain height they would get the limb swaying and leap from the limb to the roof of the gym. From the roof it was through a skylight and down a nearby climbing rope.

Students who patronized the soda vending machine in school were confused. The bottles were stacked in channels with only their necks and caps visible. You inserted a nickel, pushed a lever, and a bottle dropped out. But sometimes the bottle was empty. The seniors had discovered that they could ease the cap off of a bottle while it was still in its rack, drink the contents through a straw, and then replace the cap.

Graduation day brought a lot of reminiscing. Someone retold the story of the incredible shrinking man. In the summer of 1951 I was the drum major with the Father Harty Drum Corps. We went to Poughkeepsie for a parade; all decked out in new green and white uniforms. As luck would have it, it rained, but we kept marching. As it turned out the uniforms were not shrink-resistant. At the end of the parade I looked down to find my trousers had shrunk until they split up the back. They had shrunk until they were like knickers. I was quite a sight to behold. Al Iannone, who was along on that disastrous march, recalled:

"We were the only outfit in the parade that had its drum major start out in one uniform and finish in another. Roger had the only air-cooled Bermuda shorts in the parade."

My senior year I branched out from working at Lachmann's Bakery and picking mushrooms. Eric Ericson took me on as an apprentice carpenter. He also taught me how to play pinochle. The previous summer I had worked for him for about $1.25 an hour. He knew his trade and kept challenging me to keep up with him. I did, and in the process earned about a thousand dollars. He built solid houses.

He would invite me to pay pinochle, but never could understand why I preferred to pass on pinochle for a visit to Ed Buckley's Sweet Shop or to go to the movies with his daughter, Nancy. She was a blue-eyed blonde and one of the prettiest girls I knew.

But of all my summer jobs, picking mushrooms was the most lucrative. I would work in those mushroom caves on the Hudson River from six until two o'clock in the afternoon. The pay was about sixty-five dollars a week. From the caves I would go to the Sweet Shop or the bakery afternoons and evenings, and on the weekends I was working alongside Mr. Ericson. It made for long days and a long summer, but nothing gave me as much pleasure as when I handed mother my week's earnings.

The giant limestone caves where we harvested mushrooms were about ten miles south of town. You could drive a two-and-one-half ton truck around in the caves. Pals Lenny Sweeney, Jerry Brice, Jackie Bartells and I were on the same picking crew. The rest of the pickers were experienced. Most of them were Germans, Poles, Russians, Latvians, Czechs or Lithuanians—all displaced from World War II and all spoke broken English. We called our workplace "The Zoo" and were amused at some of the nicknames of the foreign-born—"Dead Spider," "Snow Ball," "Cookie." The younger ones were likeable and made friends easily, but some of the older folks clearly had had a difficult time adjusting to life in America. And, I am afraid, associating with us didn't make the adjustment easier.

Five or six of us made up one team of pickers. A team could

Growing Up In Saugerties • 37

pick as much as nine hundred dollars' worth of mushrooms in a day. We received a straight salary, but after a time we began competing with the other teams. The objective was to pick fast enough to stay ahead of the others but carefully enough so that we didn't knock off the mushroom caps. If the cap became separated from the stem it went to the cannery. The rest were sent to market as fresh mushrooms.

Pickers wore miners' helmets. The lights on the helmets let us see what we were picking. The mushrooms grew in large, shallow boxes stacked in tiers. Bricks separated the tiers so the workers could reach in with their hands to pick.

It was amazing how fast the mushrooms grew. We would return to the same place we had picked the previous day to find more mushrooms awaiting harvest. The smallest were called button mushrooms. These were put to one side for special packaging. Overnight a button mushroom would be twice its original size. I quickly understood how the expression "to mushroom" came into the language, to mean something fast-growing.

Veteran pickers worked all day without knocking off so much as a single cap. My team members and I spoiled a lot of mushrooms through carelessness, mostly. I suppose the job required more finesse than most teenagers possessed. But the foreman needed pickers and we were willing, if not able.

Picking mushrooms was monotonous work, so we jumped at the opportunity to drive a small flatbed truck through the cave. It would hold about forty crates of mushrooms—a day's harvest for one team. Outside the cave a refrigerated truck waited to take the crates to the market or the cannery.

Once, to make the winding run through the cave challenging, we decided to turn off the truck's headlights. We thought we knew the twists and turns in the dark. I was standing on the running board, giving directions to whoever was driving. It was thrilling. We knew there were deep pits just off the roadway, as we rolled down the ramp in the pitch-black cave.

"Curve ahead," someone said.

38 • Growing Up In Saugerties

"Little more to the left!"

"No, right!"

"Turn, turn!"

"No, not yet!"

Crash!

We had run into a giant stone pillar that was one of the roof supports in the cave. When we turned on the headlights it looked like it had rained mushrooms. They were everywhere. We had wiped out nine hundred dollars worth of them.

One of the foremen, Val Carpenter, was running down the ramp. He was also Lenny's uncle. He knew immediately what had occurred, and how. He didn't ask us to explain, but he looked angry enough to kill us all.

We were pretty sure we were finished as mushroom pickers. We began picking up the scattered mushrooms and replacing them in their crates. They all went directly to the cannery. Our wages were docked but we were allowed to keep on picking. It was more than embarrassing when I had to explain my "short" paycheck to mother.

Often times, when daddy was still alive, he would talk with me about what I might want to do "when I grew up." During these visits I would tell him I wanted to be a doctor. He gave me a lot of encouragement and I continued to be serious about it. Now I can see that my thoughts about having a career in medicine were solely focused on curing my cancer-stricken father. Even after he died I didn't completely abandon the idea and it was the motivation to study Latin. My weakness in mathematics was apparent and soon my interest in medicine waned.

Inheriting my father's love of the outdoors, I enjoyed mountain climbing, fresh air, and sleeping on a blanket of pine needles. I liked animals and guns. I owned a Savage single-action .22 rifle, which I found at a pawnshop for nine dollars. I was thirteen at the time. Mother, who didn't want guns around the house, didn't know about my rifle. I kept it in the cellar.

Some months after the Korean War started, I wanted to leave

high school and enlist in the Navy—to see the world and get a piece of the action by serving my country. This idea was short-lived. Mother nixed it immediately and sought my oldest brother Paul's support. His words still resonate in my mind. "Roger, finish high school, go to college—there will be other wars." Reluctantly I reset my compass to the course that mother and Paul advised.

I enrolled at the New York State College of Forestry at Syracuse University. There I thought I would specialize in wildlife management or landscape engineering. Since it was a state school there were no tuition worries, but I still needed cash for textbooks and board, until I could find work.

I raided my egg-money savings account and Paul made me a loan. I left Saugerties in high spirits, but apprehensive. Dressed in my new clothes I tried to look and act like a college man, and not a gangling kid from the country. Mother knew better. The look on her face told me she would double her prayers for me, and she was already praying pretty intensely for her youngest boy.

Roger as a Boy Scout in Troop 36, Saugerties.

Brother Gerard and Roger as Altar Boys, St. Mary of the Snows Church.

40 • Growing Up In Saugerties

Those Syracuse Girls

Autumn, 1952 . . .

Some days are luckier than others. My first day of job-hunting was successful beyond my wildest dreams. I was now headwaiter in a sorority house!

My main objective had been to find a job with access to food. The cafeterias and sorority houses were the best possibilities and a sorority sounded more interesting than a cafeteria.

Mrs. Grace Gilham from Ossining, New York answered my knock at the Zeta Tau Alpha house. I liked her manner so much that I decided Zeta Tau Alpha would do very nicely.

"I'm very glad to see you," she said. "I'm in a predicament."

She explained that all of the ZTA waiters had either graduated or left. She needed an entire new crew.

"If you want the job, you're hired," she declared. "And when I get the four of you together I'll choose one as head waiter."

She hired three other boys, Zack, Jacques, and Tom. Maybe because I was first hired, she put me in charge. As headwaiter I didn't have to do as much waiting as the rest, but I was responsible for seeing that they reported for duty on schedule. And if one of them was sick, I took his place.

I settled into my college routine. I found a comfortable dorm, Skytop M-8, which was a Quonset hut where forty of us lived, two to a room. My roommate was Bob Edgar from Ohio, and we became good friends.

I enjoyed working for Mrs. Gilham and the cook, Mrs. Katherine Kelly, who treated us like sons. Katherine was a typical Irish grandmother type, always cheerful as she scurried around the kitchen.

"Don't forget to check the washing machine," she would call out. That was her coded message that she had baked an extra pie just for us. She learned that I had a weakness for lemon meringue pie with graham cracker crust, and frequently that was what we would find hidden in the washer. She had other pie-hiding places as well, so the girls wouldn't find *our* treats.

We were expected to walk the straight and narrow in the sorority dining room, because we were hired hands. And it was understood we were not to date any of the girls. But we were not above what you might call "playful harassment." We spent idle time thinking up pranks. We would stack rolls of bathroom tissue atop a door that was slightly ajar. When a girl opened the door a half dozen or so rolls of tissue tumbled down. It worked every time, evoking screams of girlish fright. Once Mrs. Gilham became our unintended victim, and for our trouble we were lectured on how an innocent prank can lead to an accident.

Occasionally on a Saturday we would show up at the ZTA house after Mrs. Gilham had departed. The kitchen would be filled with pajama-clad girls making coffee and toast and frying eggs. At our appearance in the kitchen there would be shrieks and squeals as the girls ran for cover. We always proceeded to devour the food they left behind.

The greatest trick of all was our bat caper. Little brown bats lived in a nearby cave. We harvested the furry creatures and took them to the ZTA house on a sorority meeting night. We let the bats out of the bag in the basement after dinner, opening the doors leading upstairs. Then we withdrew to a stone wall across the street—and waited.

The entire sorority was on hand, not just the current residents. There were probably seventy girls in the house planning whatever Zeta Tau Alphas do. The sorority house erupted, volcano-like. Through the window we could see girls with tennis rackets chasing those poor bats. Most of the girls were piling out of the house amid a chorus of screams.

We had only introduced four bats into the house, and they flew off in short order. But we were the only ones who knew that, so the girls were awake half the night on bat patrol. The next morning they were sleepy-eyed and not too happy. We were immediately accused of having created the havoc of the preceding night. We denied everything. We must not have been very convincing, however, and in due course the girls got even.

The policy of not dating the girls didn't apply when a group of them went somewhere, such as the student council club. We were allowed to accompany groups of ZTAs.

A few days after our bats broke up their sorority assembly one of the girls extended an invitation.

"Hey, Rog, let's go have a beer," she said.

I had about seventy-five cents in my pocket. That was enough for one beer, I decided. Upon arrival at the student council club it was obvious those present were celebrating someone's birthday, and the girls insisted we all stay. They wouldn't let me spend so much as a dime, and the beer was flowing. I think maybe I had five beers, which was three more than I had ever consumed at one time.

"Who's waiting on table tonight, Rog?" one of the girls asked.

I was woozy, but suddenly it came to me. It was Saturday and the other three boys had the day off. I had table-waiting duty that evening. I took leave of the beer party and made my way to the sorority house. I was light-headed, but having realized what they had been up to, I resolved to go them one up.

Mrs. Kelly could see I was not my normal self.

"You don't look well, Roger," she declared.

"No, ma'am," I answered. "I don't feel well at all. Some of the girls tried to get me drunk this afternoon, but they won't get the best of me."

Mrs. Kelly had prepared spaghetti and meatballs. Because I was alone, I had to move faster than usual to dish out the food while it was still hot. This meant carrying five plates at a time, three on my left arm and two on the right. I had done this previously without a problem.

Mrs. Gilham was always served first. Five plates in hand, I headed toward the housemother. In an instant I went sprawling. I landed in Mrs. Gilham's lap, both of us covered with spaghetti and meatballs. The dining room exploded in laughter, except for one

Those Syracuse Girls • 43

girl, who was rubbing the spot on her shin after she had tripped me.

Shaking off most of the spaghetti, Mrs. Gilham excused herself and went to her room. She returned after a few minutes in another dress, calm and composed.

Meanwhile Mrs. Kelly and I had policed up the remnants of five dinners and I resumed serving the meal. Mrs. Gilham waited until the following day to confront me.

"Roger, that was an unfortunate thing last night," she began.

"Yes, ma'am," I replied. "And I'm sorry."

She had smelled the beer on my breath. "There goes my meal ticket," I thought. But I deserved whatever came of it. It wasn't Mrs. Gilham's fault.

"Don't let it happen again," she warned.

And that was the end if it.

When it came to waiting tables and my studies, I was a better waiter. I had forgotten the good study habits learned at the family dining room table. So I was given a year's leave of absence from school. Better to drop out for a year than hang by a thread, was the theory. I was on notice to shape up and get serious about higher education.

I was pretty disappointed with this turn of events as I stood on the highway trying to catch a ride home. I was unsure what I was going to do with the rest of my life. I still liked the possibilities of becoming a landscape engineer, but I knew whatever happened, it was up to Roger to prove himself.

As I stood there, thumb in the air, a shiny red pickup braked to a halt. The driver, who looked old enough to be retired, nodded to me to climb in. His name was James Patrick Hopkins Healy, and as we headed down the highway west of Oneida he asked what I was doing. I explained how things had been going in my life and he chuckled. Then I mentioned my interest in landscape engineering.

"Landscape engineering," he said. "Know what business I'm in? I have a nursery at Sherrill, near Oneida. I'm a landscape engineer."

He said he was en route to a large nursery in Massachusetts to

44 • 7hose Syracuse Girls

get trees to transplant to his nursery. We continued talking about the landscaping business and at one point he made me a tempting offer.

"I'll pay you ten dollars a day, six or seven days a week," he proposed, "and you'd be learning the business."

"That's a lot of money," I replied. "That's big money."

"Sure it is," he agreed. "But I need someone who can *work*. I need someone who can keep up with me."

I guessed him to be sixty or maybe sixty-five years of age. At nineteen, I was ready to take on the world.

"I'll take the job," I said on the spot. We shook hands, and just like that, I had embarked on a new career.

Those Syracuse Girls • 45

The Uniform Beckons

Winter, 1953 . . .

Working alongside "Pop" Healy, I realized what a dynamo of a man he was. It seemed he never stopped. I managed to keep up with him, but it was a challenge. Pop Healy knew the landscaping business inside and out. He taught me more than I imagined I could learn. True to his word, we put in a six-day week. We even worked on Sunday when he had a big job to finish.

Pop became like another father to me. His love of the outdoors was second only to daddy's. In the evenings, we sat around, talking. We did a lot of talking. Pop never missed an opportunity to encourage me to get back in school and finish my degree.

The best conversations I had with Pop were the ones in which he shared his experiences in the Navy. He had been an enlisted man during World War I and served with the Seabees in World War II. Naturally he was partial to the Navy, and whenever I expressed an interest in the service he would tell me to consider trying for an appointment to the U.S. Naval Academy.

It seemed my fascination with the Navy had been a passing phase from my high school days. Lately I was dreaming of flying, and thought the U.S. Air Force might be the place for me. It was the same journey that two of my brothers, Jack and Gerard had taken . . . perhaps I too would walk this path to Lackland Air Force Base in San Antonio, Texas.

Finally, on December 16, 1953, I enlisted in the Air Force at Albany, New York. With high hopes I completed the in-processing and looked forward to "seeing the world." To my surprise we were not put on an airplane, but on a train! We did not head south, but north. Well, wherever they were taking me it didn't matter. I was happy, and proud. Now I had joined the ranks of all the Donlons and Howards who had preceded me in the service of our country. I repeated the Oath of Enlistment over and over to myself.

The train rolled to a stop at Samson Air Force Base on Lake Geneva in upstate New York. Presently the booming voice of a seasoned drill instructor put the fear of God in each new recruit. As we followed him into the dark, cold, winter night I wondered if I would survive to join the rest of the men in my family as proud veterans.

Orientation the next day covered everything from A to Z. While touring the chapel I picked up a bulletin so I would have the mass schedule. I was sure I would need the prayer and solace that weekly mass would provide. Later that night I took the folded bulletin from my pocket. The title of a small article caught my eye:

Philosophy of Life

Believe it or not —

Once upon a time the Devil decided to go out of business. He offered his tools for sale to whoever would pay the price.

On the night of the sale, they were all attractively displayed, a bad-looking lot. They were Malice, Hatred, Envy, Jealousy, Sensuality, Deceit, and all the other implements of evil. Each was marked with its price.

Apart from the rest lay a harmless looking wedge-shaped tool, much worn, yet priced higher than any of the others. Someone asked the Devil what it was.

"That is Discouragement," was the reply.

"Why do you have it priced so high?"

"Because," replied the Devil, "it is more useful to me than any of the others. I can pry open and get inside a man's conscience with that when I could not get near him with any of the others, and once inside, I can use him in whatever way suits me best. It is so much worn because I use it with nearly everybody, as very few people yet know it belongs to me."

It hardly needs to be added that the Devil had such a high price on Discouragement that it was never sold. He still owns it and is still using it. Beware of it!

48 • *The Uniform Beckons*

The words hit so close to home for me! Even though I was seemingly happy with the new choice I had made, a cloud of remorse still hung over my head because of my college failure. I cut the article out of the bulletin and placed it in my footlocker. This "Philosophy of Life" reminded me of something daddy used to say, "Roger, remember, after any setback in life, get up quickly. Never let yourself become discouraged."

Upon completing boot camp I was retained at Samson and joined the cadre team as a drill instructor. I began with a small detail of recruits, progressing until I became a flight leader with ninety recruits to supervise. My superiors supported my desire to apply for the newly established U.S. Air Force Academy. I took the competitive exam, and passed. Perhaps my dream of flying would come true after all! I was excited about the prospect of being in the very first class to graduate from this new institution.

For administrative reasons my reporting date was delayed. During this time I was sent for a second physical exam. The words the doctor wrote on my record devastated me.

"The left eye of this patient may have the beginning of cataracts." Aloud he said, "Scratch roster number nineteen."

Another dream crushed! I was a wounded and disappointed young airman. Back in my barracks I dug into my footlocker and reread "Philosophy of Life." After some prayer and contemplation I reset my career compass. Maybe I could not fly, but I could still serve. I decided to apply for the U.S. Military Academy at West Point.

I set out for the Academy's prep school at Stewart Field in Newburgh, New York, to take the entrance exam. My score was not high enough for entrance in 1954. It was suggested I remain at Stewart, attend the winter prep school session, and try for acceptance the following year. That is what I did, and was assigned to Headquarters, Eastern Air Defense Command, at Stewart, as an airman third class. I would begin with the next class in 1955.

Meanwhile, I decided on a more direct approach. I was granted a three-day pass and boarded the train to Washington, D.C. Once I had reached the capital I obtained a roster of the Senate and House

The Uniform Beckons • **49**

of Representatives, plus the Senators from the territories of Hawaii and Alaska.

I began knocking on congressional doors. That first three-day pass was unproductive, so I returned on subsequent leaves until I had called at every single Congressional office on Capitol Hill, checking off names as I worked through the long list. I made up my mind that if a Congressional appointment to the Academy was available anywhere, they would know I wanted it. It was a determined assault, but it didn't work. As I reached the end of my list of Senators and Congressmen I realized there were a lot of polite ways to say "no."

Reflecting on my strategy, I suppose it was presumptuous for a twenty-year-old airman third class to tackle the entire Senate and House of Representatives as I did. At the time, it seemed logical enough, and once committed I remained steadfast to the end. It was the way I operated. Once, on a mountain climbing expedition with Troop 36, we were confronted by a blizzard. Most of the Troop wanted to turn back, but Joe Lahoud and I struggled to the summit. It was that same resolve that prompted me to tackle the Congress.

Representative J. Ernest Wharton, from Richmondville, New York, was my Congressman at that time. He told me he deeply regretted he could not be of more help. His allotted number of service academy appointments had already been announced. He gave me some alternative suggestions, showed me around the House chamber, took me to lunch in the congressional dining room and gave me passes to the Army-Senator Joseph McCarthy hearings. He pointed out the hole in the wall where a bullet struck above his head as he sat at his desk on March 1, 1954, when Puerto Rican terrorists wounded five Congressmen in an assault on the House of Representatives.

I even called at the office of Vice President Nixon, who wasn't in at the time. I considered trying at the White House, but decided against it.

What I was unable to accomplish by Congressional appointment I finally obtained on my own. I returned to the academy prep school

50 • *The Uniform Beckons*

at Stewart and on the second try, passed the entrance exam. On July 5, 1955, I was discharged from the Air Force and admitted to the U.S. Military Academy. It wasn't the first time I had marched across the parade ground at West Point, however, or worn a cadet uniform, for that matter. Prep-school students were permitted to use the academy's gymnasium, and I was among those selected to don uniforms and march as "cadet extras" in some of the scenes during filming of the movie *The Long Gray Line*.

My first day at "Beast Barracks" is one I will always remember. Upperclassmen kept us plebes on the run almost continuously. A battery of commands, many contradictory, besieged us. I remember thinking we were always supposed to be someplace else—in a different uniform. It was intentional organized confusion, and that was that. It was impossible to please our cadet captain, whom we called our "king of the beasts," and that was also part of the strategy.

One day early on in my freshman year I was standing at attention, chin flat against my throat and not a muscle moving, as we waited for an inspection by the commandant of cadets.

The commandant of cadets stopped and addressed me.

"Do you know who I am? he demanded.

"Yes sir. The commandant of cadets."

"Do you know who this is," he said, gesturing toward the acting cadet captain.

"Yes, sir. The king of beasts."

To this day I don't know why I said it. It just came out. I received a lecture on the inappropriateness of my description of the cadet captain that left me thinking I had come within an inch of having committed treason.

I had one advantage over the other plebes. I was twenty-one, and a couple of years older than my classmates. And I had had the benefit of nineteen months of prior service. For one thing I discovered that upper classmen who had also had prior service were more willing to help me out. It didn't cut anything if you happened to be out of line, though.

One day we plebes were lined up in South Area, where we were

The Uniform Beckons • 51

billeted, awaiting orders of the day from upper classmen before we were released to stand the next formation. Well, a young woman who I remember was a particularly "good looker," happened to be passing by.

This was an opportunity for upper classmen to ogle, provided they were not in formation at the moment. Plebes, on the other hand, may not even so much as move an eyeball while outdoors in formation. I was convinced that upper classmen had some sixth sense and could hear a plebe's eyeballs move.

For whatever the reason, our cadet commander gave us a right face command, so every eyeball was directed at this feminine vision. Maybe it was because he had gotten to West Point through the enlisted ranks. Then he gave us a left face and dismissed us. I came to realize it was a gesture typical of him, and unquestionably one we all appreciated. Afterward I approached him.

"Sir, may I ask a question, sir?"

"Yes," he responded. "What's your question, mister?"

"You think my sister Adrienne is pretty sharp, don't you?"

"Mister," he exploded in my face, "report to my room."

Again, I'm not sure why I loaded my foot into my mouth. It just happened that way. This little bit of familiarity, unintentional as it was, cost me extra duty as a "B.J."—Bold Before June. June is that wonderful month when a plebe transitions into a yearling and can finally relax—a bit. He can even speak without asking permission and others can actually address him by his first name.

Being called "Roger" or "Pete" or whatever was something we simply did not hear outside our barracks. It was "mister this" and "mister that" and we detested it. But it was all part of the academy experience. Finally, on the day before graduation, the firsties came through the ranks and shook hands, saying good-bye, calling us by our first name. You weren't sure until that moment that they even knew you had a first name.

We were informed we could try out for any sport we thought we could manage. Having lettered in six-man football, I decided I would go out for the football team. On the first day of practice I knew this hadn't been one of my better ideas.

"Okay, men, we're going to have some blocking practice," someone announced.

But there weren't any blocking dummies to be seen. Then we realized what blocking practice entailed. We were to throw blocks at one of the coaches, Felix "Doc" Blanchard. This legendary two-time All-American was known as "Mr. Inside." Blanchard stood there, grinning. We discovered that trying to block him was like trying to block a granite pillar. You just bounced off. If you were big, fast and experienced, he simply sidestepped.

There was an advantage to the plebes who went out for a sport—eating in the corps squad area with the other athletes. They weren't into hazing. Mealtime in the corps squad area was *peaceful*.

Well, I decided I wanted to tackle something out of the ordinary after my momentary brush with West Point football, so I signed up for lacrosse. I had little knowledge of the game and hadn't played it, but most of us were in the same boat.

One football player, All-American end Don Hollender who became one of Army's great quarterbacks, would run laps with us to keep in shape during the off-season. I remember thinking it was like running with one of the Greek gods. One day we were doing hundred-yard wind sprints when he challenged me.

"Beat me and I'll buy you a pint of ice cream," he offered. "Yes, sir!" I replied. I beat him by a stride. I'm not sure if he let me win, but I don't think so, because I was able to beat him on a couple of other occasions, with no ice cream in the balance.

Coach Touchstone was taking it all in.

"You're pretty fast," he said. The next thing I knew I was assigned center midfield, the lacrosse position that goes to the fastest man, since he roams the entire field. Lacrosse, I am told, was devised by the Indians to train their braves. I enjoyed the experience. Plebes played only intramural lacrosse. It was called "the intra-murder league." Our company won the corps squad championship in lacrosse. I also ran cross-country that first year at "the Point."

But in the classroom, where it counted, I was confronted by my

The Uniform Beckons • 53

old nemesis, mathematics. I was managing my other subjects, but algebra, analytical and spherical geometry and calculus were my undoing.

I saw the handwriting on the blackboard and, along with a couple of other plebes, withdrew in June 1956. I moved to New York City. It was my plan to try for re-entry in January. The three of us found Doc Silverman, a wonderful gentleman who had once worked with Albert Einstein. Doc Silverman made a career of tutoring young men like us. We moved in with Doc, who lived on Clay Avenue in the Bronx. Again, my brother Paul became my banker.

Silverman was the typical kindly, patient professor. He spoke with a thick German accent. Early in the morning he would knock on the door of our third-floor room and call out, "Vake up, boys. Time to r-r-rise undt zhine! The sun's ar-r-isen!"

After a breakfast of juice, milk, cereal and coffee we were bombarded with math. Professor Silverman knew his math, and for the rest of the summer he did his best to pound it into us.

I became fascinated with the Clay Avenue neighborhood where we were boarding. So many different nationalities, with everyone speaking their native language, punctuated now and again with a few words of English. Ethnic differences were never brought home to me more clearly than the time I strode into a delicatessen and ordered a ham sandwich.

"This is a Kosher delicatessen," the proprietor responded, chuckling at my gaffe.

Eating was always a problem. Food was expensive and we were always short of money. Professor Silverman loaned us a hot plate, which helped stretch our funds, but we existed on a diet of mostly peanut butter sandwiches and beer. We would accumulate empty beer bottles until we could turn them in for the deposit money. When we could afford to splurge we would head for a Chinese restaurant.

Our budget allowed us a quart of beer a night. We divided it three ways and sipped, during study breaks. For diversion we would open a window and jeer at the children who were playing in the street below. These were street-savvy youths and they replied in kind. What we hadn't bargained for was that they were laying for us the next day, ready to pounce on us with buckets of water. Once as they cut loose with their bucket barrage we sidestepped and their salvo inundated some worshippers emerging from a synagogue. Doc Silverman came to our defense. He said it was all the fault of "dose brats" who kept pestering "mein boys."

Only once did he ever loose patience with us. It happened at the end of a several days period when it seemed that we just couldn't absorb anything. Our slide rules weren't sliding and we found ourselves questioning whether we could even add two and two. We stayed awake studying so late one night that none of us responded to the professor's wake-up knock. He opened the door and entered our room.

"Ach! Gott im Himmel! No vonder you don't learn," he declared. "Look at all der beer you been drinking!"

It did look like we had had a helluva party the night before. There were beer bottles everywhere. Twenty-one "dead soldiers." Eventually he accepted our explanation that those twenty-one empties represented three weeks worth of rather moderate sipping.

Sundays were our only free days, and we took to roaming the beaches. Girl patrol. But our real objective was not so much feminine companionship as it was food. We would look at these young women not from a perspective of possible romance but on how good their mothers might be in the kitchen. Later we would compare notes on our "cuisine conquests."

We went to Governors Island in August, took the re-entrance exam, and passed. We bid good-bye to Professor Silverman and headed our separate ways. I needed to work until the start of the second semester and was lucky to land a job as a ticket agent with Eastern Airlines at their East Side terminal in New York.

Upon re-entering West Point I was assigned to my original company, C Company of the First Regiment. Things went much better in the classroom and that is where I put my focus. My time under Doc Silverman's roof had developed good study habits.

The Uniform Beckons • 55

As the semester progressed I began to realize that at age twenty-three I was very old to be a plebe. After all that I had been through to gain entrance to, and remain at West Point, the unthinkable was about to happen. I resigned in April of 1957 for personal reasons. It has come to be the one decision that I made in my life that I regret the most.

Airman Basic Donlon
Samson AFB, New York
1953

Cadet Donlon
United States Military Academy
West Point, New York
1955

A Civilian Life?

April, 1957 . . .

A little bitter and very unhappy that spring of 1957, I was angry at myself . . . angry at the world in general. But it is hard to stay unhappy or angry at the age of twenty-three. Harder still to be wrapped up in yourself around my Aunt Lilly Enders who offered me a temporary place to live. Aunt Lilly was my mother's sister, and like mother, one of the most unselfish people I have ever known. Her home, in New York City, was a happy, holy place and it changed my outlook on life as I searched for work in busy Manhattan. Aunt Lilly is gone now, but in her younger years she was a top-flight designer and seamstress by day. At night she worked into the wee hours making church vestments for which she never charged a penny. During her lifetime she made enough vestments and altar cloth, down to the last stitch of embroidery, to outfit an army of priests. And for no earthly reward . . . only prayers, which always seemed to be answered.

Hired by the International Business Machines Corporation as a demonstrator in their data processing "library," I showed customers what the machines could do, and helped them set up their own programs. It was great fun, and I liked the idea of being a white-collar worker, strutting around the big city in a suit and tie.

When I was introduced around the office, one girl caught my eye. Her name was Carol and she was one of the young "elite," a programmer who understood the machines enough to set up the entire basis on which they did their computing. Carol was a brunette, my own age, very pretty, and intelligent too! Soon I was walking her home, taking her to parties, and on dinner dates. She was a native New Yorker through and through, born on Long Island and a graduate of Queens College with a degree in political science. Carol was wonderful to be with. She was trim and athletic and enjoyed tennis, hiking, swimming, sailing and similar sports.

It was an idyllic summer. On the weekends we would get away from the sweltering city. I took her home to Saugerties a couple of times, and we also visited with her parents on Long Island. My brother, Paul, had rented a beach cottage on Long Island with some of his friends and they invited us there as well. Carol and I were falling in love.

Toward the end of June we began to talk about marriage. Carol was not a Catholic, although her mother had been, and she wanted to join the Church. She began taking instructions at St. Patrick's Cathedral.

It was a happy day for me when Carol was baptized. I had visions of the life ahead of us, perfect in every detail. We began to make plans for our wedding. After talking with our families we set the date for the wedding, Columbus Day, October 12, 1957.

The marriage would take place in a church near Carol's home. Carol looked beautiful coming down the aisle in a white gown. I was a typically nervous groom, uncomfortable in striped pants and cutaway. The church was full of relatives and friends, mostly relatives in my case because of my large family. Carol's father was everywhere with his camera, recording the loss of his only child.

We finally broke away from all the festivities, changed into traveling clothes, and waded through a hail of rice to our car. It was booby-trapped, of course, with tin cans and old shoes, and a sign proclaiming, "Just Married."

Even though Carol was very close to her family we decided to relocate to another part of the country. And so, off we went in the flashy black and white 1949 Chrysler convertible with the red upholstery that we had chipped in to buy.

Carol had good job prospects in Baton Rouge, Louisiana. She knew IBM machines thoroughly, and had even written a technical manual for one of the biggest. I was confident that I, too, would find work and had no qualms about being able to provide for Carol and myself.

The Esso Standard Oil Company hired Carol as a computer-programmer. I accepted a job at Louisiana State University helping to set up an expansion of the LSU library for computing data. We found a small garage apartment and life was good. It was full of Cajun food and strong coffee. We attended LSU football games where everybody stood up and sang *"Dixie,"* and took an occasional trip to New Orleans.

On the day of my interview with the president of LSU, I pondered over his name, Troy H. Middleton. As I was ushered into his office, and introduced, I couldn't resist.

"Excuse me, sir," I said, saluting sharply, "do you happen to have a son named Troy H. Middleton, Jr., who is a captain in the U.S. Army?"

"He's a major now," growled the retired General Middleton, who had commanded a Corps in Europe during World War II.

"Son-of-a-gun!" I responded. "He was my commanding officer at the Academy Prep School. It's a small world!"

Over the next few months, while working at LSU, I chatted about military matters a couple of times with General Middleton. The tug toward a military life still haunted me. I also struck up an acquaintance with an Army recruiting sergeant. He discussed the various programs with me, especially my chances for attending Officer Candidate School.

I don't remember exactly how the subject came up, but one night Carol and I discussed OCS. I shared with her how I was aching to get back into an Army uniform. We both knew that as an officer I would be better able to provide for us, and more importantly, for the baby that was now on the way.

Not unhappily, Carol said, "I always thought you would go back in. If that is what you want, go ahead and do it."

And so, I made plans to catch a bus to New Orleans. Carol would join me later at Fort Chaffee, Arkansas, where I would be sent for basic training. Before I left she gave me this poem by Douglas Malloch:

A Civilian Life? • 59

Be the Best of Whatever You Are

If you can't be a pine on the top of the hill,
Be a scrub in the valley—but be
The best little scrub by the side of the hill;
Be a bush if you can't be a tree.

If you can't be a bush be a bit of the grass,
And some highway happier make;
If you can't be a muskie then just be a bass—
But the liveliest bass in the lake!

We can't all be captains; we've got to be crew,
There's something for all of us here,
There's big work to do, and there's lesser to do,
And the task you must do is the near.

If you can't be a highway then just be a trail,
If you can't be the sun be a star;
It isn't by size that you win or you fail—
Be the best of whatever you are!

The Uniform Beckons . . . Again

February 5, 1958 . . .

It was a long eighty-five mile ride to the Federal Building in New Orleans. I was already missing Carol, and feeling pretty guilty about leaving her alone in Baton Rouge. I consoled myself with the thought that it would not be long before she would join me at Fort Chaffee. I knew that my officer aspirations would be beneficial to us in the long run and to the baby that was due in a few months.

I took the Oath of Enlistment for the second time, and was soon on my way to Arkansas. When my records were checked upon my arrival at Fort Chaffee, I was made an acting platoon sergeant based upon my prior Air Force service.

That indirectly landed me in the hospital for three months. Trying to be first at reveille formation, I rushed out of my barracks and slipped on a brick. I tore all the ligaments in my right ankle and spent most of February, and all of March and April trying to get it to heal. This happened just a few days after Carol arrived and she was left to fend mostly for herself.

It was an unhappy situation. Even if I had not been in the hospital, I would have been living in the barracks. This meant that Carol had to find an apartment for herself in town, somewhere cheap, as money was in short supply now that she was not working. Another garage apartment was the solution, but I could tell that she was certainly not thrilled with the arrangement.

The day I was discharged from the hospital they gave me a "physical profile," classifying me as a "permanent three." This meant the ankle was permanently flawed and I would have to have limited duty for the rest of my career. I argued with the personnel sergeant that I was perfectly all right for full duty. I requested assignment to a regular platoon, pending transfer to advanced infantry training at Fort Jackson, South Carolina, and action on the request I had submitted for officer training. He finally agreed to send me to the platoon, but he insisted the limited-duty profile had to go into my records.

"All right," I said. "I'll take it over there myself."

He gave me a fishy look. After a moment's hesitation, he handed over the piece of paper.

It was a windy day, as I recall. Somehow, on the way to company headquarters where my records were, the paper slipped out of my hand. I don't know where it went. At headquarters, nobody asked about it, and I never mentioned it. As far as I know, nothing about limited duty was ever put in my records.

Because of my hospitalization I was "recycled" and began basic training sometime in May. Spending most of my time in the field, I hardly saw Carol at all. In early June I was in the field again when Carol went into labor. It was a difficult birth, but Linda Lee Donlon was finally born on June 4, 1958.

Word was sent to the field that I had become a father, and I was given a few hours to visit the hospital. Going back to my training duties, I did not see Carol and Linda again until the day I brought them home. Then it was back to the field again for another round of training. A few days later I was called into the company commander's office.

"Do you know how to make a formula?" he asked.

"A chemical formula, sir?"

"No. A baby formula."

"Heck, no, sir. I haven't been in the business long enough to know that!"

"You are going to have to learn fast," he said. "Your wife is back in the hospital, hemorrhaging. She's going to be all right. But they can't keep the baby. They can't put her in the ward with the mother and she's too young to be put in a ward with other youngsters who are sick. So they're sending her home. And you, my friend, are on administrative leave as of right now."

I went to the hospital, comforted Carol as best I could, and took

62 • *The Uniform Beckons . . . Again*

Linda home. A nurse came along with pre-mixed formulas good for a couple of days. The nurse showed me how to wash and change Linda, how to heat the formula and test it on my wrist, and so on.

Now we were on our own, Linda and I. She was so tiny, and perfect in every detail. I spent hours marveling at her little fingers and toes. When she was asleep I would tiptoe to her crib and carefully put my ear to her chest to hear her little heart beating. Not every father is totally entrusted with the care of his newborn child, and I became very bonded to this wonderful little miracle. I felt that love for her would cause me to burst with joy.

Finally, after a hectic couple of weeks, Carol was released from the hospital. She was pale, and tired easily, so one of her relatives came to help care for both her and Linda.

When my orders for Fort Jackson came through in mid-August, we decided I would have to go ahead. Carol would follow with the baby when she felt stronger. I took the car and a rented trailer, filled with some of our household goods. After reporting in at Fort Jackson I started looking for an apartment. But then Carol wrote that she was still feeling weak and wanted to go home with her mother. I put the furniture in storage. It was the beginning of the end.

During the eight weeks I was undergoing rigorous training in advanced Infantry tactics I focused all of my attention to the duty at hand. Never a great communicator, I'm sure my weekly letters to Carol were inadequate. What little pay I was drawing prevented me from making any lengthy phone calls. I could see things gradually slipping away, but I seemed powerless to stop it.

I stayed on after my eight weeks were completed. My duties were as an instructor in various "acting" capacities, like acting platoon sergeant, but still a private. My orders to OCS should have come through by then. When I checked, I discovered I had indeed been selected for officer candidate school, but *those* papers were lost. I submitted new papers and waited, wondering if I was ever going to leave Fort Jackson, become an officer, and reunite with my little family.

Finally the new orders did arrive. I left Fort Jackson in January of 1959 and enrolled in OCS at Fort Benning, Georgia. Over the next six months I concentrated all my efforts on obtaining my commission. My letters to Carol grew fewer and farther between. In my heart my goal was to succeed for all of us. Somehow I was never able to get this message across.

By this time I'm sure that Carol had grown weary of the separations, and my lack of attention to her and Linda. Even though I was now a second lieutenant, she was reluctant to join me at Fort Jackson. She knew I was lost in my work. A divorce seemed to be the only answer.

When next I saw Carol it was in her lawyer's office. I tried my best to explain that as a lifelong and devoted Catholic I could not agree to a divorce. Carol said she understood, but would go ahead with the necessary paperwork anyway. She agreed to let me see Linda, and the three of us went for a walk on the beach.

Just a little over a year old then, Linda was a suntanned and chubby cherub. She had golden hair and blue eyes. She was so perfect I could hardly believe she was part of me, or even of this world. She was full of surprises and quick changes of mood. I knew I would cherish this visit for the rest of my life. Linda was the good that came from this marriage. Nothing could ever change that.

I returned to the U.S. Army Training Center at Fort Jackson. My promotion to first lieutenant came on Christmas Eve, 1960. I progressed in jobs from company officer through instructor and company commander to staff officer.

Early in 1961 I received word that the divorce had been granted. I was still very much in love with Carol but it was time to move on. I was pained by the distance between Linda and me, and would have liked to visit with her more often. I was afraid she would grow up not knowing who I was.

My fear turned into reality the next time I saw Linda. It was in September 1961, and I was on my way to a new assignment in Alaska. Linda didn't know me. She was three years old, and I was just a nice man who came around that day. I played with her in the

64 • The Uniform Beckons ... Again

park, on the swings and seesaws; bought her a big doll, some toys and clothes. Soon, I sped away in a little Volkswagen, which had replaced the big old Chrysler convertible I had turned over to her mother two years before.

By going to Alaska I would be even farther away from Linda. I consoled myself by the thought that it would not be forever. I would return in a couple of years. Little did I know, but it would be nineteen years before I would see Linda again.

**Daughter, Linda Lee Donlon
Age 3**

North to Alaska

September, 1961 . . .

Sightseeing every mile of the way, I drove across the continent. The beauty of the land and the feeling of pride and love of our country helped to ease the anguish I was feeling over my failed marriage. Although I looked forward to my new assignment in Alaska, I felt empty without Carol, and especially without Linda.

When I reached Seattle, I put the VW aboard a ship bound for Seward, and flew to Fairbanks. My duty would be at Fort Jonathan Wainwright; I would be a platoon leader in E Company, 1st Battle Group, 9th Infantry. The *"Manchus,"* as they were known, was a unit with a long combat history. Their motto was *"Keep Up the Fire,"* which seemed appropriate for Alaska.

This was my first experience with a line company. I realized it, since up to that time all of my battles had been fought in the classroom.

After six months with the 9th Infantry, in typical Army fashion I found myself back in school, this time at the Cold Weather Operations and Ski Instructor Course. I loved it! I learned to ski without breaking anything and I enjoyed the snowy mountains.

One day I received a message to report to the office of the commanding general at Fort Wainwright. The first thought that entered my mind was some emergency back home. I answered the urgent summons as quickly as my skis and a ride hitched on a truck would deliver me to headquarters.

Upon arrival I was informed the general wanted to talk to me about becoming his aide-de-camp. Well, Brigadier General Lester L. Wheeler evidenced no particular surprise when I said I was not the best man for the job.

"Sir, I am pleased and proud to be considered for this position, but I am not cut out to be an aide," I said. "Besides," I protested, "I don't even know what an aide does. Sir, you should know that I washed out of West Point twice and even failed in keeping my marriage together. I'm just not a smooth type. I'm a field soldier, sir, I love being in the field with my men."

We talked for a while before I left General Wheeler's office, intent upon hitching a flight back to Fort Greeley. Colonel Frank Naughton caught up with me.

"You've got just fifteen minutes to report to the general," he announced.

"I want you for my aide," General Wheeler said. "Do you want the job?"

"Yes, sir," I answered, much to my own surprise.

My return flight to Fort Greeley was aboard General Wheeler's helicopter. Three weeks later I graduated and for the next year or so I served as the general's aide. Looking back on the experience I would have to admit I came to like the assignment.

It was an honor to have worked for General Wheeler. He demonstrated a rare combination of intelligence, courage, dignity, and humor. A 1935 graduate of West Point, he saw action in the Pacific during World War II and Korea. Along the way he was decorated with no less than two Legions of Merit, two Silver Stars, two Combat Infantryman Badges, and five Bronze Stars with V for valor. He is the essence of what every good officer should be.

Complementing this quintessential general was one of the most gracious women I have ever known. The term "lady" could have been created for Dottie Wheeler. Coming from a family with service dating back to the Revolution, Mrs. Wheeler was totally committed to the Army community. They were a formidable team, and everyone loved and respected them.

Of course, being the general's aide meant I had a lot of interfacing to do with Mrs. Wheeler. She was the most patient of women, and under her gentle tutelage the rough-hewn lieutenant learned the ropes of proper etiquette and decorum.

As the months lengthened into a year, it was nearing time for the general to leave Alaska. Having spent all of his tour in command, he had not taken the time to enjoy the opportunities for hunting and

68 • North to Alaska

fishing. I knew the general really wanted to go bear hunting, and so I arranged his schedule to include a few days of leave.

Since I was the impetus for his hunting trip, it was I who got to climb the mountain and rout the sleeping bear from its den. With one shot, the general felled the huge black bear.

With General Wheeler was his good friend, Jim Messer, a high ranking local civilian. As I watched them climb toward me I recalled how the Indians killed bears as a rite of passage to manhood. But they also respected and revered the bear in legends and religious ceremonies. To the Indians the spirit of this bear represented intelligence, strength and courage.

When the general and Mr. Messer reached the spot where I was sitting alongside the bear, it dawned on me that as the junior member of the hunting party I would probably have the honor of skinning the bear.

Up to this time, skinning a squirrel or rabbit had been my only experience. The general and Mr. Messer talked me through the process, and when I had properly disposed of the bear, I took the huge hide upon my back and started down the mountain.

"Roger, you look like a six-foot bear coming down the mountain," the general said. "Better turn the hide inside out before someone else takes a shot!"

Well, the general proudly displayed that bearskin on his wall for many years. When he and Mrs. Wheeler finally retired to a smaller home, he sent the "bear" to me. It was packed in the same box that I had used more than twenty years before!

In June 1963, General Wheeler was assigned to Third Army at Fort McPherson, Atlanta, Georgia, as chief of staff. His new duties did not rate an aide-de-camp, so he asked what I might like to do.

"Special Forces, sir," I responded. I explained that I had expressed a preference for Special Forces three years earlier, before I left Fort Jackson. I had also put in for communications school and Alaska. When I was granted those two I asked that my Special Forces request be held up, not wanting to jeopardize the Alaska assignment.

"You're sure Special Forces is what you want, Roger?"

I replied in the affirmative.

"Okay, then, let's see what we can do about getting you into Special Forces."

I departed Alaska with mixed feelings. I had come to thrive on the frontier experience. The people, both military and civilian, were friendly, and we lived and worked harmoniously.

When General Wheeler retired from active duty in August of 1965 he gave me one of the proudest and most meaningful experiences of my life. Along with his two sons and son-in-law, I was asked to stand with him as part of his ceremonial staff. All of us were in uniform, the general's younger son Tom wearing his military school uniform. Three of us were serving on active duty as officers in the Army. In his closing remarks, the general referred to us as he said, "This is my legacy to the Army; use them, they are well prepared."

Brigadier General Lester L. Wheeler was the closest thing I had to a father in my adult life.

Brigadier General Lester L. Wheeler, Mrs. Wheeler, Captain Donlon, and President Johnson at The White House December 5, 1964.

The Quiet Professionals

Spring, 1963 . . .

The seed of my dream to join Special Forces had been planted in 1958. At the time I was a young enlisted soldier at Fort Jackson, South Carolina. Don Lunday, another young enlisted soldier, served with me in the G-3 proficiency-training group. Later we would go on to OCS together.

As our friendship grew we found ourselves sharing stories about other members of our respective families who had served in uniform. Don spoke with such pride and respect of his brother, Bob, who was serving with Special Forces. It was evident that Don's brother was his idol and role model, just as my brother, Paul, was mine. Both of our brothers were combat veterans.

After OCS, when I inquired about Special Forces, I was disappointed when told that as an officer, I needed to be a very senior first lieutenant or captain.

Now, twenty-nine years old, I was about to be promoted to captain. The experience in the Arctic had raised my self-confidence to new heights. This new found confidence was a combination of all the training the Army had invested in me to date . . . it was high time to give something back.

In the Arctic we faced bitter cold, and came to respect and plan for what could be devastating effects on men and machinery. These experiences had impressed upon me how *teamwork* could and would lead to victory over the elements. Teamwork was the by-product of tough, realistic training—a lesson that transcends all climatic conditions.

I knew the true value of training was to overcome the obstacles, no matter what, and that ninety per cent of any battle is won in the mind. The soldier who is disciplined and determined, aggressive and tenacious, goes into battle equipped to win. The rest is a combination of skill and experience.

To earn the right to wear the Green Beret meant tough training. Training tougher and more demanding than any I had ever undergone before. I was ready for the challenge, and if I survived I would join the ranks of the Army's best . . . U.S. Army Special Forces.

Following his inauguration in 1961, President Kennedy expressed concern about the guerrilla capability of our armed forces. He came away from a briefing concerned that there were only 800 men in the Army's Special Forces with a behind-enemy-lines mission capability.

President Kennedy directed that the 2,500 authorized strength of Special Forces be increased to 5,000, with special emphasis on counter-insurgency. In doing so he added the primary role of guerrilla warfare, and the broader role of nation building.

He visited Fort Bragg on April 11, 1962, where he witnessed a Special Forces demonstration. The President departed Fort Bragg convinced we were moving in the right direction, in combating what the Communists termed their "wars of national liberation."

That spring day in 1962 President Kennedy wrote the Army:

"Pure military skill is not enough. A full spectrum of military, paramilitary, and civil action must be blended to produce success. The enemy uses economic and political warfare, propaganda and naked military aggression in an endless combination to oppose a free choice of government, and suppress the rights of the individual by terror, by subversion, and by force of arms.

"To win in this struggle, our officers and men must understand and combine the political, economic, and civil actions with skilled military efforts in the execution of this mission.

"The Green Beret is again becoming a symbol of excellence, a badge of courage, a mark of distinction in the fight for freedom. I know the United States Army will live up to its reputation for imagination, resourcefulness, and spirit as we meet this challenge."

With these very words Special Forces took on new meaning. With the support of the President and under the direction of Secretary of Defense McNamara, the Army accelerated training in counter-insurgency with Special Forces at the "point" position.

President Kennedy became "the titular father of Special Forces." Their headquarters at Fort Bragg is named the U.S. Army John F. Kennedy Center for Special Warfare. There you will see a bronze bust of President Kennedy, enshrined in a memorial building built entirely with private funds, mostly from Special Forces personnel.

The President elevated Special Forces to a new level and officially gave them the distinctive Green Beret. The history of Special Forces predates the Kennedy Presidency. Their traditions are rooted in our Native Americans, who became skilled in the art of hit-and-run guerrilla warfare, and in Rogers' Rangers and the other pioneers who overcame the Indians.

There was Lieutenant Colonel Francis Marion, the legendary "Swamp Fox" who went up against British Regulars and Tories in the Revolution. There was Colonel John Singleton Mosby, the "Grey Ghost" of the Confederacy. Marion and Mosby understood and used the same strategy and tactics, which would later be adopted by China's Mao Tse-tung, Cuba's Ernesto "Che" Guevara, and North Vietnam's Truong Chinh and Vo Nguyen Giap.

World War II saw Americans by the thousands operating as guerrillas. There was Captain Donald Blackburn, trapped behind enemy lines in the Philippines, who rejected surrender and formed guerrilla units that battled until final victory in 1945.

There was Colonel William J. Donovan's Office of Strategic Services and Brigadier General Frank D. Merrill's 5307th Composite Unit (Provisional), which gained fame as the "Merrill's Marauders" of Burma.

The U.S. Army's first attempt to develop an entire unit capable of unconventional and extraordinary military action came with the establishment of the American-Canadian First Special Service Force, fighting in Italy and France under Lieutenant Colonel (later Major General) Robert Frederick.

The Rangers performed with distinction in North Africa and Italy under Colonel (posthumously Brigadier General) William O.

The Quiet Professionals • 73

Darby, and as airborne units in Korea. American advisers are credited with helping Greece and the Philippines turn back Communist guerrillas after World War II.

When the Army organized Special Forces in April 1952, it wanted paratroopers trained in day and night assault. It wanted men who were experienced ground troops, capable of amphibious assault, able to fight in mountains and jungles in the best guerrilla tradition. And moreover, they would be adept organizers and instructors, able to step onto unfamiliar soil and mold the indigenous personnel into an effective guerrilla army.

The first unit, the 10th Special Forces Group (Airborne) was formed at Fort Bragg together with the Psychological Warfare Center, moved to North Carolina from Fort Riley, Kansas. Colonel Aaron Bank, first commander of the 10th, and author of the book *From the OSS to the Green Beret,* looked back on the unit's formation:

"Unofficially on the nineteenth of June, 1952, I was assigned to the 10th Special Forces Group and activated the unit that same day with an effective strength of one officer, one warrant officer, and seven enlisted men. Our strength rapidly increased, and within approximately nine months we had a muster of over 1,000 personnel, of whom about 350 were officers."

In 1953 the 10th Special Forces Group took up station at Bad Tölz, West Germany. It left behind a cadre, which organized the 77th Special Forces Group (Airborne) at Fort Bragg. On June 1, 1957, a cadre from the 77th arrived on Okinawa to organize the lst Special Forces Group (Airborne). The 77th was redesignated the 7th Special Forces Group (Airborne) in June 1960. Two years later elements of the 7th deployed to Panama, activated as the 8th Special Forces Group (Airborne). Four additional groups were activated at Bragg; the 5th, 6th, and 3rd Special Forces Group (Airborne) and the Special Warfare Center Special Forces Training Group (Provisional) designated Airborne on April 10, 1963.

When I joined Special Forces, it was in a major growth mode. And I was ready to move as well. I flew off to Seattle, Washington, and on to Pontiac, Michigan. I bought a shiny new 1963 station wagon and headed for Saugerties, stopping in Chicago to see Adrienne and in New York to visit Paul. In August I reported to Smoke Bomb Hill at Bragg, where I joined the 5th Special Forces Group (Airborne).

I had read everything I could find about Special Forces. The following, while aimed at enlisted men, applies to all:

"So you want to wear the Green Beret? It takes a big man to wear it.

"Not big in size, but in courage, dedication, and in ideas. Let this be clear to you at the outset: Special Forces service is limited to those few soldiers who want to be nothing less than the best . . . and who can prove it both physically and mentally. In short, Special Forces is for special men only. Men who love their country and the ideals it stands for. Men who take deep pride in being members of the United States Army. Men who can teach as well as fight. Men who can think for themselves.

"The job of a Special Forces soldier isn't easy. You may be asked to go into action anywhere in the world to help defend freedom. You may have to work alone, or with a small group of men for long periods of time. You will be expected to solve some of the toughest problems that ever faced fighting men anywhere.

"This is why it takes a big man to wear the Green Beret. This is why it takes dedication and maturity; brains as well as brawn. This is why only a comparative few make the grade. But to those who make it, there's nothing like it. There is team spirit. There is important work. There's room for promotion. And there's a knowledge that says: I have served my country and the cause of freedom and I am proud of it!

"Those who wear the Green Beret are proud men, and justly so. Do you think you have what it takes to become one of them?"

The Quiet Professionals • 75

I was prepared to prove I had what it took. I had jump school and mountain training under my belt. While I had been weak in foreign language skills and had missed out on Ranger training because quotas were filled when I applied, I nevertheless believed I was ready for Special Forces and set my sights on earning the Green Beret.

At the Special Forces Center I was moved from the 5th to the 7th Special Forces Group (Airborne) because of my previous training in Alaska. That was where the 7th was to deploy. So in two short months after I said good-bye to Alaska, I was back for a three-month stint as adjutant to Special Forces C Detachment. The C Detachments were composed of 24 officers and senior NCOs, and constituted the primary command and control unit in the field, directing from three to eight B Detachments, each with 23 officers and senior NCOs. The B Detachments in turn exercised command and control over from four to twelve A Detachments, otherwise known as A Teams.

The A Team is the basic operating unit. Twelve men capable of taking on fifty of the enemy and trained to teach 1,500. We are not talking theory. An A Team is trained and equipped to organize a guerrilla force of 1,500. By its very name it must operate as a team, not as two commissioned officers and ten NCOs.

It is an Army truism that veteran NCOs run the unit and the officers—the successful ones—keep an eye on things and after a while they're able to run things a little, too. This was never truer than in Special Forces, due to the depth and variety of NCO training.

The two officers on an A Team operated as commander and as executive officer. The ten enlisted men were specialists: two each in operations and intelligence, communications, demolitions, weapons and medics. This enabled the twelve-man team to split into two six-man teams and perform double duty. Moreover, each man is trained in the other specialties, prepared to take over in the event of injury or death. Officers were expected to know as much as possible about all of the specialties.

The Special Warfare School was open to not only Army

76 • *The Quiet Professionals*

personnel, but also to Navy, Marines and Air Force officers, plus some U.S. Government civilian employees and selected officers from friendly foreign countries. Special Warfare School training focused on the three primary fields of special warfare: counter-insurgency, psychological operations, and unconventional warfare. The Special Forces Training Group (Airborne), considered the backbone of the Center, was tasked with training replacements for Special Forces.

Starting with a week devoted to orientation and training in methods of instruction, students move to specialty training: Eight weeks each for weapons and operations/intelligence, ten weeks for demolitions, sixteen weeks for communications and thirty-seven weeks for medics. All take five weeks of training in ambushes and raids, psychological and air operations, immediate-action drills, escape and evasion, and familiarization with strategic villages. It all comes together in a two-week field training maneuver that brings all of one's newly acquired skills into use.

It is no wonder—nor was it a disgrace—that the attrition rate was fully one-third. But the men who stuck with it, and with the advanced courses—eight weeks of intelligence training at Fort Holabird, Maryland, and fourteen weeks of engineer training at Fort Belvoir, Virginia—emerged with enviable skills. Major General William P. Yarborough, who commanded Special Forces for three years, called them "the finest soldiers anywhere."

Moreover, Special Forces were in the fore exploring new tactics, such as Sky Hook, when a man is snatched up by a cable attached to a balloon and snared by a passing aircraft, or HALO (high altitude, low opening) parachute jumps not unlike skydiving.

Special Forces are deployed around the world. They distinguished themselves in Laos, where Special Forces Captain Walter Moon (posthumously promoted to major) was captured and tortured and shot to death on his third escape attempt. Their efforts with the *montagnards* of Vietnam prompted General Chester V. "Ted" Clifton, military aide to Presidents Kennedy and Johnson, to say:

"In Vietnam villages, they are delivering babies, digging wells

The Quiet Professionals • 77

and fighting the Viet Cong. The fact that we're still there is at least half because of them."

This is what I was signing on for after the relatively soft life of a general's aide. My first assignment was as a C Detachment adjutant. My goal was to attend Staff Officers School and learn about the detachment's organization. Later I hoped to take unconventional warfare and counter-insurgency training, gaining knowledge of guerrilla and counter-guerrilla tactics while getting physically ready for overseas assignment, possibly in Vietnam.

It took a little getting used to wearing the Green Beret with its red flash, indicating the 7th Special Forces Group (Airborne), but I wore it proudly. The same went for the black and silver Special Forces crest. Its motto: *De oppresso liber* ("To free the oppressed"). The teal blue and gold Special Forces shoulder patch with its arrowhead, represents the craft and stealth of the Native Americans, bearing an upturned dagger crossed by three bolts of lightning, emblematic of speed and strength by land, sea, and air.

Members of the 77th adopted the Green Beret in 1954. They chose it because, like the berets worn by British commandos, it symbolized the ultimate in skill, esprit and dedication to duty. It was worn publicly for the first time at the retirement ceremonies on June 12, 1955, for Major General Joseph P. Cleland, commander of the 18th Corps and Fort Bragg. The 77th issued orders on December 30, 1955, that the beret was to be worn by all its personnel with all uniforms. That order was rescinded within weeks by higher headquarters, but Special Forces elements overseas continued to wear it.

On the occasion of President Kennedy's 1961 visit, the officers and men of the 7th and 5th, led by General Yarborough, stood inspection wearing Green Berets. Two days afterward the President sent this message: "I am sure the Green Beret will be a mark of distinction in the trying times ahead." Finally, on December 8, 1961, the Department of the Army made it an official component of the Special Forces uniform.

The color of the shield-shaped flash on the beret distinguishes

78 • *The Quiet Professionals*

the units: red for the 7th; green for the 10th; black with white border for the 5th; yellow and blue for the 8th; red and black for the 6th; red, black, yellow, and white, in quadrants for the 3rd; the Center and Special Warfare School, black, gray, and white with gold border; the Training Group, white; the Reserves and National Guard, teal blue, and Special Forces Vietnam, yellow with red stripes. The 1st was originally yellow. A black border was added in memory of President Kennedy following his assassination.

For a time Special Forces were dubbed "Kennedy's Rifles," indicative of his interest and support. Upon his death, the family requested their presence at the funeral. An honor guard comprised of forty-three enlisted men and three officers, commanded by Colonel William P. Grieves, the deputy commander, started immediately for Washington, D.C.

Three Special Forces soldiers stood vigil beside the President's casket in the East Room of the White House. Thereafter at least one was beside the casket at all times. The Special Forces honor guard lined the path leading to President Kennedy's grave in Arlington National Cemetery as the horse-drawn caisson bore him to his final resting-place.

As the burial rites were coming to a close Sergeant Major Francis J. Ruddy, of Scranton, Pennsylvania, senior NCO of all Special Forces, requested Mrs. Kennedy's permission to place a green beret on the President's casket. She gave her approval and this was done.

After the committal ceremony and after the throng of mourners had left, the Special Forces honor guard remained in final vigil. As they silently moved off, the eternal flame flickered over the grave and their tribute . . . a Green Beret.

"He gave us the Green Beret," Sergeant Major Ruddy said, "and we thought it fitting to give one back to him."

The Green Beret on the grave of President John F. Kennedy, Arlington National Cemetery, November 25, 1963.

Team A-726

January 1964 . . .

I believe it was on Monday, January 13, that we had the first meeting of Detachment A-726, C Company of the 7th. I had just returned from Alaska in December following maneuvers with the Eskimo Scouts of the Alaska National Guard, intent upon more schooling. Along came a crash program to organize and train more "Go" teams for deployment to Vietnam.

So there we were, gathered in the room where we stored our equipment and held our meetings—"the team room." It was not a big room, but the twelve of us crowded in. These men who were assigned to my team studied me and I looked back. What I saw pleased me but I wasn't sure what they might be thinking.

"I don't know you and you don't know me," I began. "That has its advantages and disadvantages. During the next months of pre-deployment training we're going to live together and work together. We are strangers now, but we will end pre-deployment training as a team. That's our job."

They were all professionals and took me at my word. We all accepted the challenge before us. We had no more than a week to prepare and then we were off on a tough training exercise. There were nine other A detachments—seven other Go teams like us destined for Vietnam and two buffer teams providing emergency backup. We were told we would parachute into Uwharrie National Forest in North Carolina and hike back to camp—a 100-mile hike, and we had a week to do it, carrying full packs that contained everything we needed for the entire exercise.

In that too-short week of preparation we managed three conditioning hikes of three, five and eight miles. I took charge, driving the team and maintaining attention to the slightest detail. I reasoned that they might complain about my insistence on absolute perfection, but when the chips were down and they reacted instinctively, it would pay big dividends.

That approach didn't push me to the top of their most favored list. Several of the ten enlisted men had a great deal of maturity and expertise. My exec, First Lieutenant Julian M. Olejniczak, had a more current troop record, as far as the men were concerned, than I did.

Lieutenant "O" at twenty-four, was a 1961 graduate of West Point. He went to the academy upon graduation from Mount Carmel High School in his native Chicago. He had both Airborne and Ranger training at Fort Benning and had served in Korea with the 1st Battle Group, 31st Infantry, before being drafted into Special Forces in May 1963. Unlike enlisted men, not all Special Forces officers were volunteers.

"It was okay by me, though," he explained. "When I was in Korea I was on levy to go to Vietnam. I didn't put in any particular preference for my next assignment. As Airborne and Ranger qualified I was a natural for Special Forces." And Jay had previously trained two cycles, on both a B detachment and a C detachment.

Of the remaining ten team members, seven had been together on A-55, a buffer team in the previous cycle. Buffer teams did everything the Go teams did except ship out. And they had no officers—just ten enlisted men. Being on a buffer team was a test of morale, not knowing whether you were training for a mission or just going through the motions. In the case of A-55, three of them did ship as replacements for Go team members who dropped out due to injury, illness or whatever.

Walking into the team room for our first meeting, I suppose I felt something like a trainer entering the cage with eleven wary tigers. It was my assignment to get them to do what I wanted. I had joined Special Forces to get an A team. Now I had one and we were headed for Vietnam.

I knew that Lieutenant O, with his prior experience, would be invaluable. The men would respect him for where he'd been, and he was a super guy to boot. I also knew that if I was going to run the team the way I thought it should be run I would have to be something of a martinet. I would apply more pressure, work them longer and harder than the other teams, run them farther and critique them more. That meant my executive officer would have to be the team's safety valve, someone they could turn to to let off steam.

I wasn't trying to be crafty. Call it instinct—whatever. I knew it was for the good of my entire team and I intended to have not just a good team, but the best team in Charley Company, where all of the Go teams were assigned. I knew it would improve our overall performance in Vietnam, and might save lives as well.

"Top" was a cornerstone of my team. My top sergeant—precisely, the operations sergeant or team sergeant—was a silver-haired veteran of World War II and Korea. At forty-five he was also the oldest on the team. He had been in the Army since 1940, except for twenty months following postwar demobilization.

He was christened Gabriel Ralph Alamo, a native of Newark, New Jersey, liked by everyone. Top had been around. He was the one the rest turned to for advice. He was among the first paratroopers and knew the Army forwards and backwards. Alamo could be jolly and gentle. Like the rest of us he had his self-doubts, but he hid them and outwardly was a no-nonsense, gruff trooper.

Alamo had been on the A-55 buffer team with six of the others, including Ray Whitsell. The moment I saw Whit in the team room I wondered if he might not pose a special challenge not of his own making. Special Forces teams must operate as a tightly knit, "gung-ho" type of unit. Whit was black, the only black on the team. He was also an ex-Marine and a perceived loner as well.

Staff Sergeant Raymond B. Whitsell was quiet and "self-contained" during our first meeting. Really good Special Forces men are that way. Given the scope of their training, they damn well know they're good. They don't have to prove it to themselves or to anyone else. That was the way Whit was, only more so, perhaps because of his circumstance of birth.

Whit had enlisted in the Marines in 1956. He was eighteen. He saw his first Special Forces men in Germany. Whit did his four

Team A-726 • 83

years and returned home, but he remembered that Green Beret. To him it spoke of a man's qualifications as a professional soldier and had nothing to do with his race, creed or color. So he joined the Army, his cap set for Special Forces. Whit was, as they say, lean and mean. In truth he was tough and wiry, standing five eight and 160 pounds, savvy and studious. He joined Special Forces in December 1962, after finishing jump school at Fort Bragg. After demolition training on Smoke Bomb Hill he took the fourteen-week advanced engineering course at Fort Belvoir. Whit was a well-qualified combat engineer when he joined Team A-55 toward the end of its training cycle.

Sergeant First Class Vernon L. Beeson, like Whit, was on the quiet side. He operated with a calm detachment, no matter what. A real "cool hand Luke." Bee quit high school in High Point, North Carolina, joining the Army in 1948, shortly before his eighteenth birthday. He earned the parachutist badge and served with both the 82nd and 11th Airborne Divisions. He went into combat in Korea with the 187th Airborne Regimental Combat Team, served a tour in Germany and joined Special Forces in February 1963. He was with A-55 before coming to us.

Beeson was a five-nine 170-pound dynamo, our operations and intelligence sergeant. He was the third-ranking NCO on the team and Alamo's assistant. His was an important job, and I would come to rely heavily on his training and experience. I promised myself I would get to know him better, but understanding it would have to be on his terms and in his good time.

Sergeant First Class Thurman R. Brown and Staff Sergeant Merwin D. Woods were my weapons experts. It is doubtful any two soldiers could have been more unlike, but when they went into action they were as smooth as the inside of a mortar tube. I remember Brownie as taciturn and laconic—and the most qualified all-around soldier I had known to date.

His 170 pounds were spread on a five foot, ten and one-half inch frame. He had a flat nose, a legacy from his regimental boxing days, and the only Purple Heart on the team, for hand and leg

84 • Team A-726

wounds in Korea. Brownie was always counting, cleaning and checking weapons, reading field manuals and studying tactics.

He had been reared on a farm and had worked with all types of people, he would explain. "I can get along with anybody," he asserted. "I mind my own business. I do my job. And so long as no one bothers me, I don't bother them."

Brownie was born at Lewisburg, Kentucky, in 1929. He never made it to high school. Like countless others, he got his diploma after he joined the Army. He joined as soon as possible, when he was seventeen, in 1947. After a year as a "straight-leg" or non-parachutist, so called because his trousers are straight and not bloused around a jump boot, he qualified for Airborne. From December 1950, to April 1953, he was with the 187th in Korea. He was wounded in May 1951, on the spearhead of an attack into North Korea. He joined Special Forces in September 1954, for his own reasons.

"It was a new outfit. Nobody would talk about it. You had to have a 'Secret' clearance to get in. I was curious, so I just thought I'd try it," he explained.

Brownie was in a different world in Special Forces. He changed his Military Occupation Specialty (MOS) from wheeled vehicle mechanic to light weapons. During training he switched again, to demolitions, and then to heavy weapons, and eventually back again to light weapons.

He left Special Forces in 1956 to spend eighteen months with the 36th Nike Battalion, assigned to protect the Annapolis, Maryland area with ground-to-air rockets. Why the change? For the same reason as before. "It was a new unit. I was curious. I thought I'd try something new. But I didn't like it. So I came back to Special Forces."

He was assigned to the 1st Special Forces Group (Airborne) on Okinawa. He was on three training operations to Thailand and one to the Philippines. Then he was in Vietnam for six months, where he set up a camp in the Mekong Delta swamps and did his share of wet-foot patrolling. We turned to Brownie with a lot of questions about Vietnam when he joined A-26. He responded with general answers, since his time had been spent in the swamps and we were destined for the jungles and mountains of the highlands.

Staff Sergeant Merwin D. Woods was the big man on our A Team campus. He towered six feet three and carried 205 pounds well except for his paunch. We kidded him about his "permanent reserve" because it had something of the size and shape of a reserve parachute, perpetually in place. Woody said it was the Army chow. He was always in good spirits, including that never-to-be-forgotten night at Nam Dong.

Woody weighed in at Pekin, Illinois, in 1927 and was reared in Canton, Illinois. He also had the Army to thank for his high school diploma. He enlisted in the Navy at age seventeen and was on board the aircraft carrier USS *Benning*. World War II drew to a close before he saw any action. By late 1947 he was out of the Navy and in the Army. He completed jump school, serving with the 82nd Airborne for four years. He went to Korea with a quartermaster unit, once again arriving after the shooting was over.

Woody joined Special Forces in 1954. He spent four years with the 77th at Fort Bragg, and another three years with the 10th in Germany—and then he hung up his beret. After three months he realized he had made a mistake. Two requests and fourteen months later he was back, serving with the 5th for a while, and then with the 7th. He joined A-26 after buffer training with A-55.

Staff Sergeant Keith E. Daniels was small, quiet, and strong. Originally from Union City, Michigan, he called Battle Creek home. Dan was a month shy of his twenty-seventh birthday on our first get-together in the team room. He was usually expressionless and his sharp, weathered features left you thinking he was an older man.

He also owed his high school diploma to the Army. He had left school during his senior year to work as a grease monkey in his father's garage. In 1955, anticipating he was about to be drafted, he enlisted. He tried his hand as a baker and then switched to the Military Police Corps, serving in the States and on Okinawa before he joined Special Forces in 1961. Dan was qualified as a parachutist and radio supervisor. He was chief communicator first with A-55 and then A-26.

Dan's assistant was John Lucius Houston, a tall, stringbean of a sergeant from Fort Knox, Kentucky. John passed up two college football scholarships for a career in the Army. Although just twenty-two, he had served five and one-half years, including a year in Korea. He joined Special Forces in 1963 after finishing jump school and came to us from the Training Group.

Sergeant Thomas L. Gregg was our chief medic. He was friendly, and liked to talk about medicine the way other men talked about their children. He was fascinated by and totally dedicated to the subject. He left junior college at Stephenville, Texas, near his home in Rising Star, Texas, midway in his freshman year. He was eighteen when he joined the Army in 1956. He was an excellent student and walked away from a full scholarship, deciding to try the Army for four years.

"I was on the honor roll at college and not even studying," he confessed. "I played saxophone and clarinet and sang a little in a band at dances, to pick up pocket money. I was always running out of money. The scholarship took care of school fees, but it was the extras. I got disgusted."

Our assistant medic was Sergeant (E-5) Terrance D. Terrin, twenty-two years old, from St. Johns, Arizona. He was big, husky, and liked to talk. He joined the Army in 1961, completed jump school and signed on with Special Forces the following year. After the forty-four week medic course he joined the Training Group and then the 7th in August 1961. He also had buffer training with A-55 before being assigned to A-26.

Sergeant (E-5) Michael Disser was Whitsell's understudy for demolitions and engineering. He was also the youngest member of our team, having just turned twenty-one when we came together as A-26. He had been in uniform a little less than two years when he joined us, but he had seen his share of Army posts. His father, Lieutenant Colonel Ralph K. Disser, was an infantryman.

"I had gotten out of high school, but I had no desire to go to college," he explained. "I was working in a sissified job as a buyer-trainee in a dry goods store." He saw no possibility of advancement and concluded that since he had been an Army brat all his life, why not try it on his own? He entered the Army in 1962, took basic and advanced infantry training, went to jump school and Special Forces school, and served with the Training Group and A-55.

Those were my eleven tigers. Seven had just finished pre-mission buffer training with A-55—Alamo, Beeson, Daniels, Disser, Terrin, Whitsell and Woods. Taken together we had experience in three services and all three of our country's wars in this generation. Collectively we had a broad range of specialized military training, as well as a background in medicine and engineering. On our first day together we were still twelve individuals. Time would tell if we could intermesh as a team—a great team.

Well, I was impressed with them, and while I had tried to be my sharpest, most professional self, I was falling short of my intended mark with my men.

"Sharp-looking guy, the old man, but he's a nitpicker."

"Yeah. All those questions. Holding school on stuff we've covered time and time again. Piddling detail."

"Cripes. We're senior NCOs. We know our assignments, and if we don't, we find out."

"And he keeps us longer than the other teams. That's fine for him. He's a bachelor. We'd like to see the wife and kids as much as possible before we ship."

On the last of our three conditioning hikes, the eight-miler, we lost Beeson. He limped home, his boot full of blood. Blisters had opened on one foot despite Gregg's first aid on the march. The doctor looked at his foot and said he was not to jump and not to hike for some time. He was furious over the possibility of not making the "shakedown" 100 miles!

Teamwork!
The 100-Mile Hike

January 19, 1964 . . .

It was a bright, cool, sunny Sunday morning in January 1964, when we jumped into the Uwharrie National Forest. We dropped into a plowed field, all of us except Alamo and Whit. Somehow they got separated from the rest of the team on the way down and landed in a lake. We had to pull them out and dry them off before we could get underway.

The Protestant chaplain, a Baptist, happened by about that time. He took note of their misfortune.

"Doggone it," he chuckled, " If I'd gotten here a minute sooner we could have baptized them."

"Oh, no," I said. "They're both fish-eaters, like me."

"That's all right," he replied. "I could have converted them."

We had five days to hike the 100 or so miles back to Fort Bragg. Taking into consideration our heavy load, our physical condition at that stage of our training and the mountainous terrain, I set a fairly easy pace. We walked along the shoulder of the road when it was paved and right down the center of the road when it wasn't.

Whenever we came upon a source of water we filled our canteens. Occasionally we would come upon a soft-drink stand and I treated the team to sodas. When we did pause we took long rest periods; to give the medics, Gregg and Terry, time to treat blisters. During these breaks we had an opportunity to cross-train in our specialties. We had no thought of setting any record for completing the long walk, and no thought of trying to get back ahead of other teams. We were getting acquainted, functioning as a team and generally trying to improve ourselves overall.

We were not alone on the trail. Seven other Go teams and two buffer teams were pounding the same terrain. By the end of day two the ten teams were strung out along the road for about thirty miles. Dan and Houston kept us in touch with the others by radio. They made two or more contacts a day.

There was not a man on the trail without blisters and aching muscles. Brown was in the best shape and suffered least. He had been working out at home for weeks and running two or three miles a day. He also had been on longer treks including one of 120 miles in 1955. He had humped from Camp Lejeune, and had only a couple of blisters on one toe as a souvenir.

We operated like so many musketeers—one for all and all for one. At night when we stopped we dug in. Everyone, officers and men, used an entrenching tool. We took equal turns at the watch—in actuality only a fire watch—and everyone on the team helped set up our big radio antennas.

"D'you see that? The old man digging ditches."

"Yeah, okay, but he's still a nitpicker."

"Well, he was enlisted. Maybe that's it."

"Yeah, but he was Air Force. And training recruits."

Our medics and communications specialists had the heaviest load. We were all loaded down, since everything we needed for six days was in our backpacks. But the commo and medical personnel were at an additional disadvantage because of the weight they shouldered. So, at critical times, we passed the extra load around. The additional twenty-six pounds of radio generator was the real backbreaker and it was passed among us quite often. Teamwork was paying its dividends. Team spirit was evolving.

By Tuesday morning we had reached Candor Airport. We were all hurting, but we were starting to get broken in. No one wanted to chuck it in. We were watching Papa Alamo. At forty-five he had more than the weight of his gear pulling him down. He kept moving along, never complaining, but at times he looked pretty pooped. The rest of us figured if old Pappy could hack it, we could hack it.

Lieutenant O left us Tuesday morning. There was a "dining-in" or formal banquet Tuesday night and all but two of the officers on the hike were ordered to be there in dress blues. I learned about the dining-in and arranged to be one of the two who stayed with the men. So technically I was in charge of four Go teams and a buffer. We stayed in touch with the other officer and the five teams.

For Gregg, it was his first long self-sustained march. He had brought along all manner of training aids, intent on sharing his medical knowledge, thus cross-training as many of the team as possible. I thought he had enough gear to perform major surgery on the entire team and have supplies left over. He arrived at the same conclusion, and when Lieutenant O flew back to Bragg he had about twenty-five pounds of extra medical supplies that Gregg had been carrying.

As Jay was preparing to board the helicopter to return to Bragg, we completed some strategic plans. We agreed that when he rejoined us at Mott Lake on Thursday he would not come with empty hands. I gave him the money for two six-packs of cold beer, and off he went to his dining-in.

The temperature compounded our problems. Terrin made it for about two hours with that radio generator on his shoulders. Finally the heat took its toll and he almost passed out. We took a longer break that afternoon, but we still had some seventy miles left.

When we resumed the march Gregg had the generator. He had shed twenty-five pounds of medical gear, but with the generator riding atop his pack he was no better off. He was not a big man to begin with, and after about an hour he was "walking heavy."

He was on the verge of asking someone else to take the generator when in the distance we saw our objective, an abandoned church where we planned to overnight. It was just a mile and a half down the trail. Gregg kept silent and we pressed onward.

We were within a couple hundred yards of the church when Gregg abruptly halted. His right foot emitted a loud "pop!" The pain shot up his leg and he called out, "Hey, captain! I've got to get out from under this generator!"

Alamo took Gregg's rucksack and Gregg took his. As we bedded down in the church Gregg had a pained look on his face. It was his blisters. But he tended to the blisters of his teammates before he took some of his own medication to reduce the pain.

The following day was our fourth on the road. It started off badly and got progressively worse. Any old injury or minor chronic problem like hemorrhoids, started giving us trouble. Gregg hopped along with the rest of us, occasionally popping another pill when the pain became intolerable. He never complained. Woody, who developed a swollen knee, never complained. Nor did any of the rest of us.

Our team nickname came out of this march. It was getting late in the day when I studied the map. I remembered an old store somewhere up that long road. If we could reach the store we could spend the night there. One of our NCOs calculated that the store was approximately 2.6 miles ahead. No sweat.

We started off again, and we walked. And walked. We walked 4.6 miles and still no sign of the store. The guy who had estimated our distance from the store was getting an earful of ribbing.

"More like twenty-six than two-point-six," someone kidded.

We began to laugh, and the banter continued until we finally reached our destination. It had been closer to 6.2 than 2.6 miles. But we now had our team name.

Whenever someone called for us, one of our number would sound off "Two-point-six!" It represented our determination to reach our objective. Then someone added a "7" for the 7th Group, just before we shipped out, and we were henceforth A-726.

As Thursday began we were thirty-two miles from Mott Lake. All of us brightened up as we started out. We knew that from the lake it was only another fifteen miles to Smoke Bomb Hill.

We were not the first team to reach Mott Lake. We paid no heed to the jeers of the other teams and marched past them until we saw Lieutenant O, who had ridden out to meet us with Beeson who was still under orders to avoid extended walking.

The lieutenant had hidden our beer in the lake, tied off by a line. One by one he took the men down to the water's edge, presumably to soak their feet. Nothing in the regulations prohibited our little

92 • Teamwork! The 100-Mile Hike

beer break, but there was no need for the other teams to know about our stash of suds.

That cold beer was an instant catharsis for mind and body. Coupled with the pain pills we had been taking, we were on top of the world. Even Woody, who had been grumbling about his knee, was seemingly back at full power.

A staff officer who had come out to check on the teams told me we could go the remaining fifteen miles that evening if we chose to. I shared the word with the rest of the team.

"How about it?" I baited them. "Do you want to be the first to arrive?"

The answer seemed to be mostly moaning and groaning, but nothing definitive. Finally Woody spoke.

"What the hell," he said. "It's only about fifteen miles. Let's go on in and get it over with."

"While we're warmed up," Brownie chimed in.

Woody began pacing back and forth in front of the men, limping on his bad leg, almost taunting the rest to get moving again.

"Well, let's move on down the road, anyway," I suggested. "Let's just move out and see how far we get."

As we more or less dragged ourselves down the trail we were a sorry looking lot. Each of us was experiencing his own special pain. Woody and Dan were nursing bad legs. Gregg was struggling with his foot. I had my back problem. Everyone had blisters in spades. But spirits were excellent. We could hear other teams bedding down along the road as we passed. Brownie had a piece of chalk, which he used to leave a message on the road for the other teams as we passed: "A-26 Was Here"

We had somehow managed to recharge the batteries that kept us pushing, pushing, and Smoke Bomb Hill kept getting closer and closer. Finally, around 2330 hours, we hauled our weary bodies into our team room and more or less collapsed.

Gregg was last in, limping more than ever. His face was chalk-white.

"It happened again," he said. "My foot popped again."

We policed up our gear, checked it in, and we were gone. Upon reaching my cabin I soaked in a hot tub until falling asleep. Somehow I managed to drag myself out of the water, pull on a pair of drawers, and collapse into an armchair. That's how the maid found me in the morning, with my clothes scattered on the floor.

"Sure do look tired," she said, "like you've been on a 500-mile hike."

"Only a hundred," I replied.

I gave the men Friday off. When I reported to the Old Man, I got a chewing out for bringing the team in a day early. He said we hadn't had permission to return before Friday. As word got around that we had finished first—all of us—I was not the most admired man of the hour in the company. I didn't care.

Gregg had covered seventy miles with a broken foot. We had successfully completed the formidable task at hand. The men had accepted me as their leader.

Finally, we were becoming a team.

The Devil's Wedge

March 1964 . . .

We found out we could march a hundred miles. Now we were preparing for Field Training Exercise Cherokee Trail II. All would not go well, and team morale would suffer as a result.

From the outset we knew we were going to Vietnam, but not where. Finally, about halfway through pre-mission training, we got the word. We would provide physical security, plus health, welfare and other "civic action" services for the approximately 5,000 peasants living in the Nam Dong valley. Nam Dong thus became our focus.

I learned from others who had returned from Nam Dong that little French was spoken there. So one of our first strategies was to shift our language training. The plan had been that six of the team would study French and the others would concentrate on Vietnamese. Now eight worked on Vietnamese and four on French. Our objective was not to become fluent but to acquire a working knowledge. *"C'est une grenade"* was better than nothing.

Returnees from three teams that had spent six months at Nam Dong briefed us on all aspects of the area, answering our questions until we felt like we knew what we would find once we were there.

Cherokee Trail II was the capstone of our training. It ran for two weeks, with men of the 82nd Airborne Division representing the South Vietnamese we would one day be training as our strike force. The "Viet Cong guerrillas" were officer-students from the Special Warfare School. The job assigned to A-26 and other Go and buffer teams in this counter-insurgency exercise was to build camps, ostensibly in Viet Cong territory, and guard them against infiltration and attack through a combination of aggressive patrols and a strong perimeter defense.

Our attempts to make it look realistic turned out to be bad news for one "guerrilla," a young second lieutenant. We took him prisoner on three occasions, once as he was wandering alone down a path in his underwear.

Terry and Gregg constructed an underground dispensary that brought words of praise from the group surgeon. It was constructed with forest timbers and was complete with floodlights, medicine cabinet, and operating table.

"Your dispensary was the best we saw," the group surgeon told me afterward. "It was an example of a couple of medics who were not afraid to work, took pride in what they were doing, and used imagination and ingenuity to do it."

Our efforts with the hapless lieutenant brought us grief, however. We interrogated him in disguised voices. We blindfolded him and strung him up in a tree in a cargo net. He was bewildered and, wearing only his drawers, was also cold. After a time we lowered him from the tree and took him to the Cherokee Trail headquarters. As we rode along in the jeep he spoke rather bitterly about the way he had been treated. He did not realize he was talking to his captors and, believing he was no longer part of the exercise, he told us everything we had sought to get out of him during his blindfold interrogations.

He filed a formal complaint over his treatment and the following day there were lots of people looking us over. They said we had violated the Geneva Convention on treatment of prisoners. I said we had merely improvised a POW cage with the materials at hand, and that was the end of the matter.

We received a pretty good chewing for not keeping graphs and charts so that we could brief inspecting officers. It was a valid criticism. We had focused our attention on setting up a secure camp, and not worrying about paperwork. We were surprised at the criticism and that didn't help our morale, which seemed to have been slipping since the 100-mile hike.

It was Alamo's task to maintain the graphs and charts, and he was awake most of two nights working on them. I rode him pretty hard, constantly testing him, forcing him to know more about the team and its abilities than either Jay or I. If either of us was unable to command Alamo would be in charge. I was impressed with his spirit amid adversity on the hike and had the utmost confidence in him. He saw my constant pressure on him as the opposite.

We went for a walk one evening and talked it over.

"This stuff is getting to me," he confided. "I don't know if I can put up with it or not."

"I believe you can," I answered.

"I'm thinking seriously about asking to be replaced," he said.

"You're going to have to get really screwed up for me to let you go," I said. "You can do it. You know damned well you can."

He turned away, shaking his head.

"Sure you can," I repeated. "You're as much a stubborn wop as I am a thick mick."

His grunt of a response was very close to a chuckle.

"Yeah," he agreed. "We sure knock heads together, don't we?"

"That's right, Pop."

As we looked into each other's eyes I could see Alamo's eyes were no longer clouded. They were clear, almost twinkling.

"You know what I want," I said. "I want the best."

"I know," was his reply.

"I'm not a whiz kid," I continued. "I'm just a captain, and a junior one, at that. You men are the experts. You have the training and the experience and the knowledge. You have to train the lieutenant and me."

"Sure," he said. "We can do it."

Our conversation helped lift Alamo out of his depression. Nevertheless I perceived a decline in team morale. The medics on a team have the additional responsibility of monitoring team morale, so I asked Gregg and Terry how they sized up the situation and what they thought should be done. They confirmed my fears. Sort of a schism had occurred, with Ray Whitsell on one side and the rest of the team on the other. They recommended we have a team meeting to talk it out, so the situation wouldn't deteriorate further.

We held team meetings toward the end of each day. They would

The Devil's Wedge • 97

last minutes or several hours, depending on the complexity of the latest problem. We discussed the day's progress or lack thereof, we planned, we cross-trained, we had the opportunity in all of this to get to know each other better, and let off some steam all at the same time.

No matter where we were, we held end-of-day critiques. At times they were beneficial, as when our weapons experts went into more detail on the arms we had been firing that day, or when the medics or communicators told us more about their special equipment. But sometimes these meetings were next to meaningless, as when everyone was talking and not much was really being said.

Whitsell didn't stay long at these team meetings. He was a conscientious student, paying attention when the meetings were productive. But when the brainstorming stopped and the bull session started, he would split. If we were at Smoke Bomb Hill he would go to his barracks where he worked on his equipment, studied field manuals, wrote letters or took a nap. When we were in the field he just walked off.

Occasionally after he had departed, we discussed administrative matters or housekeeping requirements. Whit would miss out on some of this information. As a result, other team members would be in the middle of a cleanup detail and someone would ask, "Hey, where the hell is Whitsell? He ought to be here, helping out."

Of course Whit, like every other member of the team, had responsibilities over and above his primary assignment. He was our chief engineer and demolitions specialist, and he was also responsible for logistics. During Exercise Cherokee Trail II he might be out scrounging needed materials or alone in his tent poring over his supply tables while the rest of the team was stringing fences or digging trenches. Inevitably someone would ask the familiar question: "Where's Whitsell?"

His typically quiet, withdrawn demeanor and his noticeable absences from meetings he was not obliged to attend became an irritant to his teammates. Some saw it as Whit not pulling his weight. There was the additional concern that because he was black and the only ex-Marine among us, that he was intentionally remaining aloof. Did he have a chip on his shoulder?

One or another of the team members confronted Whit at different times, expressing dissatisfaction.

"Don't worry about me," he would say. "I know my job, and I'm doing it."

Part way through Cherokee Trail the situation worsened. We were joined by a couple of men from a buffer team. They noticed right away that Whit spent a lot of time off on his own, working on his charts, or talking to black sergeants of the 82nd Airborne units assigned to us. These two new arrivals shared their observations with the team. The discontent heightened.

Whitsell was not blind to what was happening. Apparently he had encountered similar circumstances previously during his eight years in uniform. I had the feeling he might even be looking with anticipation to the impending showdown. Whit believed it was his right to protect his privacy and to act as he did, even on a team whose members would rely on one another so closely for every minute of their six months in Vietnam. As Whit saw things, he was giving a hundred per cent during duty hours but was turned off by the bull sessions. He felt he had nothing to add and nothing to gain from them.

He had no firsthand knowledge of the people or places his teammates discussed. As a black man he had no contact with such people. Fayetteville, where Fort Bragg is located, would not have welcomed a black man back then if he had accompanied other team members to a restaurant or bar in the town. And for that matter, where could he have found common ground during a bull session if Whit had tried to talk about the people and places of his own experience?

I had some time to think about my problem over the weekend of April 11-12. Cherokee Trail, our "graduation exercise," had ended the prior weekend. We were six weeks away from shipping out for Vietnam. It was absolutely essential that I pull my team together, even if it meant losing so valuable a soldier as Whit. Time was of the essence and as I saw it, drastic action was in order.

We assembled in the team room on Monday afternoon, April 13. We either stood in the ten-by-twelve-foot space or sat on the twelve storage compartments lining the walls. Thinking back on it later, it might have been better to have discussed it with Whit privately, but I had decided on a frontal approach.

"We're here to decide who goes to Vietnam and who doesn't," I began. "Sergeant Whitsell, I think this meeting is mostly called for you, about you. Most of the team members here seem to think you aren't carrying your full share of the load."

Whit said impassively, "If I were detachment commander, I wouldn't look to the man against whom these accusations are made. I would check the man who is out observing and putting out all this information. If he's doing his job, and doing it right, he doesn't have time to go around checking on somebody else."

Some muttering was audible in the room.

"There is some friction, and if it is going to develop into an abscess we are in trouble," I replied. "That's why I'm bringing it out in the open, so everybody can have his say. If we don't solve it, we are going to have replacements. It is my responsibility to make sure that when we go we are ready to go, and we go as a team, not as a bunch of individuals."

Whit appeared angry, but spoke in a steady voice.

"I do my job," he said. "Nobody can say I don't do my job. I'm not here to win a popularity contest."

Then Woody spoke, followed by Dan. They said they felt Whit kept to himself too much and missed too many work details.

"Where were you when we were painting the fences?" someone asked.

"The captain and the lieutenant and I were cleaning up the team room," Whit responded.

One by one, other team members joined the discussion, except for Beeson and Brown, who were silent. Beeson had the highest regard for Whit's abilities but was concerned about his habit of keeping off to himself. He looked disgusted at this latest turn of

100 • *The Devil's Wedge*

events. Brown was following his personal philosophy of just live and let live.

"This is the time for me to decide whether I want to go with you, not whether you want to go with me," countered Whitsell. "I want to go to Vietnam and you're not going to stop me. You don't have the power to decide my career."

The discussion dragged on for an hour. Each man had the opportunity to speak. I was praying that somehow we could rid ourselves of the problem and concentrate on our approaching mission. One thing is certain. We had a frank discussion. All who wanted to speak their piece did so.

When I would address Whit, I could see the hard look in his eyes. He in turn would glance in my direction, as if expecting I would take his side. Certainly he knew I had the utmost respect for his work. I had the feeling my silence at that point in the discussion was not what Whit hoped for. As he saw it he was one man against eleven.

"If you people don't want me to go with you, then go on without me, and I wish you all the luck in the world," Whit declared.

"I want you to go with us," I countered. "You're a damned good soldier and we need you. If we can't solve a little problem like this, then we aren't the men we think we are."

Lieutenant O rose to his feet. He had been silent up to this point.

"I've been sitting here and listening," he said. "It seems to me there is a little bit of prejudice operating against Sergeant Whitsell. To me, his work has been good, outstanding. As a soldier, in appearance and ability, he is above reproach. These gripes about his not doing his job, that isn't it. It's a prejudice against Sergeant Whitsell."

The others said that wasn't the case. No one had mentioned prejudice, they said. One by one the men said they held no prejudice against Whitsell, racial or otherwise. The look on Whit's face said he didn't believe that, but his expression was less stern, as if he might have seen the odds shift, to at least two against ten.

The lieutenant continued, uninterrupted, for about fifteen minutes.

"The first day we met in this room and Sergeant Whitsell walked in, we all looked at him and we saw he was different. One thing we saw was that his color was different. We didn't know anything about his character or his mannerisms, but we saw his color was different.

"Right there, I think, some of us might have formed a negative attitude toward him. And that has been building up to this.

"Sergeant Whitsell is different. He's got a right to be different, just as much right as any of the rest of us. If he isn't like us, if he doesn't have the same likes and dislikes we have, if he doesn't act like us, that doesn't mean he doesn't care for us. It doesn't mean he is not heart and soul a member of this team.

"Like the rest of us, Sergeant Whitsell has personality traits that might be abrasive to others. He ought to think about these things. We are going to be living close, in a dangerous situation. For the good of all, each of us must work on ourselves to eliminate faults that might jeopardize the harmony of this team.

"Sergeant Whitsell has to give a little, to quit being such a loner. A loner is bad news for any team. We have to be more tolerant of his differences, and his right to be different. There is nothing here that can't be talked out, if we face it honestly.

"All this is really insignificant. The detachment has a job to do and we are going to do it. Only a short time is left before we go over. Let's get on with the program."

The lieutenant sat down. There was silence in the room, each man thinking about what they had just heard. Then Woody spoke.

"We want him to go with us," he said. "With us, and not by himself."

Others joined in, expressing pretty much the same sentiment, but in their own words.

Whit's whole manner had undergone a transformation. The hardness was gone from his face. He had been touched by the lieutenant's words, just as they had reached into the hearts and

102 • *The Devil's Wedge*

minds of the rest of us.

"I want to go with you," he announced. "I like this team. I want to be part of it."

There was more silence. I did not speak immediately. I wanted to be sure everyone was "talked out."

"We all have to give a little," I said. "I think we will, after today. We're all going to Vietnam—as a team. Everybody that wants to."

Our meeting quickly broke up. The men seemed to leave with a lighter step than when they had entered. I felt we had all left a heavy burden behind during our two-hour session.

"It's going to be all right, captain," Gregg said. "Whit is one of the most levelheaded individuals I've ever known. It's going to be all right."

And he was correct. Whit went to the barracks and slept on it that night. On the days that followed he spent less time studying alone and more on making our team the best possible team. But if there was cussing or if discussions developed into bull sessions, he was out of there, and everyone understood.

What counted was that now he was solidly on our team, and we were every bit as much on his.

The Devil's Wedge • 103

Team A-726

Left to right, Captain Donlon, MSG Alamo, SFC Beeson, SGT Daniels, SSG Woods, SSG Whitsell, SGT Gregg, SFC Brown, SGT Disser, SGT Terrin, SGT Houston, 1st Lt. Olejniczak.

Vietnam

May 1964 . . .

We were one of eight Go teams that climbed aboard an Air Force C-135 transport on May 23 at Pope Air Force Base near Fort Bragg. We overnighted at Honolulu and Okinawa before losing a day when we crossed the International Dateline, and landed at Saigon's Tan Son Nhut Airport on May 27. Detachment A-726 would soon be replacing Detachment A-730.

The immediate contrasts that confronted us left us thinking we were in a totally different world, which we were. During the flight across on the C-135 there wasn't much to see. The aircraft, the military version of the Boeing 707, has only a few very small windows. The C-135 is referred to as "the flying submarine."

So there wasn't much to see until finally we were on the ground in Saigon, a mysterious, tense and teeming capital of a country in the grip of war. We sensed the situation in the way we landed. Instead of a long glide, we dropped in after a short dive to avoid small-arms sniper fire.

The following morning the eight teams flew to their respective destinations. We took a C-47 to Da Nang on the South China Sea coast, about 380 air miles north of Saigon. Da Nang was the main port and headquarters for I Corps, which took in the provinces of Quang Tri, Thua Thien, Quang Nam, and Quang Tin. It was the northernmost of the four corps areas, beginning at the 17th parallel, which, under the July 22, 1954, cease-fire, divided North and South Vietnam.

At Da Nang we were briefed and met our B Detachment commander. As it happened, there were two of them. Major (later Lieutenant Colonel) George A. Maloney of Queens, New York, was winding up his tour. Major Edwin T. Nance of Shelbyville, Tennessee, was his successor. The next day we flew on to our new

Vietnam • 105

home thirty-two miles to the west. Nam Dong, freely translated, means "five cents," and that's about as much as it looked to be worth when we first observed it from the air on May 29. Our base camp was previously known as Ruong Ruong, Nam Duc, Ta Ro, and Ta Rau.

Back at Fort Bragg we dealt with triangular camps, square camps, star-pointed camps and all sorts of designs. Camp Nam Dong wasn't any of those. You might have described it as almost free form. It vaguely resembled a lopsided figure eight, or possibly a butt-end slice of ham, with the inner perimeter as the bone.

The camp's inner perimeter, more or less oval in configuration, was marked off by a four-foot fence of five strands of barbed wire. This inner perimeter was about eighty by one hundred-twenty yards. At the center were two houses, each about sixty by twenty-four feet, with thatched roofs and rattan walls. The first of these two key buildings contained four rooms—the U.S. Special Forces Orderly Room, the Vietnamese Special Forces Joint Operations Center, quarters for five U.S. Special Forces personnel and quarters for interpreters and other Vietnamese civilian workers. Directly in back of this building was the other long house containing three rooms— quarters for the Nung tribesmen who were our special "Swiss Guard," a supply room and a communications center. There were smaller buildings of similar construction in a cluster around the two central buildings. On one side were five—the Vietnamese Special Forces mess hall, their partially buried communications bunker, their quarters, the Vietnamese camp commander's headquarters, and quarters for four Vietnamese nurses. Four buildings on the other side were the U.S. Special Forces mess hall, a partially underground communications bunker, more quarters for the Nungs and the Nungs' mess hall.

Another long house, to the rear and perpendicular to the others, was the dispensary.

A snaking trench marked the outer perimeter with another four-foot barbed wire fence running along one side of the trench. The area was roughly 250 by 350 yards. Situated randomly in this area

106 • Vietnam

were maybe twenty-five thatch-rattan buildings. These were quarters for the three Vietnamese strike forces, their mess hall, and a beer and pop stand, which was privately operated by the wife of one of the members of the strike force.

The village of Nam Dong and the camp were connected by a hard-packed dirt road. This road ran south through a gate in the outer perimeter fence and a gate in the inner perimeter fence. A helicopter landing pad was to the west of the road as you entered camp, between the inner and outer perimeters. To the east, a bit farther on, the inner and outer fences came within about thirty yards of each other. There, surrounded by barbed wire, were our three main ammo bunkers. Also on that side, just beyond the outer fences, was a landing strip. The Navy Seabees built it using crushed gravel taken from the riverbed.

"Well, we're in VC territory now," I thought, as our helicopter settled onto the landing pad.

We knew that the Viet Cong were all around us. We knew they may even have infiltrated the camp, posing as mechanics, interpreters, laborers, truck drivers, or even as members of the three Vietnamese strike forces. Personnel at Nam Dong, like many other such camps in Vietnam, were practically sitting ducks, if the VC were willing to pay the price for attacking. We were isolated and without any supporting artillery, and questionable air support.

Our camp was built on a slight knoll (YC 868840) in a north-south valley of the Annamite Mountains of Thua Thien province. We were approximately fifteen miles from the border of Laos. Altitude was less than 1,000 feet above sea level. Mountains on both sides rose to about 3,000 feet. As we scanned the terrain beyond our outer perimeter that first day we pondered what the green foliage in the distance might conceal. It was under the protection of similar cover and on such heights that the Viet Minh guerrillas assembled the manpower and firepower that toppled the French at Dien Bien Phu on May 7, 1954—just ten short years ago.

Our leaders had decided that Nam Dong was worth the risk. The 5,000 people in this valley were sorely in need of medical and hygienic assistance. The original population of native *montagnards,* or mountaineers, had mushroomed in recent years due to the numbers of lowland Vietnamese and more recently by the arrival of *montagnard* refugees from high ground along the border with Laos. The Vietnamese had responded to central government urging to leave the coastal cities and relocate in the high plateau. This program called "the Strategic Hamlet Program" was intended to give the perception that the central government of Saigon was in fact, in control of all of South Vietnam. The mountain people from farther west had either been driven out by the VC or had fled before their encroachment.

We learned that the mingling of two types of *montagnards* and Vietnamese was a sociological problem all to itself. We did not see any serious trouble among them while we were at Nam Dong, but the tension was apparent, and the Viet Cong were only too willing to muddy the waters and exploit cultural differences.

Our presence was a major thorn in the side of the VC. Three teams that had previously been at Nam Dong, and in particular the one we followed, commanded by Captain John Eddy of Boston, concentrated on "civic action" programs. They helped the farmers with their rice crops, showed them how and where to dig wells, provided seed and feed, improved their livestock, treated their illnesses, and in whatever way possible worked to upgrade their living conditions by teaching and by example.

Their efforts contributed to undercutting VC propaganda against the central government and the "foreign devils" supporting it. But moreover, Camp Nam Dong was a base for hindering the VC guerrillas who were infiltrating from North Vietnam. These guerrillas were moving down from training camps above the 17th parallel, walking the Ho Chi Minh trails which fed through Laos and into our valley and other infiltration routes along the border.

We were present to continue the program of providing physical security and improving living conditions for the peasants in nine villages in the valley. We were technically advisers to the camp, then commanded by *Dai-uy* (Captain) Nguyen. His troops included

108 • Ⅴietnam

a six-man Vietnamese Special Forces team and a strike force of three Civilian Irregular Defense Group companies, each intended to have one hundred fifty-four men. But we found the strike force battalion far below strength. Its largest company numbered only eighty-nine.

We anticipated we would spend no more than a few weeks or a couple of months at Nam Dong. The plan was to turn the camp over to the Civil Guard. We would move on to Ta Co, nearer to the Laotian border in Quang Nam, the province adjacent to ours to the south. At Ta Co we were to establish a new camp with the same mission, helping the natives and performing interdiction of infiltration routes.

We committed ourselves to maximum effort every day of our tour. We invested six months of our lives preparing for this mission. We were determined to accomplish whatever had to be done.

It is difficult to put into words the feelings we had—a mixture of desire, dedication, confusion, uncertainty, the disappointment of expectations that things would be better than they possibly could be under present circumstances. One good man did find the words.

On May 17, 1964, shortly before we left Fort Bragg, the *New York Herald Tribune* published excerpts from letters of James Polk Spruill, an Army captain who was killed April 21 in IV Corps, in the Mekong Delta. Captain Spruill, a native of Winston-Salem, North Carolina, had been writing to his wife who with their two small children was living in Suffern, New York. His widow sent excerpts to the paper. They were later published in a pamphlet.

Captain Spruill knew why he and thousands of other Americans were in Vietnam. He knew why his country had sent him there and he was equal to the task. He spoke for all who served alongside the courageous Vietnamese people, as he did, in their bloody struggle for freedom. He wrote:

"There are many moments of frustration in Vietnam. Ineptness, dishonesty, lack of spirit, confusion, and laziness cause them. But that is exactly why we are here. It is exactly in places and in

circumstances such as this that communism gains its foothold. Communism is the scavenger of the upheaval that comes with modernization and the age of rising expectations . . .

"Above all, this is a war of mind and spirit. For us to despair would be a great victory for the enemy. We must stand strong and give heart to an embattled and confused people. This can not be done if America loses heart. At the moment my heart is big enough to sustain those around me.

"Please don't let them back where you are sell me down the river with talk of despair and defeat. There is no backing out of Vietnam, for it will follow us everywhere we go. We have drawn the line here, and the America we all know and love best is not one to back away."

During our area studies we were all impressed with the history of the Vietnamese, which showed they, too, were not the sort of people "to back away." Our primary reference book was *The Village in Vietnam,* by Gerald C. Hickey.

Vietnam's civilization is among the world's oldest, dating to several hundred years before Christ. Originally the Vietnamese occupied southern and southeastern China and the east coast of Vietnam almost as far south as Hue, some fifty miles northwest of Da Nang. The Chinese conquered them in 111 B.C., and except for a few rebellions, maintained control for the next thousand years.

The most famous of these uprisings was led by two sisters, Trung Trac and Trung Nhi, in A.D. 39. They raised an army of 80,000, mounted on elephants. In one short year they overthrew the Chinese governor and were proclaimed queens of the country.

Peace reigned for about seven years. In A.D. 46 Chinese regulars overwhelmed the rebels when the Viets made a stand in a field against the cliffs of the River Day. Rather than surrender, the Trung sisters drowned themselves in the river. The scene of this battle was not far from the spot where, some 1,900 years later, French forces were annihilated by the troops of Communist Viet Minh General Vo Nguyen Giap under similar circumstances. Hopefully the mistake will not be repeated, which is why we chose to roam the mountains, jungles and rice paddies, by day and by night, pursuing the Viet Cong.

The Vietnamese overcame their Chinese conquerors for good in 940, and in 1284 made another stand for independence, turning back the Mongolians of Kublai Khan. Once in control, the Viets pressed to the south and, with Hue as their capital, spread all the way to the tip of the Ca Mau Peninsula jutting into the Gulf of Siam.

As they moved south the Viets overran the once-great kingdom of Champa and forced the Khmers (Cambodians) westward. About 30,000 Chams remained in Vietnam, unassimilated and speaking their native language in fishing villages near Phan Rang and Phan Ri, midway down the coast. Enmity between the Vietnamese and Cambodians continued into this century.

Towards the end of the eighteenth century French colonials settled in the area, as well as the British, Spanish, Portuguese and the Dutch. Fighting erupted again in the mid 1800's, but French control prevailed. On June 6, 1884, Vietnam accepted the French protectorate, and together with Laos and Cambodia, comprised what was known as French Indochina.

After the fall of France on June 25, 1940, Japan invaded. Their occupation continued until March 10, 1945, when Japan, facing imminent defeat at the hands of the Allies, declared Vietnam's "independence" under puppet emperor Bao Dai. He proclaimed the end of French rule.

Ho Chi Minh and his forces took control and forced Bao Dai to abdicate on August 25, 1945. Among Ho's followers were many who had fought with the French resistance against the Japanese. Some belonged to Ho's Indochina Communist Party and many did not, but they shared a determination to solidify their independence from France. Fighting broke out on November 20, 1946, ending eight long years later in a French defeat.

Ho's move to take over all of Vietnam was opposed by Ngo Dinh Diem. In 1955 a referendum declared South Vietnam a republic with Diem as president. The Communists unleashed guerrilla warfare against Diem with cadres left behind after the 1954 Geneva Accords divided the country at the 17th parallel, and the North and South exchanged refugees. The Communists formalized their terror and aggression by creating a "National Liberation Front" in 1960. When President Diem's position began disintegrating a year later, President Kennedy ordered the massive buildup of U.S. advisers—military, economic and political. Diem's assassination and the overthrow of his regime on November 1, 1963, resulted in political instability, including a series of coups.

Such was the unsettled history of the people we were committed to helping. Some years before I had been given a poem which I now posted on our team bulletin board. It challenged us all to . . . "Be the Best of Whatever You Are."

We were surprised to see just how far South Vietnam still had to go to become a nation in the best sense of the term, despite its great agricultural wealth, which made it "the breadbasket of Asia." The country starts in the north as mountains and rain forests and ends in the south as lush delta and mangrove swamps. The climate is either hot and dry or hot and wet.

The fourteen million South Vietnamese people were concentrated in the cities and villages of the lowlands. The highlanders included ethnic Vietnamese who had relocated there at their government's urging and some 600,000 native *montagnards*. There was a great chasm between the French-taught Vietnamese in the cities and the darker, shorter people of the mountains whom they looked upon as *moi*, or savages.

About thirty per cent of the people were Buddhists, ten per cent Catholics, and the rest Confucianists, Taoists, Animists, or members of assorted offshoots and sects. They communicated in Vietnamese, French, Chinese, English, and the numerous languages and dialects of the thirty-four basic *montagnard* tribes and subgroups.

Our field of operations was the land of the Katu tribesmen. We accompanied Captain John Eddy and his team on a tour of the camp and they briefed us on our responsibilities. I had known John since

112 • ᐯietnam

we served as privates at Fort Jackson, and later as classmates at OCS.

They showed us the two 60-millimeter and the three 81-millimeter mortar pits within the camp's inner perimeter, and the machine gun positions to be manned by the Nungs. We took stock of the ammunition and reserve small arms, the dispensary, and the command and communications areas. Captain Eddy told us his engineering projects had been the airstrip, concrete ammunition bunkers in the mortar pits, and a giant hole in the ground near our main gate. The hole was fifteen by thirty by eight feet deep. We called it "the swimming pool." Earth that had been excavated formed a mound on the outer side of the hole. Some handmade cinder blocks were stacked nearby. The objective was to construct an operations center and dispensary in this excavation and cover it with dirt. The central buildings were fortified against attack by five-foot walls consisting of two rows of logs with earth packed between.

Communications trenches, about two feet across and eighteen inches deep, were big enough for a man to crawl in with a degree of safety—and to fight from. These trenches ran strategically through the inner perimeter and extended to key points in the outer perimeter.

There were civic action programs ongoing in seven of the nine villages in the valley. North from our camp these included nearby Nam Dong, Ta Lu One and Ta Lu Two across the Ta Trach River; Ta Rau, Nga Hai, Qua Hop, and the divided village of Mu Nam, consisting of coastal Vietnamese on one side of the road and seventeen huts of *montagnard* women, children and elderly on the other side. Two villages beyond that, Truong Tra and Kha Tre, were the responsibility of the district chief, *Trung-uy* (Lieutenant) Lu, who had a 200-man outpost on the heights above Kha Tre. "Combat Alley" was beyond—the low-lying road to Da Nang. The odds against traveling that road without getting ambushed by the VC were a hundred to one.

We took up our advisory assignments with Captain Eddy and his team's guidance. They remained with us until early June, and then we were on our own. We had our own ideas about our mission, but we did not want to make any major changes in anticipation of our expected move to the Laos border. There was plenty to do and we put in long days. We greeted each new day thankful we had lived to see the sun rise over our camp.

Jay was in charge of the civic-action program and spent considerable time in the village. He covered one wall of the orderly room with a large map of the valley. He was a good artist, and with the help of a Vietnamese named Minh, he devised a color chart and symbols that helped us track where schools were needed, when the last sick call was held, and so forth.

Brown, who had been in combat in Korea and Vietnam, paced off the camp, covering every square foot and memorizing the ranges from each weapons position to various points, like a depression or brush, where attackers might take cover. Brownie was our chief weapons man. He inventoried and packed the surplus weapons in the camp—272 small arms including rifles, carbines, sub-machine guns and so on—above the customary ten per cent reserve.

We knew that many surplus weapons represented a challenge to the VC, if they knew about them. They would be willing to sacrifice a lot of men to get their hands on that much firepower. Brownie made a list of all the arms in the camp, including location and serial numbers. Surplus weapons were boxed and when he ran out of boxes the rest were tied six in a bundle. When Major Nance from B Detachment headquarters visited us on July 2, Brown gave him the inventory sheet and requested a helicopter to remove them from the camp.

Dan was having problems with his communications equipment. The camp's electrical system was also his responsibility. He checked all of the U.S. and Vietnamese radios, adjusting and repositioning antennas. He fine-tuned the portable radios for maximum range for our altitude and climate.

Whit took over where the previous team's engineer-demolitions specialist left off in civic-action construction work. This kept him in the village much of the time. He also tackled the job of completing the airstrip. And if that weren't enough he did repair and maintenance work on our buildings and put up additional defenses where we extended the camp's outer perimeter.

Gregg was the most popular man on the team as far as the Vietnamese were concerned. They already liked our medics, and Gregg was a proud husband and father and enjoyed talking about his family, and that appealed to the Viets' strong feeling for family. When the mail brought a large photo of his wife and children, he arranged for a camp carpenter to make a frame for it and he hung it in his room on July 5. Gregg worked closely with the four capable Vietnamese nurses, Co (Miss) Han, Co Gem, Co Pha, and Co Caac. One day early on in our tour a child was brought to the dispensary with a large abscess in his shoulder. Gregg knew it would kill him without prompt surgery. He proposed flying the boy to a surgeon in Da Nang, but the *montagnard* mother refused. So Gregg operated on the boy and when he checked again on July 5, the shoulder had healed nicely.

I had close contact with Team Sergeant Alamo and with Beeson, our intelligence specialist. We kiddingly referred to Beeson as our "smart sergeant"—trying to stay on top of everything that was happening. I had a portable typewriter that I had won playing bingo in Alaska, and we used it to pound out reports and requisitions to Da Nang, and for paper work within the compound. As the senior advisor in the district, everything was my concern, whether it was military, economic, political, agricultural or even social. For example, I stayed posted on a volleyball rivalry between *Trung-uy* Lu's strike force and ours. Alamo and I had a priority list, and this changed sometimes by the hour. There were never enough hours in the day.

All of us took turns on routine patrols, primarily for security but frequently to probe for any evidence of VC activity. Prior to the opening of Camp Nam Dong the valley had been a VC training ground for many years. A few days after our arrival we learned that the people in our villages were being harassed, threatened and sometimes killed. Naturally the villagers were in fear for their lives, and that made it difficult for us to gather information from the

𝒱ietnam • 115

people. And a district chief had forbidden us from patrolling east of the Ta Trach River, even though it ran within 200 yards of camp. The district chief said it was too dangerous, but we sent out patrols elsewhere almost every night and we often slept in the villages, providing security for the chiefs.

Other A-726 members worked with their seniors—Woody with Brown, John with Dan, Mike with Whit, and Terry with Gregg. We tried to improve defense of the camp and to determine where the VC were and what they were doing. At first we struggled with the Vietnamese language, but were relieved to find that after a couple of weeks we could converse well enough to understand and be understood. We pressed on with our civic-action work, constantly aware that the VC were watching and waiting, and might come out of the hills at any time, day or night, to test us.

We had an internal battle with our digestive tracts, and made the best of it. One problem was fresh water. A partial solution was to drink beer purchased in Nam Dong. Dan, a former Army cook, constructed a small outdoor cinder block oven with a 55-gallon drum for a chimney. Woody, also an ex-cook, built cabinets in the kitchen to keep the rats from sharing our food. We scrounged some chocolate flavoring for our canned milk, and bought popcorn and candy bars in Da Nang.

One day a helicopter landed on the airstrip instead of the chopper pad. Anticipating that it might be a VIP visitor, about half the team hustled out to the chopper, armed with automatic rifles, and accompanied by equally well armed Nung bodyguards. All they brought back was a carton containing a dozen boxes of pizza mix. Jay, Dan, and Woody, assisted by the native cooks, went to work building pizzas garnished with Parmesan cheese and chunks of an almost indigestible native sausage.

Five rounds of small-arms fire plinked into our camp on June 20. For most of us it was our first sniper fire. We answered with several rounds from an 81-millimeter mortar.

I decided to go after the snipers. I found Beeson in the mess hall, leisurely sipping coffee. Snipers were old hat to that veteran

Brothers Michael and Paul Donlon
U.S. Army, World War II

Brother Gerard Donlon
U.S. Air Force

LTC Donlon, U.S. Army, re-enlists his brother Jack Donlon, U.S. Air Force, Hall of Heroes, The Pentagon.

Sappers killed by Captain Donlon as they attempted to blow up the main gate.

Bodies of Viet Cong killed within the inner perimeter of Camp Nam Dong.

The blood-stained 60-millimeter mortar position where MSG Gabriel Ralph Alamo and Australian Warrant Officer Kevin Conway gave their lives.

Nurses, Eighth Field Hospital
Left to right back row: Joan Jensen, A. J. Nagelhout, Hank Walker, Georgeanne Bassman, Maryanne Dietrich, Mary Clark. Left to right front row: Julie Klebaum, Dorothy Clifford, Alice Marie Cushnil, Terry O'Dwyer, Kathy Schilling, Ruth Webster.

Nurses at Nam Dong, July 1964
Co (Miss) Han, Co Gem, Smiley, Co Pha, and Co Caac.

Nungs from the 1st Night Combat Unit present Captain Donlon with a handmade banner. It declares that he will return home with honor. Nha Trang, Vietnam, October 1964.

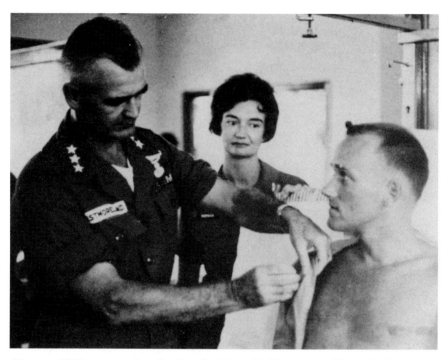

General Westmoreland pins the Purple Heart on Captain Donlon at the 8th Field Hospital. Army nurse Captain Maryanne Dietrich looks on.

Ambassador Maxwell D. Taylor and Major General Richard G. Stilwell visit with Captain Donlon.

Mrs. Marion Donlon, Captain Donlon, President Johnson, General Earl Wheeler, The White House, December 5, 1964.

Left to right: SSG Gregg, SFC Brown, SSG Whitsell, SGT Disser, Mrs. Alice Houston with son George, Captain Donlon, SFC Beeson, SSG Woods, SSG Daniels. Winter Park, Florida, April 1965.

Captain Donlon and Miss Elinor Lente, his high school Latin teacher, admire their Golden Key Awards. Atlantic City, New Jersey, February 1966.

Captain Donlon being presented the Republic of Vietnam National Order Fourth Class at the Embassy of the Republic of Vietnam. Washington, D.C., May 1966.

Daughter Linda with husband Paul and their son Griffin.

Son Damian Charles Donlon   **Son Jason Donlon and wife, Lori and their daughter Lilly.**

Son Derek with wife Melanie and their daughters Alicia, Justine and Jordan

Son Justin and his daughter Elise

Colonel Donlon places his Green Beret and Medal of Honor at MSG Gabriel Ralph Alamo's grave in a gesture of respect. Fayetteville, North Carolina.

Colonel Donlon places a wreath and his Medal of Honor at the grave of Kevin Conway. ULU Pandan Military Cemetery, Singapore.

Colonel Donlon returns to Nam Dong Valley. With him is Ted Westerman. March 1993.

Colonel Donlon with some of his former adversaries reconcile through restoration of Camp Nam Dong Cemtery. October 1995.

Ambassador Pete Peterson, Son Do and Joyce Nguyen, first Westmoreland Scholar Foundation Summer Interns. American Embassy, Hanoi, Vietnam. August 1997.

of Korea.

"The camp commander is going to take a patrol out to see if we can snatch those guys," I announced. "Do you want to go along?"

Beeson dropped his coffee, reached for his AR-15 and said, "You bet!"

However, my counterpart had a change of heart. *Dai-uy* Nguyen wouldn't leave our outpost. Despite our urgings he said it would not be possible to catch up with the snipers and there was no purpose to tiring his men on a fruitless mission. He appeared totally disinterested, mirroring the attitude that Captain Spruill had cited— lack of spirit, confusion, and laziness. Nguyen was basically a tired man—tired of war, tired of patrols, tired of killing. We had been around only three weeks. The Vietnamese had been at war almost continuously for twenty-four years.

We encountered the same problems Captain Spruill and others had contended with in trying to keep our work with the Vietnamese on an orderly basis. We were constantly double-checking to be certain there was follow-through on any agreement to take action. The Vietnamese camp commander simply didn't share our sense of urgency. When we did reach an understanding we wrote it out and saw that it was radioed to Vietnamese headquarters in Da Nang. We had our B Detachment check on the Da Nang end. This further complicated an already difficult situation but it seemed to be the only solution.

Despite these lapses of indifference on the part of the Vietnamese, our relations with them were fairly good. They were always friendly, if you could overlook their maddening propensity for rarely doing today what they could promise to do tomorrow.

We worked at learning their language and customs, and in turn to teach them ours. Of course we were always a pushover for the children. On one occasion we met a beautiful little Eurasian girl about nine years old. Her name was Jacqueline. Her father was French, her mother Vietnamese. The district chief brought her to our mess hall. After a great deal of coaxing she performed for us. That innocent child sang for us in a clear, sweet voice, accompanying

Vietnam • 117

herself with graceful movements of her arms and hands. From that day little Jackie was the sweetheart of Team A-726.

Our mascot was a lively seven-year-old boy named Nam. We didn't adopt him. He adopted us. He was perpetually underfoot, like a playful puppy. At night he would crawl in among the spare mattresses in the supply room. He chose to sleep there rather than go home. When his mother explained that he was playing hooky from school to be with us, we told Nam he could only hang around after school hours.

We truly enjoyed having children around us out there in the middle of nowhere. And we knew it was also a dangerous luxury. The VC liked nothing better than to use children as spies. This happened to one of the teams before us. They "adopted" a small girl, permitting her to roam at will. The VC told her father they would kill her unless he forced her to feed them intelligence information about the camp. Simultaneously they told this child they would kill her father unless she cooperated. So she became the eyes and ears of the VC inside the camp until they realized what was happening.

We worked with the Vietnamese Special Forces and the strike force battalion through the camp commander, *Dai-uy* Nguyen, until he was replaced by *Dai-uy* Lich at the end of June. But we worked directly with the Nungs. They lived with us in the inner perimeter and accompanied us everywhere as bodyguards. The Nungs were tough and tested mercenaries and they hated the VC. Thousands of Nungs emigrated from their North Vietnam homeland after the 1954 Geneva Accords. Together with others who followed them, they settled around Pleiku in II Corps. Le Tse-tung, a karate expert and veteran soldier who fought with the French against the Japanese, commanded the forty Nungs with us. Le was too old to go out on patrols but he held tight reins on the Nungs, making certain they were always ready for immediate action. He spoke French, a little English, and some Vietnamese and Katu.

On June 27 we received word of a "big sickness" in the villages, especially Kha Tre at the far end of the valley. Gregg and Terry responded immediately to see what the problem was. Gregg reported back that we did indeed have a raging epidemic. The symptoms included vomiting, headache, muscular spasms, stiffness in the neck and back, and severe pains, especially in the legs.

Gregg speculated that it was meningitis, and on a fairly large scale.

We notified Da Nang and a Marine doctor helicoptered out. He confirmed Gregg's diagnosis, with a note of uncertainty. The symptoms pointed to meningitis, but the physician said they could be prodromal, meaning the first symptoms were common to various diseases. Later the symptoms would change, and then an accurate diagnosis would be possible.

The village health workers were organized into a valley health corps. Although a surprise VC attack was possible at any moment, Gregg and Terry spent several nights in the villages, giving sulfa drugs to those who had been exposed.

Within a couple more days Gregg had a firm diagnosis: encephalitis, an inflammation of the brain known as "sleeping sickness." The medics brought the worst cases into camp for evacuation to the Da Nang hospital. To the extent it was possible, the valley was isolated to keep the epidemic from any further spreading.

By July 3 it seemed we were gaining on the epidemic. There were no reports of new cases that day, and no deaths. The first evacuees left the camp on July 4. The air-evac plane also brought Dr. Gerald C. Hickey of the Rand Corporation.

"Doc" Hickey was a real godsend. He was an authority on the *montagnards*, their languages, traditions and customs. He had been hired by the Rand Corporation to study the relationship between American and Vietnamese military personnel. Hopefully he could help us in our contacts with the villagers, particularly with respect to complaints from Ta Rau that a defoliation program had damaged part of their rice crop. The chemicals had been sprayed along the road to eliminate possible hiding places for ambushers. Our cursory inspection did not reveal any rice crop damage, and we guessed the

Vietnam • 119

VC had invented the story in an effort to drive a wedge between the villagers and us.

Doc had a pleasant manner. He was a tall, lanky Chicagoan who had the self-confidence of someone who was always in control. He quickly gained our respect.

Lieutenant O and Terry took him to Ta Rau so he could inspect the rice. That night we all gathered in the mess hall to hear Doc's stories about his experiences with the *montagnards*.

We took a half-day off to celebrate the Fourth of July. As it turned out the Vietnamese took the entire day off. Twenty additional Nungs had arrived from Da Nang, raising their muster to sixty. The Nungs helped us bury communications wire and other tasks. Meanwhile the Vietnamese were holding their own version of a picnic and volley ball game.

The twenty additional Nungs were brought in as part of our camp security guard. We were preparing for a five-day reconnaissance of some nearby caves to see if they were a possible VC headquarters. The recent epidemic had postponed this operation. Now that the epidemic appeared under control we were planning to begin our reconnaissance on July 6, with the best of the three Vietnamese strike force companies comprising the main body. Doing this would temporarily remove the best one-third of the camp's defenders.

I considered this too great a risk to take, since the surplus weapons and ammo had not yet been removed from camp—unless the camp's defenses were bolstered while we were absent. So some of us flew to Da Nang to discuss the matter with the B Detachment. Higher headquarters agreed, supplying the additional twenty Nungs.

And as a bonus someone authorized us a two-and-one-half ton truck. Unfortunately the only way we could get to Nam Dong was by driving the thirty miles through "ambush alley."

We started off, with Beeson at the wheel. Whether it was because of our truckload of Nungs armed to the teeth, or we were just lucky, we made it back unchallenged. Along the road we came upon a bus which had overturned. Passengers and baggage were scattered

120 • Vietnam

everywhere. We broke open the truck's medical kit and under Gregg's directions we did our best to give first aid. We stopped a passing Vietnamese Army truck, loaded the injured aboard and sent them to the hospital in Hue, some twenty miles distant.

Meanwhile we sensed uneasiness in the valley. Mike Disser was winding up a three-day mission with a squad of night fighters. Mike was at the far end of the valley, securing villages and setting up ambushes for any VC roaming the area. He radioed from Ta Rau that the villagers appeared to be frightened.

"They're getting me jumpy, too," Mike confessed. "Maybe we should have another squad on the other side of the river from Ta Rau." He said the villagers wouldn't tell him or his interpreter why they were frightened.

Beeson, Woods and a squad moved into position along the river. But the night passed without incident and they returned to camp the following morning, a Sunday.

Lieutenant O and Gregg took Doc Hickey on a tour of the valley Sunday morning. He wanted to see it all, and they visited each village, checking rice crops for any evidence of chemical damage. They found none.

While they were touring they planned to buy some beer, since our supply in the camp was getting low. They stopped at a small cafe in the Nam Dong village to pick up the beer. It was now late Sunday morning. A few hours later and they would have had a front row seat for big trouble.

Vietnam • 121

ROGER...AMERICA SALUTES...

This salute to Captain Donlon is the work of artist-illustrator Joe Sinnott who, like the author, hails from Saugerties, New York.

Before the Battle

July 5, 1964 . . .

About a dozen Vietnamese soldiers from Company 122 of our strike force had encircled one of the newly arrived Nungs in the street outside the Nam Dong village cafe where Jay, Gregg, and Doc Hickey had gone earlier to buy beer. They were talking in a highly agitated manner, making threatening gestures toward the Nung. One Vietnamese was acting in a particularly aggressive manner.

Whenever they seemed to tire of the confrontation the one Viet who had been making the greatest commotion would renew the hassling and that would restart the others. Neither the Vietnamese nor the Nungs were permitted to carry weapons into the villages when they were off duty, so up to this point the incident had been a war of words.

Finally they began to disperse and started walking back to camp. Along the way they continued to talk in an animated, agitated way.

It was a while before we figured out what had occurred. The Nung had found a former girl friend in the village and paid her a visit. Her current boy friend belonged to Company 122, and was jealous. The Nung decided he would resume his former friendship and the Vietnamese decided he would not. They said someone had pulled a knife, but no one knew for sure.

The Vietnamese who had been the principal agitator continued to vocalize, even more so than the Vietnamese soldier who stood to lose his girl friend. The lead antagonist was wearing black pajamas of the type worn by the VC. But black calico pajamas were as common as blue jeans back home. Everyone wore them, including some Americans.

Upon reaching the inner perimeter the Nung wasted no time in huddling with the other Nungs. The Vietnamese went to their company area near the main gate, but they continued to be unsettled.

They were milling around at the inner perimeter fence. The pajama-clad protagonist pressed his verbal attack, jumping back and forth over the fence. Next the Vietnamese were pummeling the Nungs with rocks. And then a shot was fired.

The shot sent the Nungs running toward their mortars and machine guns. The Vietnamese took cover in their defensive ditches and began firing with their carbines. They peppered the inner perimeter. Bullets riddled the huts. The more disciplined Nungs fired occasionally, waiting for their commander, Le Tse-tung, to give further orders.

Meanwhile I had been meeting with Le and the camp commander, *Dai-uy* Lich, trying to get things quieted down, when the shooting began. As we dove for cover I saw the Nungs manning their machine guns. I ran toward the fence, shouting to both sides to cease fire.

Alamo scrambled out with me, shouting and waving his arms, telling the Nungs to keep their weapons out of sight and to hold their fire.

"Down your arms!" he shouted. "Hold your fire!"

He called to the team members to take their positions.

The Nungs were getting itchy trigger fingers. First a machine gun cut loose with a short burst. Another Nung emptied the clip in his carbine before Dan could get him stopped. As Terry sought to control several other Nungs, Houston raced to a Nung machine gun squad. He aimed his .45 Colt pistol at the gunner's head.

"If you pull that trigger, you're dead," he promised.

Jay was in the command post when the firing began, updating his civic action map. Upon hearing the shots Jay reached for his M-79 grenade launcher and his AR-15. Grabbing extra ammunition for both, and with his .357 Magnum pistol strapped to his hip, he raced for the door, where he found Terry.

"VC?" he quizzed, "VC?"

"Not today," Terry replied. "Today we're fighting the strike force!"

Woody and Brown and Doc Hickey had been taking a break in the mess hall. Brown was kidding Hickey about his shirt. "The VC

124 • Before the Battle

love white T-shirts," he said. "They're easier to aim at." Suspecting the shooting had been started by the VC, they grabbed their weapons and took up defensive positions. Later, Brown kiddingly reminded Hickey of his admonition. "See all the trouble you cause by wearing a white T-shirt?"

I was able to get Le Tse-tung to calm down the Nungs. But *Dai-uy* Lich wouldn't come outside and order the strike force companies to pull back. Instead he remained in the Vietnamese mess hall, having his dinner.

We estimated some five hundred rounds were fired in the brief exchange. We called to the Vietnamese to settle down while we got the leaders to talk things out. But some of the strike force members refused to remain in the trenches. They crisscrossed in front of the barbed wire, waving their weapons and taunting the Nungs.

Terry and Mike Disser went to the inner perimeter gate with interpreters, trying to get the strike force to withdraw. Jay joined them. He told the Vietnamese that the confrontation was over. They pointed to his pistol as if to say, "If it's over, why are you armed?" Jay responded by unholstering his weapon and unloading it. Next he turned his back on the armed strike force members and walked to the center of the camp.

Later, thinking about what he had done, he confessed "It was probably the longest walk of my life."

He joined Alamo and me at the command post, where we were trying to decide how we could get the Vietnamese and the Nungs to back off. We needed to get things under control quickly, as it was starting to get dark. Unless we could negotiate an end to the matter no one would get much of a night's sleep.

Gregg and Houston arrived, saying they had taken care of two Nung machine guns near the back of the camp by taking away their ammunition.

"All the time Gregg was disarming that gun, there was a strike force guy with a BAR laid right on him, watching every move," Terry said. "It wouldn't have helped Gregg any, but I would have had him if he'd fired."

I strode out of the command post and confronted *Dai-uy* Lich as he was finishing eating. I was fuming, but I spoke slowly and determinedly.

"If you don't personally go out there and get that automatic weapon turned around ASAP, I will personally kill you," I threatened the strike team commander. "And then we will get that BAR man taken care of!"

Thinking back on the incident, I am not sure if I really meant it or not. I think probably I did not. Fortunately it was not necessary for me to make good on my promise.

Dai-uy Lich took my threat at face value. He ran out the door, blowing his whistle. He ordered the three company commanders to form up their men. They complied, but the troops didn't hold formation. One man would break ranks and then the rest would disperse. A few shots were fired and more whistle-blowing and shouted orders followed. They would form up, and then the same thing would happen all over again.

Meanwhile the Nungs remained in their positions, ready to follow Le Tse-tung's orders. I knew the sixty Nungs would have annihilated the more than two hundred Vietnamese. The Nungs were better disciplined, better trained, and better equipped. They had three 81-millimeter mortars, two 60-millimeter mortars, plus machine guns, submachine guns, Browning automatic rifles and assorted other firearms. The Vietnamese, by contrast, had one hand-held 60-millimeter mortar in each company, with but nine rounds of ammo per mortar, plus a few submachine guns and BARs and carbines, mostly M1 and M2s.

I remained in full view of both sides. I was standing on a sort of parade ground—an open area near the main gate where our flagpole stood. I left my weapons behind in the CP and told the other team members to disarm as well. I was gambling that in doing so we could persuade everyone else that we wanted to avoid big trouble. Le Tse-tung was trying to persuade them to convince their men to cool it. But everyone was talking at once, constantly butting into our conversation.

126 • *Before the Battle*

Fortunately I remembered a tactic I had learned from Le. I squatted. Le and Lich squatted with me. This enabled the three of us to continue talking uninterrupted. The others stood around, but they were effectively cut out of the discussion, and stopped talking. It was the custom, and everyone respected it. It was almost as good as being in a private office.

Somehow, no one was killed in all that firing. One Nung and one Vietnamese sustained minor wounds. Gregg patched them up and led them to bunks in the dispensary.

Le and Lich said they would attempt to restore order. I called another meeting for 2030 hours in the mess hall.

I hoped to ascertain how the whole affair had gotten started. I wanted to know if it was a VC ploy to create dissension within the camp as a prelude to an attack. There were also two decisions to be made. Should we hold the morning formation with all camp personnel gathered at the flagpole in the inner perimeter, as was our custom on Mondays? And should we proceed with a five-day area patrol that was planned to start on Monday? In view of what had just transpired, neither seemed to be a very good idea now.

I was thinking about the agitator in Company 122. Was he a VC infiltrator? Were there others who had infiltrated 121 and 123? It was an old VC tactic. At other camps in II Corps and IV Corps the VC had infiltrated, caused disturbances within the camp, and then attacked in force. At Long Kanh in IV Corps, the VC succeeded in slipping three infiltrators into each of the three strike force companies. They were identified and questioned. They said they were instructed to give a flashlight signal for a night attack on the camp. The defenders laid a trap, giving the signal, but nothing happened. The following morning they found newly dug trenches and other indications of VC presence, but apparently the VC sensed an ambush and withdrew.

There were probably twenty of us at the 2030 meeting. We tried to make it appear as low key as possible. Dan baked some cherry pies. He shuttled between kitchen and mess hall, delivering pies and serving them with coffee. We smoked cigarettes as we talked.

Before the Battle • 127

Le was present with his lieutenant, a crew-cut karate expert we had dubbed "Herr adjutant" because of his crisp manner. Lich was there with his company commanders and staff. Kevin Conway, the Australian, Doc Hickey, and most of our team were present. We all sat around the tables and I did most of the talking. I said it seemed prudent to postpone the five-day patrol and to move the ceremony at the flagpole to the helicopter pad, where it would be easier for us to disperse if we came under attack.

Lich, who had not been in favor of the patrol anyway, agreed to putting it on hold. Woody and Gregg felt better about the postponement. They had been scheduled to go on the patrol and weren't looking forward to the possibility of another shoot-out between our Nungs and the strikers.

But Lich vetoed my plan to move the Monday assembly to the chopper pad. He thought it would be unwise to move from the flagpole area, arguing it would give too much weight to the shoot-out. He offered to make a speech at the flagpole, calling for unity, and urging the Nungs and strike force personnel to put the past behind them and focus on the real enemy.

I agreed, somewhat reluctantly, with the additional safeguards of doubling the strike force's outer perimeter guard overnight and having them take over airstrip security. Until now the airstrip had been the Nungs' assignment. I told Lich I didn't think it would be good to have the Nungs at the airstrip, since their proximity to the strike force might result in further trouble.

I instructed Le to triple the inner perimeter Nung guard, from five to fifteen. One member of my team was always on night guard duty, with one or two others awake and ready if needed. Beeson had begun making the rounds. Gregg left the mess hall to relieve Beeson at ten. Conway was slated to relieve Gregg at midnight and I would stand guard starting at 0200 hours.

Nighttime patrol of the inner perimeter was a lonely and eerie exercise at best. One complete swing took about twenty-five minutes. We checked each Nung gun position and the Nung guarding the gate. By design, there was no set pattern for these checks.

We had another system for monitoring the outer perimeter. We did not personally venture into the outer perimeter at night. To make sure the guards were awake and alert, the Nung at the gate would strike an empty shell casing. Responding to this makeshift gong, the companies in the outer perimeter would answer with their own prearranged gong signals. Since this compromised the guard positions, we varied this procedure. It was the Vietnamese Special Forces' responsibility to check the outer perimeter and report back.

Following our mess hall meeting, shortly after 2200 hours, Lee, Lich and I conferred at the camp commander's quarters. We continued to discuss the Monday morning ceremony, and how we might use it to eliminate any further problems between the strike force and the Nungs. We had concluded the confrontation had been instigated by the VC prior to some sort of probe. And if that was not the case and the VC learned of what had transpired, we could expect them to start something anyway.

About midnight I concluded the discussion with Le and Lich. I paced the inner perimeter, checking the Nungs and reflecting on the day's events. I was ill at ease, and with reason. We were a new team at Nam Dong, only five weeks into our tour. We had far more arms stored at the camp than were needed, and this by itself was a tempting target. We were planning a move to another camp and consequently would be somewhat preoccupied with that move. It was a holiday weekend, creating a more relaxed atmosphere. And we had scheduled a patrol that would trim Nam Dong's defenses by a third. The VC may have thought we had already begun the patrol.

Upon reaching my quarters in the command post I removed my fatigues, pulled on a T-shirt, fatigue jacket and black calico pajama pants. I stretched out on my cot before going on guard duty. It had been a stressful day. I was tired and would have liked to get some sleep, but there wasn't time. I lit a cigarette, pondered the day's events, and prayed for morning.

Woody wrote an insightful letter to his wife before falling asleep.

"All hell is going to break loose here before the night is over," he predicted. "We had some trouble today between the Nungs and

Before the Battle • 129

the strike force. I was talking about it with our Australian and we figure that was just an action to get us all riled up and the VC were going to hit us before morning."

Woody put the letter on the top shelf of the makeshift mailbox at the CP. The top shelf was for outgoing letters, and there were quite a few there. The bottom shelf was for incoming mail. No letter remained there for very long, unless the man was away from camp on patrol.

Woody undressed except for his undershorts. He placed his .38-caliber pistol under his pillow, as was his practice, and tried to fall asleep. It took about an hour for him to drop off.

Brown had taken a hot shower under the 55-gallon drum that had been rigged with a heating element and showerhead, and had turned in following the mess hall meeting. He was wearing only camouflage trousers.

Lieutenant O had posted two letters. He had written his parents in Chicago, and to an insurance company, paying a personal property premium. Jay was exhausted. He had pulled two tours of guard duty Saturday afternoon and night and took Doc Hickey and Gregg on a tour of the valley Sunday morning, and worked with Houston burying communications lines. Then he updated his map. He rolled up his fatigues and placed them under his pillow with his pistol, pistol belt and a flashlight. The key to the safe was in a pocket of his fatigues. He pulled on black pajama trousers and promptly fell asleep.

Disser was asleep in the supply room, wearing his fatigue jacket and trousers. Whitsell had missed the shoot-'em-up. He had gone to the village to talk with *Trung-uy* Lu about civic-action matters and was on his way back to camp at the time of the gunplay. He showered after the meeting, climbed into black pajama pants and fell asleep.

Dan was preparing for sleep in the communications room at the rear of the second long house. It was his usual practice to hang his AR-15 on the wall so rats wouldn't knock it over as they prowled the floor at night. Instead, he leaned the weapon against a small wooden stand next to his bunk. Next to it he placed his .45-caliber pistol. He put some AR-15 clips and belt on the floor by the bed and put extra rounds for the pistol on a shelf. Then he tuned the radio to the B Detachment frequency in Da Nang so it would be ready once it was switched on. He placed his socks and shoes nearby and fell asleep in his fatigues.

Meanwhile the two medics were at the dispensary, rehashing the incident earlier in the day. They were in their own rooms. It was easy to hear and be heard through the thin rattan that separated them. Their rooms were at one end of the forty-foot building. The remainder of the building was configured for a medical supply room and treatment room on one side of the hall, with a four-bed ward on the opposite side. There was also a receiving room lined with benches where patients waited to be treated.

Gregg was wearing a maroon boxer shorts swimsuit, having come in from guard duty about 2330 hours. Conway relieved Gregg early, explaining it was too late to sleep and he had nothing better to do. Terry was stretched out on his bunk; wide-awake even though he had gotten little sleep on the just concluded three-day patrol. They found the bodies of two Vietnamese village chiefs who had been executed. Terry was exhausted but unable to sleep.

"I don't think we'll see the sun come up," he speculated.

"I don't either," Gregg replied, "but maybe we will. Anyway, we'd better get some sleep."

Almost immediately Gregg was asleep. Terry remained awake until about 0200, finally drifting off, but not in deep sleep.

I continued to drag on cigarettes in my quarters. It was quiet outside except for the dogs. They started barking about 0030 hours and seemed more agitated, but after a few minutes they were still.

Shortly before 0200 I relieved Conway, making the rounds of the inner perimeter. There was nothing I could detect to cause further concern. Maybe, I pondered, it was too quiet . . .

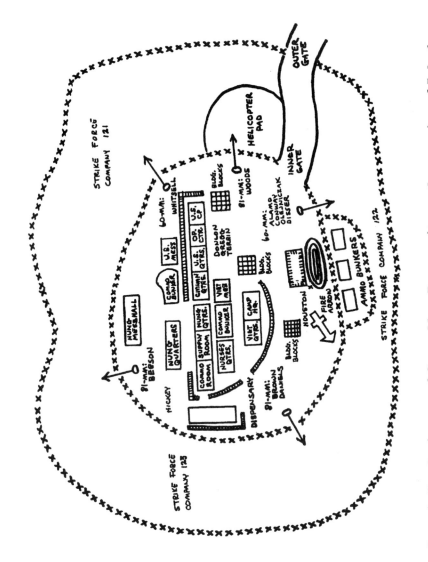

Captain Donlon's map of Camp Nam Dong as it was the morning of July 6, 1964.

132 • Before the Battle

The Battle for Nam Dong

July 6, 1964, 0226 hours . . .

As I made my rounds of the inner perimeter, the dogs were silent. Shadowing me on the other side of the barbed-wire fence was a Vietnamese Special Forces man who was walking the outer perimeter. Since he had more ground to cover I moved slowly so as to keep pace with him. Then I walked to the gate to let him back in.

"All quiet. All clear," he announced.

I unlocked the small gate so he could pass inside. This gate was just big enough for one man. After dark the American on duty and the Nung at the gate drew their weapons whenever the gate was opened. The two swinging gates across the road were kept chained and locked at night. These gates were never opened after dark. The smaller gate next to it was opened only in the presence of an American. He was to make certain the man who came through was the same man who had gone out.

Our two-gate system had been in place only a week. We made the change after a Vietnamese truck driver backed a truck into the old gate, demolishing it. We weren't sure if it had been an accident or VC sabotage. Rather than lose his job, the driver constructed a stronger gate system.

I walked up from the gate feeling somewhat relaxed. I was wearing the black pajama pants, T-shirt, and the jacket to my green nylon jungle suit. I was bareheaded, carrying my AR-15 by its handle. My pistol belt held eight AR-15 magazines, four grenades and my .45 automatic.

In something of a wish and a prayer I thought, maybe it's going to be quiet tonight after all.

It was 0226 hours as I reached the mess hall, intending to check the guard roster posted there, so I could awaken my relief at 0400 hours. It would be the last time I would open that screen door.

The roof of the mess hall exploded in a blinding flash, hit by a white phosphorus mortar shell. Two Vietnamese cooks, Onzo and Ding Dong, asleep in the rear of the hall, took the full force of the explosion. I was knocked back through the door by the force of the concussion.

My first thought was that the strike force was back in action against the Nungs. I scrambled around the anti-sniper wall and into the CP. Alamo was up, dressed in a jungle suit, and on the phone to Dan in the communications room, calling for a flare ship to light up the battlefield.

Mortar rounds continued to rain down on the compound. These shell bursts were interspersed with the lighter explosions of volleys of grenades. We were encircled by a barrage of automatic weapons and small arms fire. The mess hall was a mass of flames and the roof of the command post was on fire.

We were under heavy attack by a Viet Cong force of undetermined strength.

I formed a fire brigade of interpreters, mechanics and truck drivers and sent them to douse the fire in the mess hall.

Dan was out of the sack with the blast of the first mortar round. While his radio was warming up he put on his boots and gathered up the ammunition that he had placed on the shelf, putting it into the pockets of his jungle-suit trousers. He strapped on his holster as the explosions continued, louder. He grasped his pistol in his left hand, cocked it, and watched the door, waiting for a tone on the transmitter.

Alamo was on the field telephone, his message short and to the point.

"Call for a flare ship and an air strike! We're under attack!"

"I am," he replied.

Dan's transmitter was preset to the B Detachment in Da Nang. There was no time for code. He called "in the clear"—in plain English:

"Hello Da Nang . . . Nam Dong calling . . . We are under heavy mortar fire . . . Repeat, we are under heavy mortar fire . . .

134 • *The Battle for Nam Dong*

Request flare ship and air strike . . ."

"Roger, stand by for reply . . ."

As Dan waited the booming blasts of the mortars grew louder. When the supply room next door took a direct hit he decided the communications center could be next. He holstered his .45, grabbed his AR-15, threw on the suspenders of his AR-15 ammo belt and made a dash for the door. He took three strides and belly-flopped as far as his legs would propel him. Dan's bare shoulders and chest were a mass of small wounds from the rocks that cut into his flesh as he landed.

His flight from the communications room was not a second too soon. He felt the concussion that blew up the com center through the soles of his jump boots. The forty-foot building was a mass of fire as the thatch and rattan fed the igniting fireball.

Dan scrambled across the road leading to the dispensary at the back of the enclosure. The dispensary was also on fire. He helped Gregg and Terry drag a big steel medical chest outside. They left the fully packed M-5A kit, about the size of a foot locker, in a communications trench. Then they brought out a second chest. The medics would need the supplies stored in both before the night was over.

Hearing the first mortar burst, Gregg was out of bed in an instant, reaching for his weapon. He had a Winchester pump shotgun with a five-shell magazine. He dashed through the dispensary's back door to the protective wall where it formed an "L." Glancing around, he returned to his billet and grabbed a pair of ragged fatigues with the sleeves cut off. He pulled these over his trunks and returned outside.

The rain of mortar shells was intensifying. The sound of small arms fire was unending. The glow from the burning mess hall cast an eerie, ghostly light over the camp. Everywhere there was swirling smoke and the flashes of shell bursts.

"Damn the strike force!" Gregg swore. "Here we go again!"

He headed for an old shower room that was being used to store medical supplies. It was not far from Brown's mortar pit, near the inner perimeter wire fence. Beyond this barrier, illuminated by the fires and the moon, he observed crouched figures advancing, barely twenty yards out. He could hear bullets zinging past him as he closed on them. Backlighted by exploding rounds were the outlines of six men, seemingly floating in the half-light.

Gregg aimed his shotgun at the advancing forms. He squeezed the trigger, chambered a second shell and fired, and then a third. His salvo ripped into the VC at almost point-blank range. Only a second before they had been moving toward him at a trot. The force of his shotgun blasts carried their bodies backward as if struck by a runaway truck. Then he hurried back to the dispensary to salvage as much of his equipment and supplies as he could carry from the burning building.

Brown hit the floor when the first round landed. He saw the mess hall in flames and reached for his socks. He pulled one on his left foot but dropped the other sock at the sound of additional explosions. Then he pulled on his jungle boots.

It was Brown's habit to sleep with his .357 Magnum revolver in a leather cartridge belt and holster that he wore around his waist. His AR-15 was nearby. He had three magazines taped together, end to end, for continuous firing, plus a magazine pouch attached. He grabbed the AR-15 and raced to his mortar position near the dispensary.

As he rounded the protective wall by the camp commander's *hooch*, Brown stopped short. He observed grenades coming his direction from the general area of his pit. Positioned on top of the concrete bunker at the rear of the pit were at least two VC grenadiers.

A round struck the wall a few feet away. The wall exploded in a shower of debris. The blast lifted Brown end over end for about ten yards. He landed on the parade ground, picked himself up, and, still clutching his rifle, ran to the CP for hand grenades.

The CP was a mass of flames, as if someone had drenched it in gasoline and lighted a match. Alamo and I were attempting to remove ammunition, arms, radios and other equipment stored there. Brown joined other team members and we passed what we could rescue,

136 • *The Battle for Nam Dong*

hand to hand, stacking it away from the flames.

At that point Brown returned to his position, carrying an armload of grenades. A scant few yards in front of him one of the Vietnamese interpreters, George Tuan, was running for cover. Another 57-millimeter round exploded in front of him, hitting the very spot where the first one had flattened Brown.

"Cover me!" Brown called to Doc Hickey. He ran to the communications trench where Tuan had fallen. The interpreter was attempting to raise himself to a sitting position. Brown dragged Tuan out of the ditch, only to see that both of his legs had been blown off below the knees. There was nothing that could be done. Brown laid him gently down. Within thirty seconds Tuan was dead.

Brown scrambled back behind the protective wall. He raced between burning buildings toward his position. Another mortar round landed close behind him. For a second time the impact catapulted him through the air. He thought he had been hit this time. Looking toward his mortar pit, he could see no one. He raced to the pit and jumped in.

Looking up, he found himself staring into the muzzle of a submachine gun held by one of two VCs who were lying on top of the concrete ammo bunker. He raised his AR-15 in lightning fashion and the man with the submachine gun rolled off the bunker. Then Brown fired from the edge of the pit, killing both of the VC.

When he looked inside the bunker Brown saw two Nungs preparing ammunition for the 81-millimeter mortars. The poor Nungs were between a rock and a hard place. They couldn't get out of the bunker and the VC couldn't get in. The two VC that Brown shot apparently were trying to blow up the bunker, because they had explosives with them.

"Illumination rounds!" Brown shouted. The Nungs broke open boxes of illumination shells. Brown intended to fire them to light up the area until the arrival of the flare ship.

An automatic weapon cut loose as Brown started in the direction of his mortar. A cluster of slugs ripped into the bunker inches above his head. Before he could make it to the bunker another burst of fire found its mark. Bullet fragments and bits of concrete ripped into the left side of his neck and across his shoulders. He managed to tumble through the door of the bunker, bleeding and in shock. When he tried to stand, he could not. Then he realized his right leg had no feeling in it—and he couldn't see it!

"O my God, I've lost it!" he thought. And then Brown realized he was sitting on the leg. Shaking off his momentary disorientation, Brown returned to action with his mortar.

His thoughts flashed back to Korea, where he had seen some hot and heavy action. But Korea didn't compare to this. Mortars, hand grenades, automatic weapons, 57s, small arms, and all at point-blank range.

He fired round after round of illumination shells, lighting the battlefield so we could see the enemy. In just five minutes time he had helped fight a fire, seen a man die, killed two others, and survived four brushes with death.

Beeson was roused from his slumber by the chatter of machine guns. His first thought, like the others, was that the Nungs and the strike force were knocking heads again. He pulled on fatigue trousers and shoes, reached for his AR-15 and scrambled to the CP. He was thinking about all of the ammo stored there. It needed guarding.

He saw the fireball that had been the mess hall and sparks beginning to eat into the thatched roof of the long house. Mortars and grenades were exploding a scant twenty-five feet away. Now he knew it was the VC.

Bee helped us rescue ammunition and supplies from the burning CP. Flames seemed to be all around us. Alamo and I felt the searing heat as we hurried to remove what we could.

Bee and I struggled with a CR-25 radio that was a link to Da Nang. It was on a desk, but the radio's antenna prevented me from passing it through the window to Bee. I ripped off the antenna. Beeson cradled the CR-25 in his arms and stashed it under a nearby truck. The flaming roof of the CP was about to collapse. It was impossible to rescue anything more from the building.

Bee raced to his quarters, grabbed an ammo belt with its AR-15 magazines, and made a dash for his mortar position on the far side, where the Nungs were breaking out ammunition.

"Illumination!" he shouted, firing off the light rounds one after another.

Woody had been sleeping with his head toward the door in the team's quarters when he awoke to the first mortar burst. He said later the fireball of white phosphorus seemed to have "fourteen thousand different colored flames shooting out of it." For an instant he wondered if he was dreaming.

"For God's sake, what is it?" he screamed.

"I don't know," Conway answered.

Then another shell exploded.

"Damn! What is it?" Woody shouted.

"Hell, I don't know," Conway repeated.

Woody rolled onto the floor with the .38 Smith & Wesson Special that was his constant companion.

"Woods is hit," Conway said. Someone else called to him.

"Woods, Woods, are you hit?"

"Naw, I ain't hit," he responded.

"Well, what the hell are you doing on the floor?"

"I'm strapping on my damn pistol!

With small arms rounds zinging through the room, Woody reached for his AR-15 and began crawling out the door in the direction of his mortar position. He was wearing only his GI drawers. Aware that the rocks were cutting his knees, he rose to a standing position and ran for the gate.

"Hey, Woody! Come help us get these weapons and ammo and everything out of here." Someone had called to him from the burning CP.

As he was removing supplies from the rear of the CP, Woods glanced through a window in time to see the second hit on the mess hall. Suddenly the mess hall was enveloped in flames and big chunks of the burning building were raining down on the roof of the CP. At that point Woody dashed barefoot through enemy fire to his post overlooking the chopper pad to the west of the gate.

The Battle for Nam Dong • 139

Whitsell and Disser had been asleep in the supply room next to Dan. They were out of the sack with the first explosion. They heard the intense small arms fire and the whistle of shells coming through the flimsy rattan walls of their room. Like the others, their first thought was that this was strike force and Nungs back at one another again.

Whit was on the floor on all fours. Still only half awake, he hurriedly dressed in his fatigues and a pair of tennis shoes. He reached for his AR-15 and cartridge belt.

Disser pulled on his camouflaged fatigues and boots. His weapon of choice was his Smith & Wesson .357 Magnum. It "could knock down a horse or an elephant at a thousand yards," he would say. He strapped on a BAR belt with seven magazines in it. In his haste in the dark he didn't realize it was upside down. Grabbing his AR-15 and two hand grenades, he was ready to move out.

Two Vietnamese helpers appeared. They had been asleep at the other end of the supply room.

"I don't know what the hell's going on," Whit shouted, "but we got to get out to our mortars."

The door was secured at night and took too much time to unlock, so Whit and Mike crawled out a window. They hot-footed it toward their positions near the gate. They were racing past the mess hall when it took the second direct hit, but neither man broke stride. Just then the supply room, where they had been moments before, shook from the impact of a mortar burst.

Scrambling down the steps into his mortar pit, Whit found three Nungs had positioned the weapon but it was still covered. He tore off the cover and began firing illuminating shells one after another, bathing the area in light.

One of the Nungs was chattering excitedly. Finally Whit realized what he was saying, and what they were facing.

"VC! VC! VC!"

Whit broke open a container of high-explosive shells. He was keeping his area illuminated, alternating with high explosives whenever he saw a target.

140 • *The Battle for Nam Dong*

Disser fired an illuminating shell over the airstrip. Six Nungs were in the mortar pit, firing away at the ammo bunkers with their carbines.

Disser raised himself until he could see over the edge of the pit. On a hill beyond the runway he observed muzzle flashes from four mortars and a recoilless rifle, dug in behind camouflage. Then he saw them—hundreds of men, some advancing through the high grass of the inner perimeter! He was looking at the main assault force of a reinforced VC battalion—some 800 to 900 strong—that had silently encircled the camp in the night. There was heavy support fire from the hills in the southwest, north, and northwest. They were rapidly advancing on Disser's position, their lead elements barely thirty yards away.

Disser continued to chain-fire his mortar. He saw Australian Warrant Officer Kevin Conway who was walking down the steps. Mike thought there was a look of amusement on Conway's face. He had faced guerrillas in Malaysia and Borneo. Was a smile his way of saying, "take courage" to Disser?

A moment later the Australian fell forward down the steps. Mike saw a hole, smaller than a dime, in his forehead. He had been hit almost directly between the eyes. No blood was coming from the wound, but the back of his head revealed a massive, ugly exit wound. He was still alive but unconscious and moaning with each breath.

Alamo had suffered a painful burn in the collapse of the CP. He found a clear path to Disser's position through the incoming grenades and small arms fire. He had no set post, but in the event of attack he was to bring his 57-millimeter recoilless rifle to bear wherever additional firepower was needed.

Alamo was at the front of the pit when Conway was hit. He had been firing his AR-15 almost point-blank at advancing VC. His recoilless rifle wasn't operating. The problem, he learned later, was a bent barrel. But it didn't matter at the time because there were no targets big enough for it.

The first mortar burst had also awakened Lieutenant O. Hearing the successive mortar explosions he knew at once the camp was under VC attack. His bunk was three feet off the floor, resting on bamboo stilts. He had been intending to lower it but hadn't gotten around to it. He reached for his fatigue trousers and boots. The "lucky cap" he had worn during Ranger school and his fatigue shirt were hanging on a support pole for his mosquito net. He strapped on a first aid kit and his combat pack. He had a poncho, mosquito net, smoke grenades and hand grenades, his AR-15, a M-79 grenade launcher, and extra ammunition. Already armed to the teeth, as he moved to the door he picked up additional grenades and some hand-held flares.

He fired off three flares before running to the CP to help evacuate the ammo and supplies stored there. Moments before the roof collapsed he gathered up grenade-launcher ammo and a carbon dioxide fire extinguisher which he stashed under one of the trucks.

His assignment was to protect the communications room. It was already blazing away. So he headed for Disser's mortar pit. Conway was sprawled near the steps. Alamo was in front of him, blazing away at VC near the three ammunition bunkers thirty yards away. Disser, his AR-15 resting across his forearms, was launching a continuous barrage of illuminating rounds.

Jay examined Conway's wound and bandaged it. Removing his jacket, he rolled it into a makeshift pillow, which he placed under the Australian's head. He covered him with the poncho from his combat pack. Mercifully, Conway lived only about thirty minutes. Then Jay positioned his M-79 launcher and began lobbing grenades among the ammo bunkers. He and Alamo were making things pretty unhealthy for the VC in that area.

What had been our CP was a roaring mass of flames. The only ones still there were Doc Hickey, Woody and me. I told Doc to take cover under one of the trucks. He thought about it for a moment and decided that wasn't where he wanted to die. He rounded the truck and was running toward the dispensary. A mortar landed close by. The blast lifted him into the air. Checking himself for wounds, he found none, and continued on. Woody made it to his mortar position near the gate.

142 • *The Battle for Nam Dong*

My customary alert position was in the camp commander's *hooch*. I had no clue as to *Dai-uy* Lich's whereabouts, or if he was dead or alive. Not much was left of the *hooch*. It had received several direct mortar hits. I raced across the parade ground, very much aware of the firepower that was raining down on us. As I passed near the flagpole I was suddenly tossed into the air like a rag doll. Disoriented and minus one boot, I managed to crawl into Woody's pit.

Two Nungs were helping him, preparing ammunition. Woody and I both reached for illuminating rounds, which we fired in rapid succession. But nothing happened. We looked at one another in disbelief. There couldn't have been two failures in two shots. Then Woody realized what had happened.

"The timing," he screamed. "This is an 81. You've got to set the damn timing on an 81!"

Suddenly he was on his hands and knees in the dark, searching for a timing wrench. By a stroke of fortune he found one. Grabbing another casing, he gave a quick turn with the wrench and slipped the shell into the mortar. This time the shell arched high above, lighting the chopper pad, the road, and the portion of the outer perimeter occupied by Strike Force Company 121.

Woody was standing, which is the only way to fire the 81. That made his large frame an easy target. But the bulge of the concrete bunker to his rear masked his figure. Otherwise he would have been backlighted by burning buildings. Woody was poetry in motion operating that mortar, alternating between illuminating rounds and high explosive shells.

Houston's voice came from the direction of the "swimming pool."

"They're over here!" he called out. "In the ammo bunker!"

I crawled out and started toward him. He was on a seven-foot mound of earth on the outside of the hole, facing the three ammo bunkers. He was kneeling on the inside of the mound, pouring fire from his AR-15 directly into the bunker. He was by himself, blazing away with his weapon and shouting.

The Battle for Nam Dong • 143

"John!" I hollered. "Don't cut up the strike force! You're firing right into them!"

"No! No!" he answered. "It's them! VC! VC!"

As I was running toward him a mortar shell hit close by, knocking me off my feet. I lost my pistol belt, my other boot, and all of my equipment except my AR-15 and two clips. I crawled to the edge of Disser's mortar pit and asked for ammunition and a report on the men. Mike tossed several magazines toward me.

"Conway's hit and Alamo's hit," he said. "Conway's hit bad."

Just then I noticed movement at the gate, just twenty yards away.

"Mike!" I hollered. "Illuminate the main gate!"

The illumination round revealed three crouching VC moving along the road on our side of the gate. I squeezed the trigger on my AR-15 and cursed. It was on full automatic and I was too short of ammunition for that. I put it on semiautomatic, knelt, aimed, and fired about six times. Two of them fell. The third crawled off into the grass. I sent a grenade sailing in his direction and there was no more movement.

They were a demolition team. They were wearing fatigue jackets, shorts, sandals, and broad-brimmed bush hats. Each of the VC had satchel charges of dynamite on his back, an entrenching tool, and other demolition gear. Apparently they were well-trained, hard-core guerrillas. I learned later one was a VC captain.

I became aware that I had been wounded. My left forearm was cut and bleeding and I had a shrapnel wound about the size of a quarter in my stomach, belt-high and to the left. It was also bleeding. My face was cut and powder-burned. Despite these wounds I was not in a great deal of pain, and my legs were okay. I looked over to see how Houston was getting along.

John had been jumping back and forth along the mound, hoping to confuse the VC into thinking they were under fire from more than one man. He was doing such a great job that he was keeping most of them pinned down among the ammo bunkers. None of them had succeeded in breaching the wire between him and the bunkers.

Terry was on the opposite side of the big hole, directing a stream of supporting fire. They had been a team from the outset of the firefight, each backing up the other. When an explosion in the communications room flattened Houston as he tried to remove radio equipment, Terry ran to help him, only to be knocked unconscious himself. When he came to he was in a drainage ditch by the dispensary, Houston at his side. He had dragged Terry to safety through the intense barrage that was chopping up Camp Nam Dong.

Terry continued to fire, but saw that Houston was slumped over, face down. Terry called to him.

"I'm hit," John answered. He uttered a choking sound and then he was still.

Two VC had breached the inner perimeter fence. They had flanked Houston, taking cover behind cinder blocks stacked near the fire arrow. It was a big tin arrow that could be lighted at night to indicate the location of any attacking force, as a guide for the flare ship and an air strike. The two VC shot Houston with a BAR. One slug nicked his heart and lungs. He was dead in a matter of seconds.

Terry advanced toward him. The AR-15 was blown out of his left hand. Terry's hand was laid open at the heel. Hundreds of tiny pieces of metal and wood were imbedded in his left forearm. He was bleeding from the mouth and ears as a result of the earlier concussion. A hand grenade had been shot off of his belt and there were bullet and shrapnel holes in his fatigue jacket.

I observed him standing perfectly still, looking at his torn and bleeding arm.

"Terry!" I called out. "Get down! Take cover!"

"I'm hit!" was all he said.

"Don't speak English!" warned Smiley, my interpreter. He didn't need to explain. Bullets were flying all around us. It happened whenever the VC heard English. I only knew a few words in Vietnamese like *boxie*—medic.

The Nungs directed their fire at the two VC who had killed Houston. Terry, his left arm useless and dripping blood, was out in

The Battle for Nam Dong • 145

the open, fighting with one hand. He was firing Houston's AR-15 from his hip, pausing only to reload. He lobbed grenades, pulling the pin with his teeth.

Terry and the Nungs were battling on two fronts. They had stopped the main assault wave at the ammo bunkers. But the two VC with the BAR had an open shot at their flank for some thirty or so yards away. Their firepower took out the two VC. An illumination round burst overhead. I saw the VC sprawled to the side of the cinder blocks.

I saw that they were dead, and now I could move past them to Brown's position and the dispensary in the rear. I hoped to find Gregg and get him working with the wounded. I crouched and trotted up to Terry, ignoring the mortar blasts, the grenades, and the small arms fire coming from the ammo bunkers. I was really only aware of the din and confusion, and of sharp pains in my feet as I ran across the rocky terrain in my socks.

"Get Houston down in the hole!" I urged Terry. I was shouting, but it wasn't necessary. We were only a few feet apart.

He nodded agreement, and with the help of a wounded Nung, they pulled Houston's body to the edge of the big hole. Terry jumped into the hole, motioning to the Nung to stand on his shoulders, and they were able to lower Houston gently to the bottom so Terry could check him.

"It's too late," he announced. "John's dead."

As flames spread through the dispensary we were forced to abandon further salvage of medical equipment and take up defensive positions. The intense heat made it impossible to fight from behind the protective walls. When Houston and Terry went to the fire arrow and the "swimming pool," Doc Hickey and *Dai-uy* Lich took cover in a communications trench near Beeson's post at the south end of the camp. Gregg ducked into another trench and Dan joined the Nungs firing a machine gun in a U-shaped ditch between Brown's mortar and the blazing dispensary.

Dan was not comfortable with his position. The Nungs were sending out a continuous stream of lead, not really knowing what

146 • *The Battle for Nam Dong*

the target was. All Dan could observe from the pit was the inner perimeter fence a few feet away, and grass, two feet tall. When the Nungs realized they were without hand grenades they became agitated. Dan came up with five or six. The staccato of the machine gun was so great he thought it would rupture his eardrums.

Dan ran to the center of the camp, hoping to find a high place where he could establish a good field of fire. A mortar shell exploded in front of him. The blast tossed him into the air. He was dazed and bruised, but escaped serious injury. Instinctively he started to crawl away. Then he saw Brown's pit and stumbled down the steps to cover.

Brown and two Nungs were putting up a steady barrage. Brown made a habit of keeping his ammunition boxes broken open and the tape sealers on the canisters torn loose. The Nungs simply lifted out the canisters, tore off the rest of the tape, slid the projectile out and handed it to Brown.

Then Brown saw trouble. "Cover me," he said to Dan. "They're coming over the fence!"

Dan moved to the rim of the pit. He saw a dead VC draped over the barbed wire of the inner perimeter fence almost directly in front of them. Beeson had nailed him with his AR-15 minutes earlier. There appeared to be a group of VC some thirty yards out. They seemed to be preparing to charge.

Brown fired an illuminating round. What they observed was a hundred or more VC hugging the ground and crouching in the grass. About ten or fifteen rose up, shouted and advanced toward the fence in a line of skirmishers. Dan cut loose with his AR-15. A couple of Nungs had entered the pit and were firing alongside him.

Then Dan heard the boom of a shotgun. Gregg had joined them in the pit and was blasting away at anything that moved. Their combined firepower cut down the first VC wave. But another came on, and another, and another. Some of the advancing guerrillas made it as far as the fence. They were trying to climb the barbed wire in their bare feet when they were cut down.

Just then the Nung who had been firing alongside Dan shouted,

The Battle for Nam Dong • 147

turned and fired toward the top of the bunker in the back of the pit. Dan wheeled in time to see a VC, falling backward. He was holding a dynamite grenade.

As I worked my way along the protective wall and the stack of cinder blocks, I called in Vietnamese for a medic, *"Bac si! Bac si! Bac si!"* Gregg hollered back from Brown's pit. I zigzagged my way over and jumped in. Smiley, carrying a hand radio, was close behind. Two other interpreters, Tet and Minh, were in the pit.

"How're you doing?" I shouted. They continued shooting, but responded with the equivalent of "so far, so good."

"Houston is dead," I reported. "Conway's dead. Terry's hit but he's all right. There's a lot of wounded out there, Gregg. You better go see."

Gregg asked how I was doing. I replied in the affirmative and he crawled out of the pit.

I asked Dan if he had contacted the B Team. He said he had. I was puzzled that we still hadn't seen the reaction forces. The fighting had been going on for almost an hour. Da Nang was only thirty-two miles away. Where was the flare ship? Where was the air strike?

"Did you get an acknowledgment?" I quizzed Dan. "Did you hear a 'roger'?"

Dan said he had sent the message and it had been acknowledged.

"How's Beeson doing?" I asked. No one knew for sure. They had heard him firing and taking fire but he had been silent for some time.

I ran from Brown's pit to the rear of the camp's center, hoping to get over to Beeson. Inside the protective wall I could feel the ground hot through the soles of my bare feet. Every building in the camp was ablaze. Shells continued to land amid the debris. Explosions continued to come from the supply room.

Suddenly I felt a sharp pain in my foot. When I looked I found a piece of plywood with a nail in it, that I had stepped on. I had taken several steps before the pain registered in my brain. I pulled the nail out and limped back to Brown's pit.

They were putting up a continuous barrage. Brown was firing

an illuminating round, then two of high explosive, then two of white phosphorus. Then he would repeat the sequence. He fired whenever someone spotted a target, and occasionally lobbed a few rounds far to the right, just in case Beeson was out of action.

"Are you *sure* you called the B Team?" I pressed Dan again. Once more he said he had. I couldn't understand why we hadn't seen a flare ship and air strike.

Dan offered me a cigarette. I felt very tired, but no great pain. I had lost only a small amount of blood from my stomach and arm wounds. My feet were cut and burned, and it was sore where I stepped on the nail.

Just then Gregg dropped into the pit. He had been treating the wounded and was checking Brown's position before making another circuit with fresh bandages.

"You're wounded, captain," he said. "Let me fix you up."

"No," I replied. "I'm okay. Take care of the others."

Gregg left. Smiley and I left shortly afterward, moving back to Disser's position. As we passed the supply room there was a terrific explosion from within. For the third time I was blasted into the air. This time I landed hard, and for the first time I felt real pain. Shrapnel had torn my left leg, but no bones were broken. I was able to pull myself up and to reach Disser's pit.

In simple words, it was a hellhole!

The VC had overrun Strike Force Company 122 and were at the inner perimeter barbed wire in force. It was only our mortar and automatic weapons fire that was forcing them to stay low and move cautiously. But they were close enough to lob grenades and they peppered Disser's pit with volleys of grenades, five, six, seven at a time.

Mike was firing two illumination rounds to each HE. He had not a clue where the high explosives were going. He didn't take time to aim. On the right, Alamo was at the forward rim, blasting away with his AR-15. He tried to load his recoilless rifle with a canister round, but it wouldn't load. Jay was firing his AR-15 and his M-79 grenade launcher, covering the left front. He attempted to

The Battle for Nam Dong • 149

slip the canister round into the 57, but it refused to load. In frustration he disregarded safety procedures—two fingers from the back—and turned the weapon so he was facing the muzzle. It was not as awkward, but an accidental discharge would have blown off his head. And it still wouldn't load. When the first grenades went off, Lieutenant O gave up on the 57 and looked to Alamo. The team sergeant was bleeding from a shrapnel wound in his shoulder.

"You're all right," Jay told him after examining the wound.

Disser hollered, picked up his AR-15 and fired over their heads. They looked up to see a VC dressed in a jacket and bikini and wearing a camouflaged helmet, poised on the rim. When Mike fired he fell backward. As he fell, a grenade dropped from his hand and rolled into the pit. It didn't explode.

Jay heard a thud behind him. When he glanced back he saw a smoking fragmentation grenade rolling around by his feet. He jumped just as it went off. The force of the explosion was like a sledgehammer blow against the bottoms of his boots. He knew he had broken bones. Disregarding the grenades exploding around him, Jay tightened his boot laces and then tied them around his bare ankle. He hoped that would stop the bleeding and hold the bones together. He imagined his foot reduced to a bloody pulp inside the boot.

More grenades went off. Disser, who had been crouching beside his mortar, kept firing despite being wounded in the knees, arms and legs.

It was unreal. There were so many incoming grenades exploding with surprisingly little damage that the three men were almost ignoring them. When another grenade landed in the pit they would momentarily stop firing, turn aside, and resume firing after the explosion. Fortunately these were VC grenades. One American-made grenade would have wiped them out. But the ineffective VC grenades were still doing damage. Each explosion cut them up a bit more. Finally they moved to the cover of the concrete bunker at the rear, where the Nungs were.

Then a grenade fell into the bunker, landing in an ammunition box close to Disser. Jay and Alamo jumped out to the right, Mike

150 • The Battle for Nam Dong

to the left. This blast caught Mike in the foot and lower leg, but he managed to crawl back to his mortar and resume firing.

Alamo was slumped on the concrete steps. He was bleeding from his shoulder and from a new wound in his right cheek below the eye. Jay was sitting in the doorway of the bunker, passing ammunition to Disser. Lieutenant O had been hit in both legs, the left hand and elbow, his shoulders and back. The exploding grenades caused him to drop his weapons and he was glancing about, looking for something he could fire. It would be ten or fifteen seconds before the VC would follow up on their grenade bombardment and he was ready to jump the first VC who came into the pit and fight him barehanded.

A grenade exploded as I came down the steps and I was knocked down again. I fired a few rounds into the darkness, hoping to discourage an attack. Mike kept firing his mortar with the assistance of two Nungs. Jay was passing them ammunition.

"This is for Pop!" Jay cried out. Mike grabbed the shell, shouted and launched it.

Yelling and firing. Firing and yelling. We continued like that, keeping up spirits as we struggled to stand off overwhelming numbers of VC. But the pressure was getting to all of us. We were picking up unexploded grenades and throwing them back. Mike was batting them aside as if they were so many mosquitoes. Jay dropped an empty ammo box on top of one.

But it was madness beyond belief to stay in the pit.

"Let's get the hell out of here!" Mike yelled.

"Right!" I called back.

At that moment a concussion grenade exploded over us, showering the pit with rocks and debris. The blast knocked Mike and me down again. Mike's entire side was numb and he was stumbling around like a drunkard.

"Get out!" I shouted. "Back to the flagpole! Back to the commo trenches!"

Mike and Smiley were the first to leave, followed by Jay and the Nungs. Although Jay had sustained multiple wounds he left the pit

The Battle for Nam Dong • 151

the same way he arrived—armed to the teeth with two AR-15s and two M-79 grenade launchers. I covered their withdrawal to a shallow ditch we had dug for burying communications wire.

Alamo was unable to move. He was sitting on the steps, holding a 57-millimeter recoilless rifle. Pop was bleeding from the face, shoulder and stomach. I called to Mike and Jay to cover me, got one of Alamo's arms around my neck and tried to straighten up. I had made it to about a half-standing position when a tremendous blast went off in my face. I could hear myself screaming as I sailed through the air. There was the sensation of falling backward off a cliff.

I am going to die, I thought. My screaming was like the terrible wail of death. Strangely, I didn't want it to end. When it ended, I was certain I'd be dead.

My last conscious thoughts were of a beautiful little blonde girl in a pink dress. She was laughing as I pushed her on a swing in the park . . .

Victory at Nam Dong

July 6, 1964 . . .

I regained consciousness. My head and shoulders were inside the bunker. The rest of my body was outside. My left shoulder was a mass of blood and intense pain radiated down to my fingertips. My head was bloody too and throbbed with pain. The wound in my stomach was bleeding, but I was still alive and I could move.

Alamo was sprawled in the pit, motionless and bloody. He was dead.

I moved out, taking the 60-millimeter mortar with me. Thirty yards away were the cinder blocks. When I reached them I found four wounded Nungs. They looked like the fight was gone from them. One had a massive scalp wound. I talked in English and pidgin Vietnamese, but they were too shocked to answer.

Taking off my fatigue jacket and T-shirt, I tore the shirt into bandages and wrapped their wounds. I used one of my raggedy socks for a tourniquet on one man. I had a small piece of shirt left, and stuffed it into the wound in my stomach, hoping to stop the bleeding.

"Come on," I urged, "you fellows are going to be all right. You can still fight. Here's your weapon. Cover me. Do you understand? Cover me. I'm going over there. Use your weapon. Cover me!"

I left the Nungs beside the cinder blocks with their carbines. I shoved the mortar behind them and started to run back to the pit. I couldn't straighten up, for the pain. So I walked, bent over.

I found a box of mortar ammo and a couple of 57-millimeter rounds in the pit. When I returned to the cinder blocks the Nungs were blazing away with their carbines. I didn't know if they could see something in the darkness or if they were just firing to keep up their spirits. What counted was they were in action. There was still some fire in their bellies!

I gestured to the Nungs to begin firing the mortar, and back I went to the pit. I didn't want the VC to find anything there that they could use on us if they overran Disser's position. On the third trip, I found Alamo's 57. As I was taking it back to the pile of cinder blocks a grenade exploded on top of me. I felt the pieces of shrapnel bite into my left leg, and the sharp pain.

Jay and Mike continued to cover me. Jay had moved back to the 3/4-ton truck by the CP. Mike remained forward until I had evacuated the weapons and then he joined Jay under the truck. I told them to find a better position. They crawled to a trench that was at the rear of Whitsell's pit, west of the gate and helicopter pad.

"I've got the 57," I said. "It's over there by the cinder blocks. If they start a rush or we're overrun, get it! It's loaded with canister. Fire it into the main attack!"

I returned to Woody's pit, calling out my name so the Nungs wouldn't shoot, and sprawled on the rim. Woody was standing amid a pile of spent canisters and ammo boxes. He was firing illumination rounds, alternating with high explosives. I told the Nungs to pitch out some of the clutter so Woody could concentrate on firing. His feet were cut and bleeding from the spent canisters.

"Fire HE to the east!" I shouted.

"Where the hell's the east?" came Woody's response.

"Toward the airstrip!" I said, wondering why I hadn't said so right off.

Woody began dropping shells into the area Disser had been covering. Between rounds I asked him how he was doing.

"Hell, I'm all right," he replied. "But I think my right eardrum's busted. I felt some liquid running out of it. How's everybody else?"

Should I tell him? Back in training we would argue about whether it was better to lie in such circumstances if your men were taking heavy casualties. There are two schools of thought. I decided that the awful truth would just make them fight harder. I was correct.

"Alamo's dead. Houston's dead. Conway's dead," I blurted out. "Lieutenant O and Disser are wounded. Brown's wounded. Terry's wounded. I don't know how Beeson is. I can't get to him."

Woody took the news without comment. He thought it was about over for all of us. Isolated as he was, all he knew for certain was that three men of A-726 were still alive—he and I and Whitsell, out of contact but still blazing away on his left flank.

Hell, we're all dead men, Woody thought. None of us'll come out of this alive. But they're going to have to hump some to take me!

He called to his Nungs to cover him and turned to his mortar. He fired illumination rounds and began rotating his fire in a circle, lobbing HE rounds on every front. The VC were unwilling witnesses to a beautiful show of mortar marksmanship. If they failed to charge Disser's pit and if the pressure eased on Beeson and Brown, it was due in some measure to the hammering of the outer perimeter by Woody's 81.

I climbed into the pit and helped Woody shift his mortar. Then I saw a case of hand-held flares. As I stooped to pick up these flares I suddenly felt weak and tired. There was so much to do and I couldn't think clearly. And there was the unending noise. If only it would let up!

I wanted to see how the medics were doing with the wounded. I had to call the B Team for help and a flare ship. Did Dan call the B Team? Didn't he say he had called, or was I imagining that? I hurt everywhere—my head, my shoulder, my stomach, my feet. If only I had boots I could find out how Beeson was doing. Then I remembered Disser had boots, my size! I would get them as soon as I filled my pockets with flares.

I straightened up. To my horror I realized my face was inches from the muzzle of Woody's mortar, and he had just dropped in a round.

"Look out!" Woody screamed. It was too late.

The muzzle blast hit me full in the face, shoving me flat on my back. Any closer and the shell would have hit me. It could have exploded, killing us all. Woody was bending over me.

"I'm okay," I said. "I've got to go."

Exhausted and punchy, I stumbled out of the pit and started in

Victory at Nam Dong • 155

the direction of the cinder blocks. Another mortar blast knocked me down. My leg was hurting. I managed to crawl to Jay and Disser in the trench behind Whitsell's position. A number of Nungs and Vietnamese were with them, all bandaged and armed. I knew then that Gregg and Terry had been busy.

The medics had been crisscrossing among the pits and trenches and cinder blocks, disregarding the incoming fire that was raining all around them. Although hampered by a throbbing left hand that Terry had wrapped in a sling, he was rounding up the wounded and Gregg was tending them. When they had used their last bandage they returned to the trench near the dispensary where they left two aid kits. Along the way they fired at the VC, shouting encouragement to the defenders and helping supply them with ammunition. Only the most severely wounded were given sedatives. They knew as many as possible needed to be alert when the big push came.

"You're okay," they would say. "Here's a weapon and ammo. Hang on. Help is coming. It'll be daylight soon."

Terry gave Disser a Colt .45 and six shells.

"Rest easy," he urged. "But use it if you have to."

Disser looked at the chrome-plated pistol. Only Houston had a chrome-plated .45.

"Where's John?" he asked. "Where's John?"

"John's dead," Terry answered.

I pulled on Disser's boots and walked through the smoldering remains of what had been the heart of Camp Nam Dong. I moved past the supply room, which was still blowing up, and to the Nungs' quarters. The fire must have silhouetted me, because each time I started in the direction of Beeson's position a machine gun opened up on me. I didn't know if Beeson was dead or alive, but someone was operating his mortar. I doubled back to Brown's pit.

"Did you get the B Team, Dan?" I asked.

"Yes," Dan answered.

"Do they know we're under attack?"

"Damn it!" Dan shouted. "You keep asking me that! I told you. I got them!"

"Then why the hell aren't they here?"

Dan shrugged his shoulders and resumed firing over the rim of the pit.

Gregg arrived on his rounds, and insisted on examining my wounds.

"I'm all right," I said. "I'm tired, but I'm all right."

"You're all shot up," Gregg responded. "Hold still and I'll fix you up."

"No," I said. "There are a lot of them worse off than me. Take care of them and catch me later."

I started in the direction of the main gate. I thought there might be an all-out assault there. I thought I might get the Nungs to move a mortar back into Disser's pit. We would need it if we were to hold. I was exhausted and my entire body was hurting. Worse, I saw no end to all of this. We had been fighting continuously for over an hour and a half. I wondered if anyone knew what we were up against.

Finally I heard it. Above all the other noise of the battle I heard the sound of a distant airplane engine, getting louder all the time.

Then the heavens lit up. It was just after four. Finally, the flare ship was on top of us. Welcome as the illumination was, that flare ship brought more than light. Now we had a glimmer of hope. And the VC must have seen the flare ship as a bad omen. Little by little the intensity of their firing diminished. They knew an air strike almost always followed a flare ship. It seemed that they might be withdrawing, but they were far from through with us.

Then, in front of Brown's pit, a loudspeaker crackled. We heard a man speaking excited, high-pitched Vietnamese. The sound was incredibly strange amid the booming battle noises and it startled both sides into silence. Not a shot was fired as the voice carried across the camp.

Dan turned to Tet, the interpreter. "What's he saying?" he asked. Tet was shaken.

"He say lay down weapons. VC going to take camp and we all be killed!"

Victory at Nam Dong • 157

Dan, Gregg, and Brown were unimpressed.

"Over my dead body," Dan declared.

"We'll lay down our weapons when we're too dead to pick them up," Gregg added.

The silence continued. Not a shot was being fired in that sector. The silence was unnerving. And all at once it was broken again by the loudspeaker. This time the voice was in English.

"Lay down your weapons," it urged. "We are going to annihilate your camp. You will all be killed!"

"Can you pick it up by the sound?" inquired Gregg.

"I think so," Brown said. He was adjusting the elevation on his mortar. "Where to you think it is?"

"Over here," Dan answered, pointing.

Brown cut loose with about ten rounds of high explosive and white phosphorus as quickly as he could slide them into the tube and make adjustments in the elevation. These bursts sounded even louder as they broke the temporary silence of the night. The spell was broken. Nung machine guns and small arms resumed firing. They were answered by more incoming mortars and small arms fire.

To hell with your rotten brainwashing, Brown thought as he sent up his salvo of answering shells. He had a very good idea where his rounds were landing, along a ridge line running from the south-southeast corner of the camp, where he was, to the strike force outpost, some 850 yards distant. He knew, because he had measured it when he measured all of the key distances.

Maybe I don't figure to get out of here alive, Brown thought. If that's so, fine. But I'm sure not going to be captured. Not so long as there is something to fight with!

There was nothing further from the loudspeaker. Then mortar shells started coming from Brown's front. They were moving toward his pit from the direction of Beeson's position. Each burst came a bit closer.

Everyone in the pit ceased firing and listened.

"That mortar's close!" Brown said.

158 • Victory at Nam Dong

They could hear the thunk, thunk, as shells were dropped into the mortar, the small explosion of their launching and the booming impact as they landed closer and closer.

Brown moved to the rim. He remained there for what seemed like an eternity. Probably it was only five minutes. Then he spotted what he had been looking for. No more than thirty yards out he observed the muzzle flash, followed by the tracerlike arc of the round, and finally its noisy return to earth just yards behind him.

"If that's the strike force, they're VC," Brown declared, "because they're firing on us."

Brown crawled back in the pit and threw two hand grenades. As they exploded he saw one body fly through the air, silhouetted by another muzzle flash of the mortar. It was a strike force weapon that the VC had seized from Company 123 after they slipped into the outpost and slit the throats of a half-dozen Vietnamese who were asleep after coming off of patrol.

Brown's grenades knocked out the mortar and he resumed firing his mortar.

The loudspeaker came on again, this time from the vicinity of the airstrip, repeating the same message in Vietnamese. Brown answered with a barrage of HE and WP rounds. Nothing further was heard from the loudspeaker.

Brown continued to hammer the area at the edge of the airstrip as I climbed back into the pit. Dan was attempting to make contact with the flare ship with his PRG-10 hand radio, but without success. Examining the handset closely, he discovered its mouthpiece had been shot away. He tried Morse code but there was no reply.

I remembered that I had taken a radio out of the CP earlier but had no recollection of what had become of it.

Returning to the main gate, I told Woody to cover me while I returned to Disser's pit to get that mortar firing again. "Herr adjutant" and some other Nungs helped me with the weapon and the Nungs resumed firing.

I kept thinking about Beeson, worrying about what had happened to him. Woody and I turned his mortar towards Beeson's sector. I

Victory at Nam Dong • **159**

helped him aim it and Woody commenced laying down rounds precisely where he wanted them.

Beeson and his Nungs were completely cut off from the rest of us. He was firing his mortar only when he found a target. Meanwhile he was launching illuminating rounds. When he was not firing the mortar he was at the edge of the pit, his AR-15 ready for action. One VC charged to within about fifteen feet. The burst from Bee's AR-15 knocked the man back ten feet.

The VC dropped seven mortar shells on Beeson's position. They were all HE except for one white phosphorus round. They exploded on the roof of his bunker or nearby in a shower of shrapnel, dirt and rocks. There were about ten Nungs with Bee, and somehow none of them had been hit.

About the time Bee was wondering how much more shelling they could withstand, Brown spotted the mortar that was hammering Beeson's bunker. The accuracy of his two grenades took out the weapon and probably saved Bee's life.

Whitsell was also cut off but could hear Woody firing on his right. Two Nungs were firing carbines over the rim of Woody's pit and another was passing him ammunition. One of the Nungs at the rim fell back, his hand to his head. His forehead was bloody, but he was not seriously hurt. "VC! VC! VC!" he shouted, gesturing to his immediate front. VC grenades were landing at the rim of the pit.

Whit began firing his AR-15 into the darkness. He could hear men moving and they were not far off, but he could not see them. He fired in the direction of the sound, ignoring the grenades and small arms fire that continued to pepper his position. About fifteen yards out a VC rose up to lob a grenade. A Nung who was crouched next to Whitsell took aim with his carbine and shot him dead.

Whit was preparing himself for a VC charge on his position, thinking about the other members of the team and how they were depending on him to hold. I'm not running, he thought. I wouldn't leave this pit if all hell broke loose. If they find me dead, they'll know I died fighting.

160 • Victory at Nam Dong

He continued to fire into the night with his AR-15, interspersed with illumination bursts and HE. I just want them to know we're here, he thought. I always said I wanted to die on a battlefield.

Woody's mortar tube was glowing white-hot at its base, but he continued to fire until one round misfired. Standard procedure is to wait about twenty minutes to let the weapon cool or douse it with water. Then you kick it to make sure the projectile isn't stuck, lift the tube and slide the round out. Another man, standing clear, catches it with his two thumbs placed over the muzzle. The second man replaces the safety pin and disposes of the round. In this way, if the round goes off, the retriever loses only two thumbs.

There wasn't time to wait. There wasn't any water handy, and Woody didn't have trained assistants. He kicked the tube several times, the way it says to do in the field manual. Then, using some rags as gloves, he took hold of the tube at its base and gave it a quick turn. This freed the pintle from the U-shaped pintle housing. The rags began smoking and caught fire. One of the Nungs caught the round when Woody shook it out.

The Nung didn't know how to replace the safety pin. He stood there holding the hot projectile, not knowing what to do. Woody locked the tube back onto its baseplate. He took the shell from the Nung and replaced the pin. He saw that the increment charges, in plastic bags in the rear fins, were smoldering. If they had ignited in the tube the round would have been launched without benefit of a firing pin.

We're not going to get out of this alive, Woody thought, so what the hell. He rolled the faulty round to a corner of the pit. He experienced two more misfires and took care of them the same way. What the hell, he thought. Why worry?

It was now going on 0600 hours and the intervals seemed to be getting longer between the VC mortars. But the small arms fire continued without letup. I continued to make the rounds among Whit, Woody, and Brown, urging them to direct fire in front of Beeson's position. Now that the flare ship was overhead they could concentrate on HE.

Victory at Nam Dong • **161**

Whit had been holding his position for almost three hours. I crawled along the communications trench to his rear, calling out my name so as not to get shot by a Nung. Whit continued to fire while we talked. He was peppering a wide arc to his front, left, and far left, Beeson's position, and he was keeping pressure on some hills to the northwest, where there seemed to be a VC base of fire.

It was almost daylight by the time I got to Beeson. He greeted me as if I had been out for a stroll and dropped in for coffee. Terry had been there. Gregg was in the pit, treating a wounded Nung.

"Sit down, captain." Beeson spoke softly, but he was looking at me a bit strangely. In the dim light he could see I was pretty beaten up and near exhaustion.

"Naw, I'm all right," I responded.

"Sit down, sir," Beeson said, still gently, "or I'm going to have to knock you down."

I sat on an ammunition box and Bee started checking my wounds. As I sat there, relaxed, I felt the strength draining out of me. Throughout the worst of the attack I had nagging doubts, not knowing how Beeson was doing in his corner of the camp. Two, three, maybe six times I had tried to get to his position to see if he was still alive. Now I had an almost overwhelming sense of a mission accomplished. The VC seemed to be withdrawing, but I knew they might simply be regrouping.

One of the Nungs took out a pack of cigarettes. He offered one to me and I lit up.

Bee dressed my shoulder but I wouldn't let him work on the stomach wound. I wanted to make the rounds again to check on ammo resupply, to try to locate a radio, to check on the aid stations that Gregg and Terry set up, and to prepare for a possible new assault.

I walked out of Beeson's pit without trying to duck the small arms fire. I was sick of all of the hours of ducking, running, crouching, and crawling. To hell with it, I thought. A hand grenade exploded close by, knocking me off my feet. I got up and kept walking toward the makeshift CP behind the cinder blocks near

Whit's and Woody's positions.

Some thirty yards in front of Woody's pit four or five VC were hiding behind some tree stumps, throwing hand grenades. I asked Woody if he could drop a round on them.

"I never did it before, but I could damn well try," he responded.

Without using the sights, he positioned the tube almost straight up and dropped in a round. It landed on target but didn't explode. Woody cursed and tried again, holding onto the tube at launch so it wouldn't fall backward. One moment the VC were there, the next moment they had disappeared. He had scored a direct hit.

Woody looked like hell. His white GI drawers had turned a grimy gray. His body was a mass of powder burns, soot and dust. From the knees down he was covered with cuts and bruises as a result of having stumbled over discarded canisters and ammo boxes. Big red ants had attacked his bare feet. Blisters from ant bites were rising around the nails of his toes. He had an unholy look about him as he climbed out of his pit. But to Mike and Jay, and the others who had not seen him during the battle, he was a beautiful sight.

"I can't take any more of this crud," he said disgustedly.

The four Vietnamese nurses had come out of their trench near the dispensary and were busy giving shots and making bandages. They were a comfort to the wounded and the sight of their delicate figures and their fluttering *ao dai* dresses lifted everyone's spirits. One of the Nungs told me later that Co Pha picked up a rifle during the battle and blasted away at the VC.

Gregg and Terry were busy at aid stations set up behind the cinder blocks, in the trenches and behind the burnt-out Nung mess hall near Beeson's pit. Doc Hickey told Gregg that one of the nurses needed medical attention. Doc had witnessed Co Caac being hit by shrapnel. She was embarrassed because of the location of the injury and was trying to keep it secret.

"Where was she hit?" Gregg asked.

"In the butt," Doc said.

She was working with the wounded in the central area when Gregg found her.

Victory at Nam Dong • 163

"Let me take a look at that wound," he offered.

She shook her head from side to side. Gregg insisted, but she again declined.

"Now, wait a minute, girl," Gregg shouted. "You come over here. Captain Donlon's my boss and he can tell me to go away and I'll go. But I'm *your* boss, and I'm telling you I'm going to fix up that wound. And if I say you can go back to work, you'll go. And if I say you can't, you'll be flat on your back with the rest of the wounded. And that's all there is to it!"

Co Caac was embarrassed almost to tears, but she complied, letting Gregg remove the shrapnel and dress her wound. Then he let her return to work. I promised to buy her a new *ao dai* to replace the one with the shrapnel-torn bottom.

Doc Hickey's appearance at daylight, like Woody's, raised the rest of the team's spirits. Gregg and I had stumbled across him in a fighting trench behind Beeson's position, but no one else had seen him since the fighting started. We feared we would find him dead.

By a stroke of luck Doc wound up in the same hole with *Dai-uy* Lich, the camp commander. He told us he fired three rounds from the pistol I gave him and then decided it would be better to save the rest of his shells until he really needed them. Due to the crossfire set up by the Nungs in Bee's pit and the Nung machine gunners, no VC came near.

Thanks to his fluency with Vietnamese, Doc communicated with Strike Force Company 123, deployed in the outer perimeter to his front. He told *Dai-uy* Lich to call to them to hold their fire until they could see targets, and to direct their fire outward, away from the inner perimeter.

The first aircraft overhead was a U-10 light plane. The next was a most welcome sight—a twin engine CV-2 Caribou. It parachuted medical supplies, radios and ammo to us. The pilot was Captain Robert W. Clark, of the 21st Aviation Company. His first drop landed in the outer perimeter. His second was a bulls-eye, right in the center, or what had formerly been the center, of Camp Nam Dong.

164 • Victory at Nam Dong

Beeson left the Nungs in charge of his mortar and together we tried to make contact with the arriving aircraft. I made a thorough inspection of the inner perimeter, checking every trench. Then I settled down beside the cinder blocks near Woody's pit. The blocks were some protection from sniper fire. Later we spread a parachute overhead to shield us from the sun.

Brown remained wary. He could hear shots through the woods near the outpost. He guessed the VC were withdrawing along two possible routes. One was up the river beyond the outpost. The other was across the river and a stream bed, in the opposite direction. Thanks to his previous careful measurement of the distances, he laid down a mortar barrage along both routes.

Brown and Dan checked ammunition reserves as part of our regrouping to prepare for another VC attack. Each of the pits had started with about 350 rounds and some had no more than twelve remaining. Brown and Dan took a detail of Nungs to the ammunition bunkers. They found the area covered with dead VC, a testament to the accuracy of Houston and Terry and the others in Disser's pit. Sporadic small arms fire continued as the ammunition party reached the bunkers. Dan detected a movement in one and was about ready to open fire when he realized it was a goat that had taken refuge there during the siege. Brown and Dan discovered the VC had gotten away with over 13,400 rounds of carbine ammunition that they took from the bunker closest to the gate.

At eight o'clock we were treated to a wonderful sight. *Trung-uy* Lu came marching down the road and into the camp with about seventy-five of his men. He had brought them through the valley from Kha Tre. When he reached my cinder block CP he found me sprawled under the parachute canopy, looking like an oriental potentate. Beeson was nearby, talking on the radio to the aircraft.

"*Dai-uy* Donlon," he began, "is there anything I can do to help? I am sorry we could not get here sooner, but it was impossible to start before daylight. I heard the firing. We were ambushed twice along the way, but here we are, at your service!"

At 0920 hours our tactical air support arrived.

Victory at Nam Dong • 165

Lu had a good map. We studied it in an attempt to discern the probable VC withdrawal route. Lu and Beeson radioed possibilities to the Vietnamese A-1H Skyraiders, but they released their bombs from the extreme height of 5,000 feet. The bombs all fell on the far side of the ridge, where there were no VC, as far as we knew.

Twenty-five minutes later six Marine choppers arrived, escorted by four armed Army UH-1B choppers and four A-1H Skyraiders. They were led by Lieutenant Colonel Oliver W. Curtis of Miami Springs, Florida. Curtis was commander of Marine Medium Helicopter Squadron 162. They brought the first of 104 troops and five Vietnamese nurses from An Diem, ferrying them in during the day in sorties. One of the other pilots was my old classmate from Fort Bragg Special Warfare School days, Captain Robert W. Barber of Santa Ana, California. He had visited Camp Nam Dong several days earlier.

Bee calmly talked the helicopters to a landing. We enthusiastically welcomed our Special Forces relief party. Both Major Maloney, the outgoing B Detachment commander, and Major Nance, his replacement, accompanied them. They inspected what was left of our burnt-out camp and set up evacuation procedures.

Things seemed pretty much under control. Bee was on the radio. Gregg and his nurses were helping the wounded. Brown and Dan were redistributing ammunition, and the rest were preparing for a possible new attack. I could feel my wounds stiffening up. Then I realized I couldn't stand without assistance.

The thirst was unbearable. We were all parched. Lu's men brought us some water, some melons and some beer from Nam Dong village.

Woody and one of the Special Forces men in the relief party helped me to the helicopter pad. By that time Woody looked somewhat more presentable. He was wearing a pair of Gregg's fatigue trousers. They had been dug out of the embers of the dispensary, and were wet and scorched. I offered him my boots. Woody took them rather reluctantly.

"I wasn't keen on wearing those boots if we had to fight again,"

166 • Victory at Nam Dong

he explained later. "The last two guys to wear them, Disser and the captain, got pretty shot up in them."

About ten o'clock the first evacuation helicopter lifted off. On board with me were Disser, Jay, and two badly wounded Vietnamese. Lieutenant Colonel Curtis piloted the chopper. The last I saw of Terry, his arm in a sling, he was carrying a 200-pound bundle that had been dropped to us from the Caribou. Long after we had departed Bee ran into Terry.

"What the hell are you doing here?" he challenged. Terry said he had work to do and disappeared. Gregg caught up with him at the helicopter pad, helping evacuate wounded. Gregg put him on a chopper but Terry jumped off, giving his place to the wounded nurse. Finally Gregg pulled rank and ordered him out, standing by to see that he actually did leave.

We had suffered fifty-five dead and sixty-five wounded. We counted sixty-two dead VC. Some were trussed up with communication wire, as if an unsuccessful attempt might have been made to drag them off of the field of battle. The usual ratio was three dead VC to each body you found.

Most of the other VC dead were wearing only shiny red and blue loincloths. They were young and well-muscled, with the close-cut brush haircut of the professional soldier. We had been fighting hard-core professionals, not poorly trained, ill-equipped guerrillas.

The nurses moved among the wounded, dispensing encouragement and vitamins. Vietnam was vitamin-happy. Some of the wounded were evacuated without bandages because we ran out of dressings, but none of them left Nam Dong without his vitamins.

As our chopper lifted off for the hop to Da Nang I looked back at our camp. It was nothing but a mass of blackened, smoking ruins. The ashes of the supply room exploded every time the smoldering debris set off another round. Sniper fire continued as the last of the VC covering force retreated through the jungles. Pursuit forces did not catch up with them, but they found recently dug foxholes at the edge of the airstrip. These fresh foxholes were bloodstained, but any bodies had been removed. Curiously, an American magazine was found abandoned in one foxhole. It was a fairly recent issue of *Playboy*.

They had thrown massive numbers of well-trained VC at us. They had good weapons—with the possible exception of their grenades—good tactics, and excellent intelligence about Camp Nam Dong. And we beat them. We held, and we threw them back.

Healing the Wounds of War

July 6, 1964, Midday . . .

During the helicopter ride to Da Nang my thoughts remained riveted on Nam Dong. I was turning over and over in my mind the ordeal of the previous night with all of its fighting and frustrations, death and destruction.

I was tremendously proud—and more—of my team. Every man responded without hesitation again and again in a superhuman effort that ultimately was successful in preventing the camp from being overrun, as the VC loudspeaker had promised.

The training, the discipline, the ingenuity, and the courage of my team had been put to the most severe test a soldier could possibly face. And without orders, each man on the team functioned as a fighting unit.

I was informed that the relief forces were arriving under the command of a friend and OCS classmate, Captain Jerry Griffin. He was known for his courageous candor off the battlefield and his raw courage on the battlefields of Vietnam, where he would eventually serve three tours. His presence, along with his Nung company, was the best medicine I could have received as I was MEDEVACED by a U.S. Marine helicopter, H-34.

Such were my thoughts as I arrived at the Marine hospital at Da Nang. I received a preliminary examination and a hurried debriefing. Four of us were lifted aboard a C-47 transport for the 275-mile flight to Nha Trang. As Terry, Disser, Jay and I were awaiting takeoff, a big red-haired Marine colonel strode on board. He addressed us in a gruff manner.

"Who the hell did you have on that damn radio of yours this morning?" he demanded to know.

I recalled the rough talk that Beeson had thrown at the Marine choppers on my behalf after their first attempt to land was aborted.

But before I could speak, he continued.

"Well, whoever it was, he was the calmest individual I've ever known under those circumstances. His voice was calm and clear. Gave me all the details. He ought to be commended."

I breathed a sigh of relief. Beeson was the last member of the team to leave Nam Dong. He remained there overnight and left the following day. And then it took a direct order from Major Nance.

"Beeson, you're going back," the major informed him.

"Sir, I'm staying here," Bee replied.

"You're going back," the major repeated.

"Yes, sir!" was Beeson's response.

Brown, who was slightly wounded, also spent the night at the camp. As the senior NCOs, he and Beeson helped turn over what was left of Nam Dong to replacements. The camp was rebuilt in succeeding weeks and, in a ceremony that I attended on September 17, was formally transferred to the Vietnamese Civil Guard. The rebuilt camp looked nothing like its predecessor. It was triangular in shape. Instead of two perimeter fences it had a single barrier, a solid wall of timbers reminiscent of Army forts on America's frontiers of the previous century.

Dan and Gregg, who, like Beeson, were not wounded, remained until they were ordered out. Woody and Whit were evacuated in the helicopter that carried the bodies of Alamo, Houston and Conway to Da Nang for the start of their final journey.

Whitsell's hand was patched up in Da Nang. When the doctors asked Woody what was wrong with him he replied "Hell, there ain't nothing wrong with me!" Later, when he was preparing to shower, he told Whit, "Just for the hell of it, I'll have the doc check my eardrum and see why it's hurting."

The doctor who examined his ear found the source of his discomfort. "Here's what's wrong with your eardrum," he announced. "You had this sticking through it." He held up a piece of shrapnel that he had extracted.

Woody took Alamo's death pretty hard. He loved Pop, perhaps more than any of the rest of us. He cried when he climbed out of his

170 • ʄealing the Wounds of War

pit and saw Alamo's body. All of us were shaken by the deaths of Pop and Houston. The bitter irony was that, of the twelve of us, only they had expectant wives. The irony was complete when we received the tragic news that Mrs. Alamo lost her baby and Mrs. Houston lost one of the twins to whom she had given birth.

Woody was not having any more fighting in his underwear, thank you. Our first night at Da Nang we were put on alert, based on word of a possible VC attack. "Oh, hell!" he grumbled. "We just got out of one mess and now we're going to get into another one!" He drew a new set of fatigues, an AR-15 with twelve full magazines plus 400 additional rounds, and new boots. That's how he slept, with his .38 pistol strapped on. The night passed without incident, and I don't think he was disappointed.

Doctors at the Army's 8th Field Hospital in Nha Trang expressed concern over my stomach wound. They wouldn't know how deep it was or what it was until they took X-rays. They made countless X-rays of my stomach, shoulder, leg and arm, and I spent most of the next day in the operating room. The stomach wound proved to be deep, but did not go into the stomach wall or any muscles. I don't believe they ever got all the shrapnel out.

My body was so filthy I couldn't stand it that first night. After the ward quieted I eased myself out of bed and drew a big tub of hot water. I was too sore to reach the soap, but the soaking was wonderfully relaxing. I slipped once, and my head went under. I almost drowned, but it was worth it, even though the ward attendants gave me a bad time when they found me out of bed.

Woody came down from Nha Trang the second day. He, Jay, Terry, and Disser were evacuated to the States after a few days at Clark Field in the Philippines. I was beginning to feel pretty good after about three weeks and requested return to duty. Instead I was assigned to limited duty, in charge of security at the hospital with additional responsibility of S-2 and S-3, Operations and Intelligence, at Special Forces headquarters there.

I asked why I couldn't rejoin my team.

"You've got a label on you now. We don't want you picked up

5ealing the Wounds of War • 171

as a prisoner of war," was the explanation.

I had heard that I might be recommended for the Medal of Honor. It was when we were visited by General William C. Westmoreland, commander of the Military Advisory Command, Vietnam (MAC-V). He was addressing troops in a hangar at the airfield and I went AWOL from the hospital to hear his remarks. I stood behind the rear ranks in my pajamas. The general commented that some people in the hospital would be recommended for decorations requiring approval from the highest level of our government. Some senior officers came over to me and said "He's talking about you, for the Medal of Honor."

I really didn't think it would happen. We all felt honored enough when the Purple Heart was pinned to our pajamas in the hospital. We had simply done our jobs.

There were lots of visitors besides General Westmoreland. They included Ambassador Maxwell D. Taylor, Major General Richard G. Stilwell, in charge of operations and planning on General Westmoreland's staff, and Major General Joe Moore, commander of the Air Force's 2nd Air Division. I was impressed with the thoroughness with which General Stilwell debriefed us on the events at Nam Dong.

I actually enjoyed my stay at the hospital. The staff was kind and attentive. Thanks to the hospital food I gained about five needed pounds, and my fellow patients were interesting. Not enough can be said for the selfless personnel who run an Army field hospital. They seemed to never stop working, regardless of the hour of day or night. Their assignment is the slow, sometimes heartbreaking drudgery of trying to mend bodies and minds torn by battle. It calls for a special sort of caring and courage, and they were equal to the challenge. Whenever I needed someone to talk with they took the time. They helped to heal all my wounds, physical and mental. I will be forever grateful for their total dedication.

One of the Vietnamese patients in the hospital was a youngster about five years old, named Mui. He appeared to be in pretty bad shape with some sort of internal disorder. My first day there I saw

172 • Healing the Wounds of War

him lying listlessly in bed with tubes sticking out of him. It looked like he might die and really didn't care if he did.

I left my bed and approached him. "Hi, there," I said, and smiled. Then I made a face at him. He was apparently hurting so much that he wasn't aware of my presence.

Mui managed to pull through, with the help of the doctors and nurses. But he would not move in bed because it caused him too much pain when he tried. His muscles had weakened, and all he did was stare at the ceiling.

I was exercising in bed, lifting a leg and that sort of thing, and I tried to get Mui to try to move a bit. I motioned to him and used all of my limited Vietnamese and sign language, but he refused to respond. I approached his bedside and encouraged him, gently lifting his leg. But he only cried out in pain. I tried the old "handkerchief mouse trick." You roll a handkerchief a certain way, blouse it out here and there, and it looks like a mouse. There's a way to make it appear to crawl around on your arm, if you know the trick. Mui remained unresponsive. Then I borrowed a set of checkers. When I arranged the board with all the pieces on his bed, I hit paydirt. We made up our own rules as we progressed. He loved the checker board and kept it with him all the time.

After that, when I would be resting in bed, I would look in his direction, wink, and slowly raise my leg. He struggled again and again before he finally got his withered leg off the sheet. Finally he succeeded, and pretty soon he was running around the ward, challenging the others to a game of *Mui rules* checkers.

They reactivated Team A-726. Brown, Beeson, Whit, Gregg, and Dan called on me at the hospital a few days after my arrival. They picked up replacements, returned to Da Nang, and on September 4 they left on the long-postponed mission to build a camp at Ta Co on the Laotian border in Quang Nam province. The site was on top of two hills in the heart of VC country. They went in aboard Marine choppers. The landing was uneventful, but beginning the next day they were constantly in firefights while patrolling the area.

Healing the Wounds of War • 173

The beach at Nha Trang was magnificent. It was only a short walk from the hospital. I spent a great deal of time there, wading tentatively at first, and then going all the way in as my body started to heal.

There was another reason why I went there—a more important reason. The worst thing about serving in Vietnam was never seeing an American flag. At least, that's the way it was when I was there. The Army and Marine units that went in later showed the colors, but we were strictly advisers and guests of the Vietnamese. It bothered me to not see the Stars and Stripes. Then it dawned on me. U.S. Navy ships fly Old Glory! I would sit on the beach, waiting and watching. It sure made a difference.

Brown, Beeson, Whitsell, Dan, Gregg and I completed our six-month TDY tour in Vietnam and left from the Saigon airport on November 20. We came home aboard another C-135 "flying submarine" via the northern route, stopping in Yokota, Japan, and again in Ohio to refuel, before landing at Seymour-Johnson Air Force Base at Goldsboro, North Carolina. A bus took us on to our headquarters at Fort Bragg.

After a week of debriefing we were free to take leave, and we were ready! I set a course for Saugerties, arriving just in time for Thanksgiving Day with my family. When I saw my brother Paul, I apologized for losing the Miraculous Medal he had given me before I left for Vietnam. Paul had worn it all through World War II and thinking it would bring "good luck," I had taken it. Sometime during the battle it had fallen off. Now it was lost in the ashes of Nam Dong. Paul told me not to worry about it. "By the way, he added, I forgot to tell you that a Purple Heart comes with it!"

I tried not to think about the Medal of Honor. I already felt tremendously honored to be recommended for it, and to know that I had commanded one of the most decorated units in the history of the United States Army.

Alamo and Houston were posthumously awarded the Distinguished Service Cross. Olejniczak, Brown, Disser, and Terry received the Silver Star, and Beeson, Daniels, Gregg, Whitsell and

Woody won the Bronze Star with V for Valor. Nine of us earned the Purple Heart—Alamo and Houston posthumously, and Olejniczak, Brown, Disser, Terrin, Whitsell, Woods, and I. All twelve of us were decorated by the South Vietnamese government.

An endless succession of good things happened to me following my return home. There were letters from all corners of the nation, from small children barely able to write, to aged men and women who had also served their country in times of crisis long since passed. I promised myself that I would answer each letter personally, because I believed they deserved no less.

The Army sent me off on a tour of the country, making personal appearances and doing interviews, which was a new experience for me. My home town gave mother and me a wonderful parade and celebration, proclaiming December 28, 1964, "Donlon Day" in Saugerties. My mother's heart was gladdened again on March 6, 1965, when the Saugerties Junior Chamber of Commerce honored me as "Saugerties Citizen of the Century."

The children of my Aunt Ruth's sixth grade class in New York went to great trouble to reenact the White House award ceremony for me.

President Johnson invited me to be a special guest at his Inauguration in January of 1965. It was a whirlwind of activity capped off by an evening attending all of the Inaugural Balls. At the Sheraton-Park Hotel we bumped into his daughters on the dance floor. He introduced me to Lynda and Luci and put me completely at ease just as he had done at the White House, six weeks earlier.

In cooperation with the Martin-Marietta Company, I was sent to various defense plants to talk about the firm's "Zero Defects" program. I made an effort to emphasize the vital link between the manufacturer and the user of essential military hardware. With the use of such hardware coming only when all other means of problem solving have failed, I stressed the importance of those products being flawless to ensure victory and the preservation of our way of life. Just as U.S. Army Special Forces Team A-726 did on the night of July 6, 1964, I encouraged all to "Do it right the first time!"

Late one night after coming home from yet another welcome home celebration, I received a call from Vice President Hubert Humphrey's office asking me to appear with him on the Today Show. The next morning, with a raging hangover I made my way to the TV station. During a break from the taping I asked where I might get some aspirin. The Vice President, always one for a good laugh, said "You need some Chlorophyll aspirin, captain."

"What's that?" I queried. He burst out laughing as he answered "It's for stinking headaches!" Not wanting to be outdone, I countered, "Well, sir, looks like you could use some low-cal shampoo."

"Never heard of low-cal shampoo," said the Vice President.

"It's for fat-heads, sir," I said, as Mr. Humphrey laughed heartily.

It was about this time that I was approached by several organizations to write the story of Nam Dong. The result was a book, published in 1965, and co-authored by Warren Rogers. I took the title from a speech by General Harold K. Johnson, the Army Chief of Staff. He described Nam Dong as "an 'Outpost of Freedom' over 5,000 miles from our shores defended by American lives." The book was excerpted in the October 23, 1965, edition of the *Saturday Evening Post* with my picture on the cover. Later the United States Information Agency translated it into three languages, Portuguese, Marathi and Hindi. It was also condensed for *Reader's Digest Books,* appearing in the winter 1966 selections.

After *Outpost of Freedom* was published I received a call from Dr. Kenneth Wells, president of Freedoms Foundation at Valley Forge, Pennsylvania. It seems he had been reading my book and was taken by the paragraph where I had sat on the beach in Vietnam waiting and watching for a U.S. Navy ship with our flag flying proudly. This led to my being recognized with the Freedom Leadership Medal. I was immensely proud to be so honored, but the real good that came from many of the ceremonies I attended was in the people I had the privilege to meet. Dr. and Mrs. Wells certainly stand out in that category as great American patriots.

One of the most moving moments for me was the recognition by the American Legion with their Distinguished Service Medal. I was so humbled and near speechless in the presence of all the veterans from many of our country's past wars. It is to these men and women that all of us owe our never-ending gratitude.

It also gladdened my heart when I had a chance to recognize someone who had touched my life in a significant way. Certainly, with my academic background, I never thought I would be standing on a stage in front of the National Education Association at their annual gathering. But that is exactly where I found myself one evening at a black tie gala. Beside me was Miss Elinor Lente, my high school Latin teacher.

Chosen by the NEA as the Outstanding Citizen that year, I was asked to pick one teacher who had influenced me the most. Without hesitation I gave the name of Miss Lente. She taught more than Latin. Regaling us with special stories, but always keeping her finger on the pulse of the class, Miss Lente took us on an annual trip to New York City. The money we earned through out lunchtime Latin Club helped pay for entrance to museums, art movies and the Metropolitan Opera. She taught us the value of things beyond sentence structure.

It was a proud moment to be standing with Miss Lente as we were presented with our Golden Key awards. At the time she was the youngest person ever to receive this prestigious award. After retirement, Miss Lente finally changed the "Miss" to "Mrs." and married Hank Clements. Today they reside in a waterfront home near the marina in Saugerties.

My next trip to Vietnam would be to the embassy of the Republic of Vietnam in Washington, D.C. This time I was able to take my mother along. What a joy it was to introduce her to some of the culture of this beautiful country. The occasion was the presentation of the Vietnam National Order Fourth Class and the Gallantry Cross-with Palm. Mother was fascinated with the lovely, flowing *ao dai*, the national dress of the Vietnamese women and the wonderful array of French and Vietnamese food at the reception.

This was all pretty heady stuff for an Army captain. I was thankful, and kept on balance by the knowledge that what we did at Nam Dong was a team effort. I was also grateful for the generous advice and friendship I had received from some of the other medal recipients. It seems such a coincidence now, but before I left for Vietnam my roommate had been Ola Lee Mize . . . the last Medal of Honor recipient from the Korean War. Lee was particularly helpful with his recollections and how the medal can change a person's life. All of the medal holders I have met take seriously the responsibility that goes with this highest honor.

Shortly after my book was published I received a telephone call late one evening. The woman calling explained that her husband had been assigned to the 25th Infantry Division at Schofield Barracks, Hawaii. He had taken a shotgun platoon to Vietnam and was killed just one week before he was to return home. There would be a library dedication in his hometown on November 15, at the school where his mother was a teacher. She had purchased a copy of *Outpost of Freedom* to donate to the library and wanted to know if I would consent to autographing it. I agreed and she asked if I would be in Columbus on the 13th or 14th of November. She planned to stop in Columbus on her way to North Carolina, and would call me after she arrived.

As I hung up the phone a great sadness came over me. How much longer would this war go on? How many more lives would be lost? The stranger's voice on the other end of the phone had touched me deeply. I could feel her pain with each soft-spoken sentence. My thoughts turned to Mrs. Alamo, Mrs. Houston . . . and her surviving son.

Norma

November 12, 1965 . . .

The plane was full except for the seat next to me. As we sat on the runway at the Atlanta, Georgia, airport, I reminisced about the ceremonies I had attended the day before in Washington, D.C. It was a privilege to be invited by Vice President Hubert Humphrey and to watch the wreath being placed at the Tomb of the Unknown Soldier on Veterans Day.

Although it had been a quick trip to our nation's capital I did manage to visit John Houston's grave at Arlington National Cemetery. Would this stabbing pain in my heart for the men I had lost at Nam Dong ever go away?

Now, I shifted my focus to other things. I had begun the Infantry Officer's Career Course at Fort Benning in August . . . another school. Only two and a half months into the course and I was already falling behind. The demands on my time since the *Saturday Evening Post* cover story and the publication of my book, *Outpost of Freedom,* were beginning to overwhelm me.

The door of the plane closed, and I watched as the stairs were slowly moved away. Thank goodness we would now taxi and take off. It was late in the evening and I was anxious to return to my apartment in Columbus. I was grateful it was Friday, I would have the weekend to catch up with my studies.

My attention turned again to the window as the plane began to move. Suddenly the engines were turned off and the stairs reappeared. I heard the door being opened again. This flight was the last one out of Atlanta bound for Columbus that night. Some lucky soldier is going to make it after all, I thought.

Then I saw her legs. Someone was running down the terminal corridor to catch the plane. Nice legs, I said to myself.

When she finally boarded, she passed by me, quickly glancing at the empty seat. I saw her give my uniform a "look." Perhaps her mother had told her never to sit next to a soldier when she was alone.

Then a soft voice said, "Excuse me, is this seat taken?" I looked up into a face slightly blushing with embarrassment. "No, please sit down," I said, rising to let her pass.

We buckled our seatbelts and sat in silence as the plane began to taxi down the runway. I could smell her perfume. It was an exotic fragrance and matched her face.

After the takeoff she turned to me and said, "I'm Norma Irving, the widow who called you last month about your book." I was caught totally off guard; her face certainly did not match her name! Trying my hardest to remain calm and not show my surprise, I said, "Hi, I'm Roger Donlon." She looked like she was suppressing a giggle, and, with a twinkle in her eye, extended her hand and said, "Nice to meet you."

Now why did I say such a dumb thing! She already knew who I was when she saw my nametag! I tried not to look flustered as I returned the handshake. When our hands touched I felt the warmth of her skin. She felt like silk, soft and smooth. I noticed her nails were perfectly manicured. On her ring finger was a wide gold band.

As we flew into the night sky, Norma began to remove her heavy, fur-trimmed suit coat. She struggled a bit, trying to free her arm from the sleeve while sitting down. I reached across her back to assist her.

"Thanks," she said, smiling. Wow, I thought to myself, what a smile! Her teeth were so white, so small and straight. As the coat came off I had to avert my eyes; I didn't want her to catch me staring.

We started making small talk but I was having a difficult time taking my eyes off her beautiful form. She was gorgeous from head to toe!

Our flight was a short one, and in a few minutes we started our descent into Columbus. I asked Norma if anyone was meeting her at the airport. She answered, "No, I'll just take a cab to my hotel." I guess big city girls from Los Angeles didn't realize that small towns like Columbus, Georgia didn't have much of a taxi service.

"Well," I said, "I could save you the fare. It's a long ride from the airport into town."

"That would be great," came her reply. "I'm staying at the Holiday Inn on Victory Drive."

The amount of luggage Norma had amazed me. She quickly apologized and explained that she was only going to be in town for the weekend but would be in North Carolina for two weeks.

On the drive into town Norma seemed pensive, looking intently out the window. She talked softly and slowly about how she had come here to Fort Benning two years before to be married. Her late husband was a student at Airborne school. She had arrived in time for "jump week" and they were married after his graduation.

"My plans for the weekend were to get your autograph on the book and take a walk down memory lane," Norma said. "On Monday I will attend the library dedication in John's hometown. It's at the school where his mother is a teacher."

All of a sudden it occurred to me that I had not eaten since lunch. I was hungry! "Listen," I said, "I'm starving. How about going to get something to eat?"

"I'm glad you asked," came Norma's response. "I bet they don't have room service at this Holiday Inn, and I'm starving too!" I liked her enthusiastic reply. In fact, I liked a lot of things about this intriguing woman. I didn't want the evening to end.

By the time I changed into civilian clothes it was after 2100 hours. When we reached the "Cotton Palace" they were closing the upstairs restaurant and everyone was moving into the sing-along bar in the basement. Several of my classmates were headed in that direction, and after a curious, sidelong glance at the stranger with me, cajoled us to join them. I waved them off, saying we would be down after we ate. The owner was very gracious, after I explained my situation, and agreed to let us be her last dinner customers.

It was a wonderful meal. The conversation flowed between us like we had known each other all our lives. The dining room was empty except for us; it was as though we were the only two people in the world.

At dinner I had the chance to look at Norma from across the table. She was the most attractive Asian-American woman I had ever seen. The combination of her jet-black hair, clear olive complexion, large, expressive almond-shaped brown eyes, and warm smile made her a winner. She looked directly at me when she spoke, and her voice was low-pitched and sensual. I was impressed with the clarity and articulation of her words. She was, in every sense, "a classy city girl," confident, polished, and sophisticated.

I could have stayed in that dining room all night, but seeing the waiter anxious to close up we finished our food, thanked our hostess, and joined the group in the bar.

Our gang of mostly bachelors and their dates was a rowdy crew. The blind piano player encouraged us to sing with abandon as he played our favorite tunes. This night, though, I was not my usual self. I would normally lead the dancing on the tables and others would follow.

We sat with our backs to the wall, side by side, shoulders touching. For some reason I did not introduce Norma around. I wanted to keep her all to myself. Sensing my mood that this was someone special, my buddies kept their distance. Slowly, my hand found hers under the table. She did not resist or pull away.

We sat there, hand in hand, singing along with the crowd. Norma knew all the words to every song, surprising me yet again.

All too soon it was closing time. On the ride back to her hotel Norma said, "I have your book packed in one of my suitcases. Do you think you could sign it tomorrow?" Delighted to have another excuse to see her I said, "Of course. What time should I come by?"

"Why don't you give me a call in the morning," she said.

"By the way," I offered, "I'll be happy to give you a ride back to the airport when you leave."

"Thank you, I really appreciate that," she said. "My flight to North Carolina leaves on Sunday afternoon."

When we reached the hotel I waited while Norma registered. Then I carried her luggage to the room. She opened the door, and stepped aside. She did not invite me in, or to stay, so I quickly put the suitcases into the room, turned, and said, "Well, looks like you're all set."

Standing in the darkened doorway, with only the moonlight shining down on her face, Norma looked so young and vulnerable. I wanted to reassure her in some way that everything would be all right. As I started to exit the room she looked up at me with those expressive eyes and said, "Thank you for dinner. I can't remember the last time I enjoyed myself so much."

I don't know what made me reach out to her, but I gently touched the fur on her collar and leaned down to kiss her lightly on the forehead. She closed her eyes and raised her head ever so slightly. Surprised, I found my lips touching hers. It was a very brief kiss, soft, innocent and gentle. I felt as though an angel had kissed me.

Driving back to my apartment I felt light-headed and giddy. This just couldn't be happening, I told myself. Since my divorce in 1961 I had kept a rein on my emotions. It was beyond belief that I was so purely and passionately attracted to a complete stranger!

I drifted off to sleep that night with so many mixed emotions. First, I fantasized of holding Norma in my arms. Then the guilt set in. What was I thinking of? She was still in mourning for her late husband. Where was my respect? Wasn't he killed in the same war that had claimed the lives of some of my men? Could I fall in love with someone who was not even of the same race or religion?

When morning came I awoke as if from a dream. I opened my eyes and realized everything that had happened the night before was real. Then I remembered that I was to call Norma. My heart leapt for joy! Hopefully she would consent to spending the day with me.

After I had showered, shaved, and dressed, I paced around my apartment until 0900 hours. My hands trembled as I dialed the number for the Holiday Inn.

When Norma answered the phone I recalled the same soft, sensual voice I had heard last month when she first called about autographing the book. "Good morning," I said, "did you sleep well?"

"Yes," she said, "and you?"

I answered, "Better than usual. Have you had breakfast?"

"Don't tell me you want to feed me again," was her laughing reply. "Well, okay, but only if you let me treat."

I agreed, and arranged to pick her up in a half-hour.

After breakfast I talked Norma into stopping by Ed and Carol DeChristopher's house where some of my classmates were gathering to watch a football game. She fit right in. She not only understood the game, but loved watching it as well. Where had this terrific woman been all my life? As we were all leaving it was decided that the Officers' Club would be that evening's dinner stop before our usual songfest at the Cotton Palace. I looked at Norma and she nodded in the affirmative that she would go with me.

Next we went to the home of George and Pat Day. George and I had attended the U.S. Military Academy Prep School together. Just that morning they had come home from the hospital with their fourth child. Little Michael would now join his older sisters in the Day family. I loved children. Often when visiting my friend's children, I would think of my daughter, Linda, and imagine what it would be like to have her with me. Both Norma and I marveled at the wonder of this little miracle before us. I could tell she loved babies; she seemed to be so natural with them. Was there anything I would not like about this wonderful woman?

I dropped Norma at the Holiday Inn to change for our first "real" date. Since I had only one civilian suit I would have to wear it again. Thankfully, I did purchase more than one civilian shirt but they were all white, and all the same style. Boring, I thought to myself. She probably thinks I'm boring.

Dinner at the Officers' Club was an elegant affair. We then rendezvoused at the Cotton Palace for a round of drinks and a rousing chorus of *"God Bless America."*

Walking Norma to her room, I could feel her tension. We had spent the better part of the day, and all of the evening together. There was no denying the chemistry between us.

When we arrived at her door, Norma said, "Are you too tired to autograph the book now?"

"No," I replied. We stepped inside the room and she handed me the book. I sat down on the bed, opened the book and began to write. When I was finished, I looked up at Norma, and as she reached out to take the book from my hands I gently pulled her towards me.

"Please," she said, "I'm not ready for this." She sat down on the bed and silently began to cry. I knelt down on one knee beside the bed, holding her hand and apologizing.

"I'm sorry, I don't know what made me do that, I'm so sorry," I said.

The tears were streaming down her face. With a small, soft sob she said, "I'm so frightened of the way I feel about you. I can't believe this is happening. I don't want to fall in love again, and especially not to a career military man."

I did not know what to do to assuage her grief. I just knew that I wanted to put my arms around her, to protect her, to make things right for her. A chance meeting on an airplane was one thing, but to think both of us were feeling something for the other . . . was this destiny?

Finally I said, "Just let me stay with you. I promise nothing will happen. Just let me stay and comfort you."

By this time Norma was too emotional to resist. She was like a small rag doll as I gently laid her head on the pillow and removed her shoes. I took off my suit coat and tie, untied my shoes and slipped them off. Fully clothed, we lay there on the bed together. I took Norma in my arms and rested her head on my shoulder. She was still crying softly and soon my shirt was wet with her tears.

We did not speak. Words seemed unnecessary. After awhile I could tell that Norma had fallen asleep. Something inside of me knew that this was the woman I would spend the rest of my life with. I did not want to do anything to jeopardize my chances.

When I awoke the next morning, Norma had already changed her clothes and had on fresh makeup. "Come on," I said, "we're going to my place and I'm cooking breakfast."

The world's greatest chef I was not, but I could do eggs! As a matter of fact Norma told me they were the most perfect eggs she had ever eaten. About the time we finished breakfast, my roommate, Jay Olejniczak, came down the stairs. Introductions were made all around and I had Jay take some pictures of Norma and me. He reminded me it was Sunday as he headed out the door for mass.

Alone again, I said, "Come upstairs with me. There is something I want to show you."

With mock humor Norma answered, "Your etchings?"

"Yes," I teased back, "my etchings. Actually, I want to show you all the unanswered mail I've accumulated over the past few months."

Curiosity now getting the better of her, she followed me up the stairs. I opened the door to the bedroom and Norma's eyes widened as she stepped inside. What she saw was carton boxes piled waist high lining three walls. There was barely enough room for the bed and a small dresser. "This," I joked, "is the price of fame."

"Fan mail?" Norma asked.

"Not exactly fan mail," I answered, "just letters from all over the world, mostly congratulating me on being awarded the medal. Some asking for autographs, pictures and other stuff. Also, there are several proposals of marriage."

"You're kidding?" was Norma's reply. "Women that you don't even know write and ask you to marry them?"

"Well," I said with a laugh, "I need someone to answer them so I don't keep them hanging."

"Why are you telling me all this?" Norma asked.

"Because you are a secretary," I answered. "You could help me out here."

"That's impossible," Norma replied. "I live in California, remember!"

"But you could move," I said.

Norma gave me an incredulous look. "You're crazy!" she replied.

I noticed the clock on the night stand. "There's a noon mass at church. Would you like to go with me?"

"Yes," Norma said. "I haven't been to any church in a long, long time. And, I've never been to a Catholic church."

At mass I had a hard time concentrating on my prayers. I kept sneaking a peek at Norma, watching her fascination with the rituals of a religion new to her. She may not have been a churchgoer, but I could tell that in her soul she knew and felt the presence of God.

All too soon mass ended, and it was time to retrieve Norma's luggage and head for the airport. We said good-bye with a brief hug, and I made Norma promise to call me after she returned to California. I watched her climb the stairs to the waiting plane, just as she had done less than forty-eight hours before. At the top she turned and smiled . . . that wonderful smile that was now etched in my heart.

As the weeks turned into a month Norma and I talked endlessly on the telephone. When my bill came I wished that I had owned stock in AT&T! It really was the only way to communicate as I lived to hear her voice each night. With every call I tried to convince her to move to Columbus and be my secretary.

During one conversation she finally said, "Okay, Roger, you win. There are some people I want you to meet, and if you pass their inspection I will come to Columbus and help you."

Christmas break was upon us now and I had two weeks of leave from school. Both Norma and I had already made plans for the holidays before we met. She was flying Mr. and Mrs. Irving out to California and I was going home to Saugerties. Although we had talked about changing our plans to be together, neither of us wanted to disappoint either of our families. I had given Norma my flight schedule, just in case she changed her mind and decided to accompany me to New York.

While waiting for a plane change in Atlanta I heard my name being paged. Approaching the ticket counter I saw an elderly couple standing there with a young, dark-haired girl. Something about her back looked familiar. She turned around, smiling. That smile! It could only belong to one person . . . Norma.

Norma • 187

"Surprise," she said, laughing. She had a look of merriment in her eyes for she knew she really caught me off guard this time. "Roger, I'd like to introduce Mr. and Mrs. Irving. John and Ruth, this is Roger Donlon."

Automatically I shook hands with them, but I was so dumbfounded it took me a few seconds to find my voice. "Nice to meet you," I replied to their warm greetings.

"Let's go get some coffee," Norma suggested. All of us had only a few minutes before we had to catch our respective flights. Norma explained that she had decided to surprise the Irvings by meeting them in Atlanta and flying west with them. It was nice to know I was not the only one who was surprised by her! She had arranged their flight so we would all be in the airport about the same time because these were the people she wanted me to meet.

I must have passed the test because the next time I called Norma she was making plans to move to Columbus. She didn't realize it at the time but the work she would do for me would turn into a lifetime endeavor.

From January to May of 1966 Norma worked hard to get me organized. She set up an office in a small house she rented just a few blocks from my apartment. I moved all the boxes of correspondence out of my bedroom and spent each evening dictating responses that Norma would type and send.

It was a time of getting to know each other better. I found out that Norma had many talents in addition to being a great secretary. She was a gourmet cook, and loved to entertain my friends. Her house became another place to "hang out" and a regular stop after bachelor parties, to sober up and get some breakfast. Most of all I loved Norma for her caring and unselfish attitude toward others. She was the most considerate person I had ever met. Her love of God and her fellow man was second only to my mother's.

After my graduation from the Infantry Officer's Advanced Course I received orders to finish my degree at the University of Nebraska at Omaha on the Army's "Bootstrap" program. I was ready to marry Norma, but kept my feelings to myself. I could tell she needed more time before making any commitments. When she came to my marriage bed I wanted it to be without ghosts.

We continued to keep Ma Bell rolling in dough by calling each other, sometimes more than once a day. After two summer sessions of school I was ready for a break. Norma asked me to come out to California and meet her family. They had an annual reunion and clamfest at Pismo Beach. It sounded like fun. In the more than ten years that Norma's family had been having this annual reunion it had never rained. Well, that year it not only rained, but it was so cold we couldn't even go down on the beach! Of course all her relatives good-naturedly blamed it on the newcomer and I took a lot of kidding.

In September it was back to school. Although I was never a great student, maturity was now on my side. I knew this would be my last chance to get a college degree. By November I was beginning to become distracted by Norma's absence. While in Columbus I had grown accustomed to seeing her every day. Her always-cheerful disposition and great sense of humor gave me a much-needed boost. Thankfully she had relatives in Omaha and they invited her to come out for Thanksgiving.

When Norma arrived she could see that I needed more than just a daily chat on the phone. She decided to stay on until my graduation in March. Because her Uncle Woody and Aunt Chris lived on the other side of Omaha, Norma found an elderly lady just a block from my house who agreed to rent her a room.

Life now became a routine of daily mass, school, and study. Each weekday I would pick up Norma at 0600, and we would attend mass together. She would drop me at school, then spend the day at my house editing and typing my papers. In the evenings we spent a lot of time at the library where Norma helped me do research. On the weekends we visited at Woody and Chris's home. Woody was a retired FBI agent and I never tired of listening to stories of his days with the "Bureau."

March of 1967 was a month of celebration. The college degree that had eluded me for so long was finally in my hands! Norma had

Norma • **189**

helped me accomplish what I was never able to do alone. It convinced me even more that we would make a strong, lifelong team. I resolved to make her my wife and began to plan how I would propose.

While in Washington, D.C., at the Office of the Chief of Information, my promotion to major came through. It was a "below the zone" and I stood proudly as Major General Keith Ware pinned on my new rank. General Ware was a Medal of Honor recipient from World War II, and much admired by his fellow recipients. He had taken the time to give me wise guidance and counsel on being a medal holder. One statement that he made didn't sit well with me. "Roger," he said one day; "you will no longer be just Roger Donlon. You will now be known as the 'first' to be awarded a Medal of Honor in Vietnam." We lost a fine general and a great person when General Ware was later killed in a helicopter crash in Vietnam.

I was due for another "short" tour and wanted to go back to Vietnam. Rumor was that the Viet Cong had a "bounty" out for my capture so the Pentagon would not let me go back. In frustration I accepted a tour to Korea instead. I would spend two months doing public relations work before heading for the DMZ.

Shortly before my departure for Korea I received word that I was scheduled to attend an official function in San Francisco with General of the Army Omar Bradley. Wanting to surprise Norma with a marriage proposal before I left, I called her.

Explaining that I would have to attend a "stag" affair of the Association of the United States Army on a Saturday night, I asked her to fly to San Francisco early on Sunday morning. My plan was to pick her up at the airport, attend mass, take in all the romantic sights around the city during the afternoon, and then propose that evening at dinner.

I made a reservation for Norma at the Fairmont Hotel. The room was perfect. It was situated on a corner of the fourteenth floor. The windows were large and provided a sweeping view of the city. I ordered a special dinner to be brought up that evening. The stage was now set for the perfect proposal!

Norma's plane was on time and we made it to mass with minutes to spare. When I took her to the hotel she expressed surprise that I would pick something so pricey. Then, when I opened the door to her room she exclaimed, "Oh, it's beautiful!" She seemed excited about having a real "suite" with an elegant living room and separate bedroom. I put her suitcases in the bedroom, gave her a quick kiss and said, "Let's get changed and go see the city."

My smaller room was down the hall on the same floor, and after changing into some casual clothes I knocked on Norma's door. No answer. She must not have heard me, I thought. I knocked again. Again no answer. I went back to my room and called her on the phone. As soon as she heard my voice she let loose! She was angry and didn't even want to see me ever again! What on earth could be wrong? What did I do?

Finally, Norma yelled, "Did you leave the newspaper on the table so I would find it?"

Puzzled, I said "Newspaper?"

"Just read it!" she shouted as she slammed the phone in my ear.

I hurried down to the lobby to buy a paper. There on the front page was a picture of me with Miss San Francisco, "toasting" each other at the stag dinner. The whole thing was a publicity stunt. She had attended last evening's function representing the city and a photographer had posed us for a picture. I had no idea that he was a reporter and that the picture would end up on the front page!

Spotting a phone in the hotel lobby, I quickly dialed Norma's room. After I explained what had happened she calmed down. The rest of the day went smoothly and that evening we enjoyed a romantic dinner looking out at the lights of the "City of Love."

Norma accepted my proposal. Anxious not to lose her again, I suggested we drive to Lake Tahoe the next day and get married before I left for Korea. Wisely she talked me out of that wild idea, and we made plans to be married as soon as my Korean tour ended.

Shortly after I arrived at my new duty assignment with the 2nd Infantry Division I received the following letter:

Dear Roger,

We want to send you our love and congratulations on your engagement. Do you remember the weekend that you and Norma met? Well, when she arrived here, she collapsed in our arms crying uncontrollably. We had never seen her cry before and we knew that she had met someone she cared about very much.

Losing our son, John, was the hardest thing we have had to bear. Norma was a godsend; she was kind, loving, and compassionate towards us. We could not have survived this ordeal without her help. There is an old saying that goes, "A daughter is a daughter all of your life, but a son is a son till he takes a wife." Now you know why Norma is so special to us.

John and Ruth Irving

Captain Donlon, Norma, Bob Hope, Medal of Honor Convention, Los Angeles, California, October 1966.

Our Family Team

November 9, 1968 . . .

My short tour to Korea was almost half over when I took a twenty-day leave to spend Christmas with Norma and her family. Now officially engaged, it was a joyous time for all of us. One night we stayed up late watching a movie on television. I must have smoked more than usual because the next morning Norma's grandmother passed the word that if Norma married me she was going to be a young widow again! I went back to Korea and immediately stopped smoking.

On my return to the DMZ in January of 1968 the Pueblo was captured and North Korea made the raid on the Blue House. Things were heating up and all tours were extended indefinitely. There went the plans for our June wedding!

When I finally arrived back in the States it was early July. Sometime during the Fourth of July celebration an old back injury from my night at Nam Dong started acting up. The next morning I couldn't walk. Norma and her mother helped me to the car and Norma drove me to the nearest military hospital. They gave me some pills and told me to sleep on the floor for a few nights.

I was due at my new duty assignment, Fort Carson, Colorado, and was unable to sit up in the car. We made a makeshift bed in the back, and Norma chauffeured me to Colorado. After checking in I was sent by ambulance to Fitzsimons General Hospital in Denver.

Fortunately Norma had some distant relatives in Denver and they were kind enough to give her accommodations so she could stay. The weeks turned into months and slowly I got better. The doctors wanted to operate on my back but I was not convinced. In October I was released from the hospital and would convalesce for another month before returning to duty. The day before I left the hospital I was out-processing when I ran into three of my doctors on the elevator. They all looked surprised that I was leaving as they thought they had me scheduled for surgery.

"No," I said, "I decided to get married instead."

One of the doctors quipped, "Well, it will kill you or cure you!"

The dream that had begun three years before was about to come true. On November 9, 1968, Norma and I were married. It was the happiest day of my life. We had a beautiful candlelight ceremony and wonderful sit-down dinner reception. Our tiered wedding cake was cut with the traditional saber and we toasted each other with silver goblets.

We had reserved the honeymoon suite in the hotel for our wedding night and just as we entered the room a light snow began to fall, the first of the season. Silently I wished it would continue to snow so that we would not have to leave that room for many days.

Our married life began by moving into a small set of company grade quarters on post. Even though I was a major, the housing office would not allow us to have field grade quarters because we did not have children. As is usually done in military neighborhoods, someone came to call on Norma the first day we moved in. She brought a delicious casserole to welcome us along with these words, "I'm just so happy to finally meet you. I met your husband once; it was when he escorted Miss San Francisco to a dinner one night. I was her roommate and met him when he came to pick her up." That poor lady probably never understood why Norma did not return the call!

Shortly after we settled into our first home, Norma asked, "Now that you are married and can provide a place for a child to stay, do you think we can have your daughter Linda visit us?" There is nothing I would have liked more, but I explained that a few years before I made a decision to put Linda's welfare before mine.

It was at the time that I was to receive the medal. I wanted to have Linda with me at the White House ceremony. After much discussion I agreed with her mother that it was in Linda's best interest to grow up undisturbed by a tug-of-war. Carol had remarried and was doing a wonderful job of raising Linda. I was a mere stranger. I did not want to upset anyone's life, let alone my own daughter. Along with my daily prayers I would continue to send her a monthly allotment and buy savings bonds for her. Fervently I hoped and prayed that when she became an adult Linda would get to know me and become part of our family too.

My job at Fort Carson as the G-3 training officer kept me at work long hours. Norma was busy with volunteer work on the post, but more than anything we wanted to start a "team" of our own. Being aware that Norma had a genetic condition that might not make pregnancy a reality we consulted a fertility specialist. He started Norma on a regimen of fertility drugs and recommended surgery.

We also applied for adoption. The day we were to have our face-to-face interview with the adoption agency was the same day Norma was released from the hospital after her surgery. The doctor had ordered no stair climbing for three weeks, but stubborn and determined, Norma would not change our appointment with the agency. It was a painful climb for Norma to the second floor office of our counselor and my heart ached watching her take the steps one at a time.

Before we knew it, that all-important call came from the agency. They had a baby boy for us! The next day we picked up our first son. He was eighteen days old, healthy and handsome. We thought he looked just like the "Gerber" baby. When Norma took him in her arms he looked up at her with the biggest brown eyes and smiled. I thought she would melt on the spot! We named him Damian Charles Donlon.

Our days at Fort Carson were winding down and my next assignment would be a challenge . . . school again! I would be a student at the United States Army Command and General Staff College at Fort Leavenworth, Kansas. I had some leave time, so before classes began we took six-week-old Damian and toured the country from coast to coast, and even spent a night in Canada. While visiting Saugerties, my mother became fascinated with all the new gadgets Norma had at her disposal for traveling with a baby. Every time mother would be introduced to something different she would remark, "It's a Godsend!" I'm sure having ten children she could have used some of these modern day conveniences.

My class would be one of the largest to attend C&GSC and as a junior major I did not even qualify for regular on-post housing. They did offer substandard, and not wanting to commute from Kansas City every day I took the old converted World War II barracks called "Splinter Village."

One day Norma's parents came to visit. Dad looked around the quarters and said, "I'm glad to see you living like this . . . It is the same way your mother and I started out." Norma's parents were Americans of Japanese ancestry and were relocated from California to a War Relocation Center at Camp Jerome, Arkansas, during World War II. Their first home had been a tar paper barrack!

It was a good year in spite of the academics. We renewed many old acquaintances and made tons of new ones. We both enjoyed having friends over, and there was a steady stream of classmates coming and going from our modest quarters. Monday night football became a tradition at the Donlons. We would all sit on the floor and enjoy beef fondue while watching the game.

Norma worried about my class standing and began to envy the wives who had husbands burning the midnight oil studying. After graduation we were packing out of our quarters when one of those wives came up to Norma and said, "This has been the most miserable year of my life. All my husband did was study. I've really envied watching you and your husband have such a good time with your friends all year."

During the course of the year I had listened to my classmates talk about second and even third tours to Vietnam. We now had a few more Medal of Honor recipients from the Vietnam War. I didn't know how many had returned after receiving the medal, but I was determined to go back to Vietnam on my next assignment. When I told Norma that I would volunteer to return to Vietnam she said, "I know you must do what you feel is right."

I accepted a District Senior Advisor position with the Civil Operations and Rural Development Support program under William

E. Colby. After four months at the Foreign Service Institute in Washington, D.C., I would be assigned to Binh Dai district in Kien Hoa province in the Mekong Delta.

Norma chose to take Damian and live in Bangkok, Thailand, while I was in Vietnam. Damian was eighteen months old now and we both felt it was time to find him a sibling. We talked about the possibility of adopting a Vietnamese child, and I left Bangkok on January 2, 1972, hoping I could also accomplish this mission during the next eighteen months while in Vietnam.

Strange as it may seem, I did not really worry about Norma. She was so strong and independent I knew that she would adjust to her surroundings. Motherhood added another dimension to her capacity to love, and I had no doubt that she would focus all her attention on raising Damian.

Just before her birthday in March, Norma was invited to dinner at the home of Dan and Shirley Davis. The Davises had been classmates at Leavenworth who were now assigned to Thailand. Shirley was active with her church and also knew that we were looking for another child to adopt. This particular evening she was having a missionary couple to dinner. They operated a Christian Missionary Alliance Orphanage in up-country Thailand near Udorn. Shirley hoped to make a connection for us with the orphanage.

As it turned out, there was only one child with the proper papers to be adopted by an American couple—a five-month-old boy. Never one to hesitate when an opportunity presented itself, Norma inquired, "When can I come and get him?"

The next day Norma made arrangements to fly to Udorn and pick up our second son. When she entered the room where the babies were kept, a tiny boy was standing in his crib, holding the rail and walking back and forth. She thought to herself, "He is too small to be five months old, and even if he is, that is still pretty young to be able to stand and walk." When she picked him up he was as light as a feather. She gave him a hug and was surprised when he hugged back.

Norma sent me a message through the Red Cross that "Jason

has arrived." To my boss it seemed a very cryptic message and he questioned me at length about it. Not remembering that we had, years ago, made a list of baby names, I did not know who "Jason" was. I was allowed to use my boss's phone to call Norma in Bangkok. Beaming when I hung up the phone, I announced to the anxiously awaiting crowd in the office, "I'm a father again! Our second son just arrived and his name is Jason Douglas Donlon!"

In April, Norma came to Vietnam for a four-day visit. I had planned to take her south to my district, but she arrived on the same day that the spring offensive started, so we confined our visit to Saigon. We stayed in the old Continental Hotel and because of the curfew we were off the streets by 2100 hours each night. Norma could not get enough of watching the scene on the street below us. Every night trucks full of armed soldiers raced by and we could see the tracer bullets flying in the air from the nearby airfield.

Things in my district remained pretty calm until one August day mortars hit my camp. I dove into a bunker, hitting my head as I fell. The next morning I was directing a helicopter landing when a raindrop landed in my right eye. I closed the right eye and the helicopter disappeared. It was as though someone had pulled a shade halfway down on my left eye.

We did not have an ophthalmologist in Saigon, so I decided to take my mid-tour leave and have my eye checked in Bangkok. I arrived at home, surprising Norma for a change, and we made a quick trip out to the military hospital. They sent me to a Thai specialist who confirmed that I had a detached retina. I was blindfolded and immediately sent by MEDEVAC to a larger hospital in Okinawa, Japan.

I spent the next ten days flat on my back and blindfolded, going from one military hospital to another around the Pacific . . . Clark Air Force Base in the Philippines, back to Okinawa, Clark again, and finally on to Tripler in Hawaii. There a young doctor looked at my eye and said, "Textbook case of detached retina. I've never seen one except in a medical book. You need an experienced surgeon." And so I was loaded on the plane again and flown to

198 • Our Family Team

Letterman General Hospital in San Francisco.

Now that I was back Stateside the doctors decided to send me to the experts at Walter Reed Medical Center in Washington, D.C. When I finally reached Walter Reed and the surgeon checked me out, he asked, "Who diagnosed your detachment?"

"Dr. Prachak in Bangkok, Thailand," I answered.

With a smile the doctor said, "Oh, you should have had him do your surgery. He was the honor graduate in my class!"

By this time Norma was really getting concerned. Every night I had called her from a different location. She wanted to come and be with me, but I told her just to stay put. My sight was in the hands of God and the surgeons. What I didn't know was that Norma talked with the doctor and when they told her there was a good chance I might lose the eye, she went straight to the airport.

When I came out of surgery, Norma was in the recovery room waiting for me! I didn't know whether to scold her for disobeying me, or hug her for being there. Fortunately I did not lose my eye, but my sight was seriously impaired. I was ordered not to return and finish my Vietnam tour.

Norma had fallen in love with Thailand and the gracious Thai people. She asked if there was any way I could get an assignment in Bangkok. I checked with the personnel section and there was an advisory slot open. I would be assigned to the Military Assistance Command, Thailand, as an advisor to the Royal Thai Army.

A few months after my assignment to Thailand we adopted another child. This one came to us straight from the hospital after he was born. He was a tiny, dark-skinned child with a thick head of hair. Norma was in seventh heaven with a newborn. We now had three sons, the newest just thirty-six hours old. We named him Derek Paul Donlon.

These were the glory days for Norma. She was so happy being mother to three under the age of three! Both of us were totally fulfilled with our role as parents. Now that we had a family, it was time for Norma to stop all of her fertility treatments. I was no longer willing to risk her health for the sake of a biological child.

Norma disagreed. She still wanted the experience of being pregnant. But in her heart she knew that it was the wiser decision to stop all treatments in order to remain healthy for our three young sons. We had, at various times, had five doctors tell us that we would never have a biological child. Three years of fertility treatments and two operations had done nothing to correct the problem. It was time to enjoy the children God had given us.

During my second year in Thailand I changed jobs and was posted to the joint staff as the J-34, in charge of third country training. I enjoyed my time on the joint staff, especially working with officers from the Navy and Air Force.

Just weeks before our departure from Thailand our number one maid, Kobkul, got married. We felt honored to be asked to participate in her wedding ceremony by witnessing the Buddhist religious rituals in the morning and pouring the holy water in the evening. One thing we did not count on was participating in the fertility rites. Kobkul insisted we partake of the various foods set out for the bride and groom—foods that were believed to enhance fertility. Not wanting to offend her, we allowed her to bring us a plate and she and her new husband joined us at the banquet.

It was a long flight from Bangkok to Los Angeles, especially with a one, two, and three-year-old. When we reached Hawaii we had to process through immigration. The visa paperwork for our two Thai sons seemed to take an eternity. Norma's parents were happy to see us when we finally landed in Los Angeles. It was the first meeting with their two new grandsons. They took charge with the boys and I think we slept for the next twenty-four hours!

While on leave my promotion to lieutenant colonel came through. We celebrated one morning by pinning my new rank on my pajama top. Fort Benning, Georgia, would be our next assignment.

As luck would have it, we had a long wait for on-post housing at Fort Benning. For the time being we would have to rent a furnished apartment in Columbus. It was back to good old Wedgefield Court, the apartment Jay and I had shared as bachelors when Norma and I first met.

My new assignment to the Infantry Board as a test officer meant that I had to travel. Preoccupied with my new job, I didn't notice that Norma was not her usual peppy self. She kept from me the tiredness she was feeling, not wanting me to think she was having a hard time readjusting to Stateside living. Finally she went to the doctor. To her surprise she learned she was sixteen weeks pregnant!

When she told me the news, I didn't believe it. The next morning I called the doctor and asked that he retest Norma. When the new test results came in, I was in the field. Norma sent me a message: "The rabbit died!" We had a large dogwood tree in our front yard and I predicted that the baby would be born, "When the dogwood blooms."

It seemed to us a miracle that in this place where we had first met and fallen in love, God would again bless us with a new life. For the first time I would be able to witness the birth of one of our children. We began to prepare for the big event by taking Lamaze classes. Norma was determined to have a natural birth; she wanted to be awake and aware for every minute. All went smoothly, and on April 22, 1975, our fourth son joined our family team. He was a beautiful child with a perfect complexion and a light dusting of blonde peach fuzz on his head. We named him Justin Luis Donlon.

Now with four children under age five, Norma really had her hands full. Where she found the patience, I will never know, but with each new addition she was happier than ever before. Being a full-time wife and mother was for her the only choice. She never had any desire to seek employment outside the home.

Our next assignment would be a challenge for both of us. I had been selected for a battalion command and would take over the 3rd Battalion, 7th Special Forces Group (Airborne) at Fort Gulick, Panama. This meant a lot of outside responsibilities for Norma as well.

One of the areas we did not anticipate was the social arena. During my tour in Panama the United States was negotiating the treaty to turn the Canal over to Panama. There were visits by nearly every Congressman and Senator to investigate the issue. With each delegation, the commanding general would host a social gathering so the politicians could meet and speak with all the commanders. These events always took place on the Pacific side, which meant a two-hour ride over a mountainous road. I made the trip in fifteen minutes by helicopter, but Norma had to make the drive.

The situation was compounded by not being able to find a baby-sitter who could stay late enough on a weeknight. So, Norma would leave in the afternoon with the boys and drop them at the nursery on the Pacific side. After picking me up at the helipad, we would dash to the Officers' Club to change our clothes, then attend the function. Around 2100 hours we would pick up our sleepy little ones and drive two more hours back to our home on the Atlantic side. This we did over a hundred times in eighteen months.

Six months into the Panama assignment I had to return to Saugerties for a sad duty . . . to bury my mother. The words in our Christmas letter that year best describe my feelings. We wrote: "Please remember Roger's mother in your Christmas prayers. She died very quietly and peacefully on June 10, 1977 . . . in her heart was truly the spirit of Christmas."

Many times during our tour in Panama I flew over the Canal. It was such a beautiful sight that I wanted to share it with the whole family. A few days before our departure I hired a private plane for an hour and took Norma and the boys up. We still talk about that adventure.

Panama had been the most demanding assignment for our family. Both Norma and I were exhausted from meeting the needs of both job and home. We looked forward to a break at Fort Leavenworth, where I would be an instructor at the U.S. Army Command and General Staff College.

The boys were growing up and getting involved in their own activities at school, in Scouting, sports and church. Norma was happy to be at Fort Leavenworth. With my regular work hours, and no TDY, I was around a lot more to help out.

At work one day I received a large envelope with just my name, and Fort Leavenworth, Kansas, on it. There was no return address.

When I looked at the postmark I saw that it came from the small town in North Carolina were Mr. and Mrs. Irving lived. Thinking it must be something for Norma, I took the envelope home unopened. Gasping as she read the letter, Norma shouted, "Roger, come here! Look at this!"

It was a letter from Linda's grandmother telling me that Linda was hoping to meet me someday. She had just graduated from college. The picture enclosed was of a beautiful, grown-up Linda.

My promotion to colonel had just recently taken place and the celebration, or promotion party, as we called it, was in two days. Would it be possible for Linda to join us? We dialed the number her grandmother had provided. I don't remember any of the conversation but Linda did consent to making the trip to Kansas to be with us for the party.

Excitement at our house was at a fever pitch. The boys were so anxious to meet their "sister." Norma was as ecstatic as I. She was the only one who knew just how much I had prayed for this moment.

With Linda's arrival our "team" was now complete. The joy in my heart was overflowing as I celebrated my promotion with all of my family in attendance.

Everyone has grown up now, and through the years they all have continued to provide us with SEEs—significant emotional events—as we call them.

Linda honored me on her wedding day by asking me to escort her to the altar. She and husband Paul have given us our first grandson, Griffin. Damian finished his education at Kansas State University and now lives and works in Topeka. Jason gradutated from Emporia State University, married his college sweetheart and they have a precious daughter. Derek served in the Army where he met and married a German lady, they have three lovely daughters. Justin lives nearby and has a beautiful daughter with blue eyes!

**Norma and Roger Donlon
November 9, 1968
Colorado Springs, Colorado**

Beyond Nam Dong

December 14, 1988 . . .

Retirement Day. It hardly seemed possible that three-plus decades of service to our country could pass so quickly. I awoke earlier than usual that morning to put my uniform together one last time. As I pinned on each badge, tab, medal, and insignia I reflected on what they stood for, and how I earned them. My thoughts went back in time to . . .

Nam Dong, and a conversation I had with Le Tse-tung, the commander of our Nung special security force before the battle.

As a warrior, Le was naturally curious about the new AR-15 that had arrived just a few weeks before. He wanted to see and feel the new weapon, as well as test fire it. We gave him the opportunity to try it out, and he came to the conclusion that it was too small a caliber for the heavy foliage of the mountains. And it was definitely no match for the dense jungles of Vietnam. We launched into a long discussion about the weapons of war and Le shared with me his true thoughts.

Le knew that the AR-15 or any other modern day weapon the U.S. brought to this war would be ineffective. He explained to me that, in the long run, the enemy's primary weapon would be drugs! They intended to use drugs, to make drugs available on all fronts. Knowing our "tooth to tail" ratio of support to combat (ten to one) the enemy would make our rear combat service support area a high priority target. This would include training bases and educational institutions in the United States.

I must have looked a little skeptical, because Le next posed the question, "Captain, who do you believe brought drugs into China? Drugs that played a major role in the collapse of our society?"

Before I could reply, Le answered his own question. With a glare in his eyes Le continued, "It was *you!* The long nose, round eye!" Then he proceeded with a history lesson on how and when this had happened and how the opium wars had ruined China. He finished by sharing his contention that the white man would now know the insidiousness of drugs . . . "The worm has turned," he said.

After the Medal of Honor award ceremony at the White House I shared this story with President Johnson. At the time it didn't seem of any consequence and the President just shrugged it off.

Le Tse-tung, a wise and courageous warrior, was killed in action sometime after the victory at Nam Dong. His courage and that of his fellow Nungs was a genuine combat multiplier and forever remains an inspiration to service and commitment.

In Panama my assignment as commander of the 3rd Battalion, 7th Special Forces Group (Airborne) was indeed a singular honor . . . to be selected to command one of only two deployed U.S. Army Special Forces battalions. This battalion was oriented toward Latin America and stationed on the Atlantic side of the canal at Fort Gulick. We had area responsibilities that included all of Central and South America. The Panama Canal treaty negotiations impacted heavily upon our visibility and the intensity of our "in-country" training. From this experience I brought with me a renewed respect and appreciation for our Special Forces non-commissioned and new young officers. Their dedicated commitment along with their demonstrated competence proved to me that the U.S. Army Special Forces would become a major player in the painful rebuilding of our Army. I was confident that from the pits of the hollow Army of the post-Vietnam era would rise a new generation of soldier, more intelligent, better trained, and totally dedicated to the mission at hand. The men of the 3/7th rose to every training and operational challenge that we were given. They inspired all with whom they trained and worked to perform at the very highest level of proficiency. It was a genuine privilege to have served with these men.

My promotion to colonel on May 7, 1980 . . . a special day with a special pair of "war eagles." I recalled my remarks after receiving the official pinning on of my new rank:

"It is the spirit of trust and confidence, coupled with a great sense of pride, that I would like to share with you the flight of these 'war eagles.' The route they have taken is filled with milestones that epitomize duty to God and Country. The very first U.S. general I was honored to serve directly for, Brigadier General Lester L. Wheeler, USMA '35, sent these rank insignia to me. He was a soldier who gave me my first military lessons on what trust, confidence, and fidelity really mean. He has since been my guide. In General Wheeler's career there was also a soldier who was his inspiration and a living example of service . . . Major General Aubrey S. Newman. General Newman, USMA '25, wore these eagles when he commanded the 505th Regiment of the 82nd Airborne Division. He was kind enough to enclose the following instructions: 'Eagles, unlike other insignia of rank, are not identical pairs. There is a right side eagle and a left side eagle. When pinned on the correct shoulders, both eagles look in the direction their wearer is headed. If pinned on the wrong shoulders, they look where their wearer has been.' Well, as my youngest son Justin said this morning, 'the eagle has landed' and I intend to make certain that these eagles are always facing in the right direction. Thank you all for making this day so special for me and my family."

With my promotion to colonel came increased job responsibilities. I was assigned as Director, Office of Allied Personnel at the U.S. Army Command and General Staff College at Fort Leavenworth, Kansas. This was the assignment that ultimately brought me back to Leavenworth for my retirement years. It was one of the most important and rewarding jobs I had during my thirty-two years of service. I reflected back to an article I had written called,

A Matter of Perspective

The "Leavenworth Experience" offers all of us an opportunity of a lifetime to expand our mental, physical, and moral horizons as we increase our depth and breadth of knowledge, thus gaining new and valuable perspectives of the world in which we live.

Just what should one expect to accomplish in anticipation of gaining these new perspectives while here at the United States Army Command and General Staff College?

One should expect an improved capacity to view things in their true relationship or relative importance. I would like to offer some of my thoughts about the International officer community in the interest of your gaining a clearer perspective of its presence and value.

From my own perspective, I would like to remind you that the very presence of our International officers is a genuine reflection of our current national foreign policies and interests. It is through our Security Assistance Programs that we, as a nation, strive to maintain and strengthen our bonds of friendship, understanding, good will and mutual defense. Under such programs, we are able to exchange our "leaders of tomorrow" in the arenas that are designated to sharpen our military minds. A military mind is one that is continually improving its capacity to view things in their true relations or relative importance. To this end I offer the following thoughts.

First, recognize and appreciate the perspective from which our International officers view us. We represent a Super Power and are, therefore, expected to perform and project ourselves as such, thus inspiring continued mutual trust and confidence through our professional and personal actions. Coupled with this expectation is another very important fact about our IOs that must be put in proper perspective. That is that each International officer has expended the enormous mental effort required in learning our language. Through his and his family's study of our language, we as a nation and as members of our armed forces are now better understood. I am sure that our International friends' individual and collective perspective of us is generally clearer than our perspective of them. I am compelled to remind you that our collective efforts here at CGSC reflect not only our foreign policy but also the foreign policy of each country represented here. The design and scope of these policies vary from country to country, and the variation is in part a direct reflection of the actual and perceived mutual dependence that exists between our nations. This invaluable interdependence stems from understanding — be it problem solving, tactics, logistics, strategy, military or geographical history, customs or all-important values.

With respect to values, it is clear that peoples' values differ and that these differences are molded by the time and location in which and from which they are reared and educated. I ask you to reflect upon both your professional and personal values as you pursue each opportunity to sharpen your minds. More specifically, when you have your values in clear perspective, strive to gain an appreciation of the values and perspective of your International friends. For the asking, clarification is available and possibly even a significant emotional event is in store for you and yours. I am confident it will lead to your improved perspective of the world in which you live. Remember, the keys to the lock on the "Window of the World," from your perspective, are in the hearts and minds of our most distinguished International officers and their families. Reach out and improve your own capacity, as well as theirs, to view more things in our ever-growing Family of Nations.

When my three years at Fort Leavenworth were up I was sent to Fort Bragg for one of the most difficult assignments I ever had. Three schools at the same time! Five hours a day in the classroom at the Foreign Area Officers' Course. Two nights a week at Campbell University getting a Master's degree in Government and the Army War College by correspondence. If this wasn't enough of a challenge, I was also having difficulty seeing, with a large cataract in my left eye. Norma came through like the trooper she is, and earned another PHT (pushing hubby through). Without her I don't know if I would have made it. She read to me when I took constitutional law and the print in the textbook was too small. She took notes from the microfiche at the library because I couldn't see the print; helped with research for all the papers I had to write, and then typed everything for me. This in addition to making sure the carpool ran in the right direction for all the boys' activities, school, church,

Beyond Nam Dong • **209**

scouting, sports, and music lessons. There were days when our station wagon became a mobile dressing room and fast food restaurant!

We still look back on those days and wonder how we survived it all. Of course all the help from Norma did not come without a price. I made a promise to her that when the year was over I would do anything she wanted . . . a cruise, shopping trip, vacation, whatever. Well, immediately after my graduation from Campbell she hauled me down to Fayetteville and we signed up for dance lessons! On the first night we each had our own instructor. Mine was a beautiful buxom blonde named Samantha. Norma was not so lucky, and she kept giving me looks of despair as her male instructor whirled her around the room. After the instructors had assessed our dancing abilities we had a conference and it was decided that Norma really didn't need any lessons, but I was a nearly hopeless case. They recommended that I double up on my lessons and that Norma stay at home. This of course made her very happy . . . I was now going to the dance studio two nights a week to dance with beautiful Samantha! Every Friday was dance party with spouses joining in to see what we had learned during the week. Samantha and I tangoed and waltzed our way around the floor, but when I tried to dance with Norma I couldn't lead, and all she knew how to do was follow, so we were a disaster. The evenings would end up with us upset with each other, and barely speaking as we left the studio.

On the night of the last dance lesson, all the families were invited to the big show. Each instructor would strut their stuff with their primary pupil. Dance studios have floor-to-ceiling mirrors on every wall so you can see all angles of the couple dancing. When Samantha kept pulling me close to her I began to think we had had one too many lessons together. Each time she would *whisper* in my ear, "XYZ Roger." After the third attempt she finally said, "You don't know what XYZ is, do you?"

"No," I said, "I don't. I thought you were trying to give me a code to do a dance step."

She threw back her head laughing, and said, "Roger, XYZ means 'examine your zipper'!"

Perhaps the highlight of my career, from the family's perspective, was our four years at Camp Zama, Japan. It was a time for Norma to explore her roots. To journey to her ancestral home and pay respect to several hundred years of relatives buried in the family cemetery. It was a time of wonder and excitement for our boys, learning about a new culture and sharing experiences with their Japanese friends. My assignment as Commander of the United Nations Command Rear Headquarters charged me with the administration of a multinational Status of Forces Agreement. This brought me in daily contact with the highest level of diplomatic corps officers from the countries that came to Korea's call for support from the world community. Once again, good fortune had placed me in yet another multinational environment.

. . . I pinned my eagles on the correct shoulders, facing forward, and was ready for the next phase in my life and the adventure it would bring. The retirement ceremony was perfect in every detail. All my children were there plus my brother, Jack, in his Air Force uniform, and Norma's brother, Douglas Shinno. I watched proudly as Norma was recognized for her many, many contributions during the twenty years we had been married. She was awarded the Department of the Army, Outstanding Civilian Service Medal. Then it was my turn as the Legion of Merit was pinned to my uniform. I felt completely on solid ground. My career had been a triad of Infantry, Special Forces, and Foreign Area Officer; I was ready for the new challenges awaiting me in retirement.

Through the years I have given hundreds of speeches and one of the questions I am most frequently asked is why I did not suffer from post traumatic stress disorder. I believe the answer lies in the response I received when I returned from Vietnam . . . I was welcomed home. It began with "Donlon Day" in Saugerties, and continued through hundreds of recognition dinners and celebrations. Now, I wondered if I would have PTSD from no longer being on active duty.

God bless my hometown! Shortly after my retirement the

American Legion in Saugerties decided to sponsor a reunion of Team A-726 to mark twenty-five years since the battle of Nam Dong. It turned out to be quite an event lasting four days, and bringing Tom Gregg, Woody and me together with our wives. The good citizens of Saugerties named the Veterans Park the Roger Donlon Veterans Park in honor of all who have honorably served. Al Iannone, Jack Bartells, Jack Keeley, and Jim Gage, some of my old classmates "roasted" me at a wonderful dinner. And they even named the Fourth of July baseball tournament the Roger Donlon tournament. But it was the parade that took my breath away. It was a good old-fashioned Fourth of July parade in a village with a population of about five thousand. Well, thirty-five thousand flag-waving, patriotic Americans lined the streets to watch Tom, Woody and me ride by! I was overwhelmed, and so proud to be a Saugertiesian.

During the planning for the Saugerties reunion we were able to get an update on most of the team members. Jay Olejniczak retired from the Army as a lieutenant colonel. We were not surprised to hear that he had returned to his alma mater, the United States Military Academy at West Point. Today he is the editor-in-chief/vice president for publications of the *"Assembly,"* the magazine of the Association of Graduates.

Woody retired after twenty-three years of service as a sergeant first class. He and his wife Dessie have been "seeing the USA," not in a Chevrolet, but on their three-wheeler Honda motorcycle with sidecar. They see their greatest achievement as recently celebrating their forty-third wedding anniversary.

Tom Gregg became a physician assistant, served three tours in Vietnam and retired in the grade of chief warrant officer 3 after twenty-nine years. In retirement Tom continues with his vocation in the field of medicine. He was instrumental in the development and certification of the first hospital based rural health clinic in the state of Texas. Tom is the proud grandfather of three.

Ray Whitsell went on to receive a commission through the Artillery OCS program and returned to Vietnam for a second tour.

After twenty years in the Army he retired as a major. Whit also completed his bachelors and masters degree work. He now runs his own private training consulting company. Ray and his wife are proud grandparents of two.

Mike Disser received his commission as a second lieutenant of Infantry. He served a second tour in Vietnam and rose to the rank of captain. Mike's civilian career has been centered on sales, computers and real estate. Mike and his wife Judy are proud grandparents of one.

Doc Hickey has become a world-renowned anthropologist through his seventeen years of work and study in Vietnam. He served with the highest distinction in numerous senior executive analysis and studies efforts. Doc has always displayed the courage of his convictions and is much respected by his professional colleagues and friends. He is the author of five books, the last one titled, *"Shattered World,"* and is currently writing his memoirs.

Terry Terrin was medically discharged from the Army as a result of his wounds. Terry passed away in 1997. Two daughters survive him.

Vernon Beeson died some years ago and is buried in Winston-Salem, North Carolina.

Unfortunately Thurman Brown and Keith Daniels have not come up on the radar screen, but we continue to search for them.

On the day of my retirement ceremony, a reporter asked the question, "Why Kansas, colonel?"

Well, the answer was, "People, and in particular, People-to-People International." Founded by our late President Dwight D. Eisenhower in 1956, it is a not-for-profit, private sector cultural and educational exchange organization. The world headquarters is located in Kansas City, Missouri. It just so happened that the CEO heard my remarks and the next thing I knew I was serving as a trustee on the Board of Directors. I spent several years with this great organization and still continue to be a trustee.

In 1993 I was asked to represent People-to-People International as the delegation leader for the very first Mission in Understanding

Beyond Nam Dong • 213

to Vietnam. I didn't hesitate to take on the mission, but after accepting I had some sleepless nights. Norma and I talked it over and she agreed with me that it was time to put the past into its proper perspective and move forward. The United States had not yet lifted the trade embargo or named an Ambassador, but we knew in time these things would be done. Should I, or could I be in the forefront of this movement toward normalization of relations between our two countries? In many ways this return to Vietnam would prove to be more difficult for me than my second tour in 1972.

The purpose of the eighteen-day mission was for the thirty-eight delegates to gain a deeper understanding of the economic, political, and social changes taking place in Southeast Asia. We would also visit Singapore, Malaysia, and Thailand so we could see first hand how these changes impacted, specifically on Vietnam.

Eight days would be spent in Vietnam with meetings and briefings by government officials and community leaders in Hanoi, Da Nang, Hue, Ho Chi Minh City, Cu Chi, and the Mekong Delta region.

If I had handpicked the delegation I could not have done a better job. It was a vast cross-section of America with doctors, nurses, teachers, farmers, lawyers, business owners, and only one other Vietnam veteran. Each had their own reason for wanting to visit Vietnam. Most started the journey opposed to normalization.

Our first stop was Singapore. After all the briefings were completed, Norma and I took our free afternoon to journey out to the ULU Pandan Military Cemetery. It was here that Kevin Conway was buried. He was the first Australian killed in the Vietnam War. At the time of his death at Nam Dong it was the Australian custom to inter their war dead at the nearest Commonwealth cemetery. This was the first time I was able to visit Kevin's final resting place to pay my respects for his sacrifice for Team A-726. I placed a wreath on Kevin's grave and with a prayer, briefly shared my Medal of Honor with him.

Next, it was on to Vietnam. As the plane began its descent into Hanoi, the hair on the back of my neck started to prickle. The passengers were unusually quiet, each person lost in his or her own private thoughts. I looked at Norma. She was staring out the window, taking in every detail of the land. I could tell by her stoic expression that she was steeling herself against her emotions. Sometimes she was more Japanese than American.

After landing and finding our way into the terminal we were met by a senior Vietnamese general. He presented Norma with a dozen red roses. I wondered if he knew that her first husband had been killed in Vietnam.

The ride into Hanoi was like going back in time. Looking out from the window of the bus, we saw a third world country and a poverty-stricken people. Our hotel in Hanoi was clean and very presentable. The people were friendly and helpful. All of us were surprised to find everyone so hospitable. I think most of us felt that we would not be welcome in Hanoi. As the sun went down the city took on an eerie feeling, as few people had electricity and there were almost no streetlights.

We settled into the hotel and finished dinner, and I felt the need to get some fresh air. Norma opted for a long, hot bath, so I went for a walk alone. The streets of Hanoi were nearly deserted. I could see shadows of people huddling around flickering lamps in small cafes, down the alleyways, and in small homes. The purpose of my walk this night was to see the infamous "Hanoi Hilton."

Finding the prison where so many Americans had been incarcerated during the war was not difficult. As I walked around the prison, still topped with barbed wire, I thought about all the men who had suffered so much at the hands of their captors. Those who I personally knew were mostly Medal of Honor recipients, and I had heard first hand accounts of the torturous years they had spent here. Some spoke with bitterness of the lack of support from the homefront, and especially all of the anti-war demonstrations. I stood quietly in front of the prison for a few minutes, prayed for all the men and their families, and then returned to the hotel.

In the morning the streets were bustling with people again. Norma was fascinated by the thousands of bicycles in the streets, and the fact that there was only one traffic signal in all of Hanoi. The traffic

Beyond Nam Dong • **215**

circles were an amazing sight as cars, buses, trucks, motorbikes, and bicycles all came together.

My duties as the delegation leader took up the greater part of each day, but I hoped to find the time to slip away for a few hours and revisit Nam Dong. I had with me a picture of the cemetery at Nam Dong where some of my Vietnamese soldiers were buried, and I wanted to pay my respects to them. As I showed the picture around, I kept getting the response that this cemetery did not exist.

Our tour guide turned out to be a former Viet Cong captain. On the bus ride from Da Nang to the old Imperial capital of Hue, he pulled me aside at the "pit" stop. He pointed across the road and asked if I remembered the way to my old camp. I told him I did and asked if he could help me to return to Nam Dong. He said he would try, and later that evening he showed up at our hotel in Hue with a four-wheel drive vehicle. It was one of only five in the country, and after checking it out we arranged to leave for Nam Dong at 0300 hours the following morning.

Before dawn, Norma and I left for Nam Dong with a driver, Vietnamese interpreter, and two other members of our delegation, Ted Westerman and Ken Ketchie. Ted was a Vietnam veteran who had spent most of his time with the 25th Infantry Division. After retirement he had worked his way up the corporate ladder at Hughes Electronics. Ken was the owner and editor of a newspaper at Boone, North Carolina, and the youngest member of our delegation.

It was a rough three-hour ride back into the mountains on a one-lane road. There were several streams along the way, and at one spot the bridge had not yet been repaired from one of our bombing runs, forcing us to ford the racing waters. Finally we came to the end of the road. We had gone as far as the vehicle could take us. I recognized the ridge line surrounding us and knew we were in the immediate area of my old camp . . . Nam Dong.

Not being sure if there were any mines around, I left Norma in the vehicle with the driver. Ted, Ken, the interpreter and I proceeded to walk through the tall grasses toward the area of the camp. We had gone about one hundred and fifty yards when my foot hit a

216 • Beyond Nam Dong

large stone. I stopped, bent down, and turned the stone up. It was a grave marker. Carved into the stone were several lines in Vietnamese . . . then the numbers 6-7-64 . . . I knew I had found the cemetery.

As I looked around I saw several other markers lying face down in the grass. The cemetery had been abandoned. Judging from the #10 cans filled with joss sticks, someone did still come here to pray. I set the marker I had stumbled upon upright, vowing to return someday to restore the cemetery.

By this time word had filtered around the village that some Americans were in Nam Dong, and a few curious locals had begun to gather. Spontaneously I picked some wildflowers and we had an impromptu memorial ceremony. I explained to the small crowd that in America we sometimes join hands when we pray. I reached out with both hands and bowed my head. It seemed like an eternity, but finally a hand found mine, then another. I looked up and the entire group was linked together. The seed of reconciliation had been planted.

We arrived back in the U.S. with a new perspective. The entire delegation was in agreement that our country should go forward with normalization. It was definitely the best way to get a full accounting of our personnel listed as missing in action.

I was still haunted by the condition of the Nam Dong Cemetery. Knowing that the Vietnamese believe a spirit cannot rest in peace if not properly buried, I was determined to return and clean up the graveyard. I began raising money for the project.

In 1995 I was able to return to Vietnam, this time leading a small tour group. With a much more flexible schedule I set about arranging my second return to Nam Dong.

On the day we visited Hue, I had lunch with a former North Vietnamese "political officer" named Nguyen Van Thu. He had been one of the planners of the attack at Nam Dong on July 6, 1964. At first the conversation went back and forth, each of us asking questions not really answered by the other. One of the facts that I wanted to know was the true number of "sympathizers" we had in our camp. We had estimated the number at about twenty, but after the battle I guessed it was more than a hundred. This I was finally able to confirm. Now I knew why so many of my Vietnamese were found in their beds with their throats slit or their necks broken. Some even had their hearts and livers cut out.

During my first return to Nam Dong I had taken note of a large government cemetery not far from the District Headquarters. I wondered how many of the hundreds of graves were enemy casualties from the battle on July 6, 1964. Mr. Thu reluctantly acknowledged that the figure was upwards of two hundred and fifty.

My curiosities somewhat satisfied, I rose to leave. I invited Mr. Thu to accompany me to Nam Dong in the morning. He accepted.

The next day I took my group to Nam Dong. Mr. Thu came along with his former chief of staff. When we arrived at the Nam Dong Cemetery I was pleasantly surprised to find that Mr. Thu had arranged for a work party of my former adversaries. Together, we cleaned up the abandoned cemetery, cutting the grass with hand sickles and placing the headstones upright.

This time we had a more formal memorial ceremony. I had given Mr. Thu some money. He purchased a wreath, which together we placed. In my remarks I said, "Today we remember the past with some sorrow . . . but we look to the future with joy and hope. May we also strive to do our best so that we leave the world a better place than we found it."

It took a few weeks for me to "decompress" after I returned home from this second return to Vietnam. My thoughts lingered with Mr. Thu, and the conversation we had shared. I wanted to continue this dialogue in some way.

An opportunity to take part in a Veterans celebration in Springfield, Illinois, brought me together with Ambassador William E. Colby and General William C. Westmoreland. Upon hearing about my recent trips to Vietnam, they expressed an interest in starting some type of non-political, non-governmental organization to help bridge the gap between our two countries.

I have great admiration for General and Mrs. Westmoreland. They continue to serve their country and the Vietnam-era veterans.

They are always available to support Vietnam veterans and have attended hundreds of functions all across America demonstrating their patriotism. When Ambassador Colby co-founded The Westmoreland Scholar Foundation and asked me to be the first Executive Director, I accepted without hesitation.

This foundation would be dedicated to "Rebuilding Bridges of Understanding" between the *people* of the United States and the *people* of Vietnam. Today this mission is being accomplished by providing educational assistance (scholarships) to young students active in the Vietnamese-American community who have strong academic ability and a high potential for service to the larger community. In the past two years the foundation has been able to provide over $50,000 in scholarships to deserving students. Two of our scholars, Joyce Nguyen and Son Do, were sent on a summer internship to a hospital in Da Nang. They spent four weeks working, studying, and assisting with humanitarian projects. It was the first successful crossing of "the bridge."

Whenever Norma and I travel to Washington, D.C., we always make time to visit John Houston's grave at Arlington National Cemetery. Then, hand in hand, we take that long walk along "The Wall." At the start the wall is small, but by the time we reach the apex it has grown so we cannot even read the names at the top. All along the path we can see our reflection passing by the more than 58,000 names. There are three names we stop to touch. By coincidence they are all on the same panel . . . the first panel of the Vietnam Veterans Memorial.

The debt to a warrior's fallen comrades is never fully paid. May their unselfish acts of bravery continue to be a source of strength to those of us who strive to heal the wounds of war.

Rubbings from Vietnam Veterans Memorial, Washington, D.C.

Norma and Roger Donlon
1998

Epilogue

In June of 1998 I received a letter from a high school student asking me to "tell my story." The letter was a poignant request for "the truth," something the writer felt was in short supply these days.

If I may quote from that letter, "Vietnam is a powerful story, a sobering story, teenagers today want to learn about it. We want to know why Vietnam had so much impact on the world . . . and we don't want the world to forget about Vietnam. All of the people who gave their lives in Vietnam can no longer speak . . . those of you who survived must speak for them . . . "

In the preceding pages you have read my story. It is a story about "teamwork" and how we are all a team, all of us . . . all races, colors, ethnic backgrounds, creeds, religions, beliefs, cultures . . . We are a Family of Nations.

You have read about the importance of the "Philosophy of Life." This has been a major guidepost for me, reminding me that "the devil never rests," and is always trying to wear us down by using his "wedge" of discouragement.

But the real story is about love. Love of family, love of friends, love of my men, and yes, even love of my former adversaries.

Thank you for sharing this sojourn with me. I hope in some small way the journey has been of value for you . . . in your life of service to your fellow man.

In closing, let me share with you a few last words. They came to me more than thirty years ago, engraved into my wedding ring. Someday when I make that final bugle call, they will find these words engraved on my heart. They are the words my wife, Norma, and I live by. With her beside me all things are possible . . .

What we are is God's gift to us . . .
What we become is our gift to God . . .

Index

A

Ailes, Secretary Stephen T. 12, 13
Alamo, Master Sgt. Gabriel Ralph 3, 83, 84, 87-91, 96, 97, 104, 115, 124, 125, 134, 136, 138, 141, 142, 144, 149-154, 170, 171, 174, 175
Alamo, Mrs. Gabriel Ralph 4, 171, 178
Aloysius, Sister Mary 18, 24, 25
An Diem 166
Annamite Mountains 105, 107, 166
Arlington National Cemetery 14, 79, 80, 179, 219
Association of the United States Army 190

B

Bad Tölz, W. Ger. 74
Ball, Mrs. Rodney 27
Bangkok, Thailand 197, 198, 199, 200
Bank, Col. Aaron 74
Bao Dai 111
Barber, Capt. Robert W. 166
Bartells, Jackie 37, 212
Beeson, Sgt. First Class Vernon Lee 6, 84, 88, 92, 100, 104, 115-117, 120, 121, 128, 138, 147-149, 154-156, 159, 160, 162, 165-167, 169, 170, 173, 174, 213
Bitterman, Mrs. 23
Blackburn, Capt. Donald D. 73
Blanchard, Felix (Doc) 53
Borneo 4, 141
Bradley, Gen. Omar 190
Brice, Jerry 31, 37
Brinnier, Bill 34, 35

Brown, Sgt. First Class Thurman R. 5, 6, 8, 84, 85, 90, 93, 100, 101, 104, 114, 116, 124, 125, 130, 135-138, 146-149, 154-161, 165, 166, 170, 173-175, 213
Buckley, Ed 37

C

Ca Mau Peninsula 111
Cahill, Lawrence 29
Cambodia 111
Camp Jerome, Ark. 196
Camp Lejeune, N.C. 90
Camp Zama, Japan 211
Campbell University 209, 210
Carpenter, Val 39
Chidister, Dr. Hugh 15
Clark Air Force Base, Philippines 21, 171, 198
Clark, Capt. Robert W. 164
Cleland, Maj. Gen. Joseph P. 78
Clements, Hank 177
Clifton, Maj. Gen. Chester V. 11, 77
Colby, Ambassador William E. 197, 218, 219
Conway, Warrant Officer Kevin 3, 4, 8, 128, 131, 139, 141, 142, 144, 148, 154, 170, 214
Cu Chi 214
Cunningham, Mother Mary Regina 11
Curtis, Lieut. Col. Oliver W. 166, 167

D

Da Nang 105, 110, 113, 115-117, 119, 120, 131, 134, 138, 148, 167, 169-171, 173, 214, 216, 219
Dale, Charlie 15
Daniels, Staff Sgt. Keith E. 6, 86-90, 93, 100, 104, 114, 116, 124, 127, 130, 134, 135, 140, 146-149, 155-157, 159, 163, 165, 167, 169, 171, 173, 174, 213
Darby, Brig. Gen. William O. 74
Davis, Dan and Shirley 197

Day, George and Pat 184
DeChristopher, Ed and Carol 184
Disser, Lieut. Col. Ralph K. 87, 141, 150
Disser, Sgt. Michael 6, 8, 18, 88, 104, 116, 121, 125, 130, 140-142, 144, 149-152, 154-157, 159, 163, 165, 167, 169, 171, 174, 175, 213
Donlon, Adrienne 7, 18, 21, 52, 75
Donlon, Alicia 203
Donlon, Barbara (Mrs. Jerry Huff) 7, 13, 17, 20, 22, 25
Donlon, Capt. Roger H. C.:
    birth 15
    college 40, 41, 49, 189
    decoration ceremony 1-3, 5, 7, 8, 10-13, 70, 206
        citation for Medal of Honor 13, 9-11
        meeting with President Johnson 5, 8, 11-13, 70, 80, 175, 206
    early recollections: brothers and sisters 15-23, 25, 30;
        childhood friends 18, 31-37
        education 20, 23-25, 27, 35, 36, 40-43
        jobs 26, 27, 37, 38, 41, 45
        parents 3, 4, 7, 8, 15-20, 27, 39, 40, 47
        religious training 22, 23
    Medal of Honor Convention 192
    military career: Air Force 47-51
        Army, enlisted in infantry 61, 63, 67
        Special Forces 1, 69-72, 74-78, 216
            leader of Team A-726 3, 7, 81-88, 93-95, 103-109, 116, 173
            training 72-78, 88-95, 99
        West Point 49-53, 55, 56
            resignations from 54, 56, 68, 120

Viet Nam Service: Camp Nam Dong 3, 95, 106-109, 115, 116, 121, 132, 134, 141, 164, 167-170, 176, 193, 205, 206, 216-218
    and Viet Cong 1-3, 8, 78, 95, 107, 108, 114-116, 118-121, 123-125, 127, 129, 130, 134, 136-138, 140-142, 144-147, 149-151, 155-157, 159-163, 165-169, 171, 173, 190
    civic action programs 95, 113, 114, 116, 118, 119, 124
    relations with Vietnamese 117-119, 123-127, 129
    return to U. S. 172, 193-195
    wounded in battle 2, 8, 144, 149, 152-157, 162, 166, 171, 193
Donlon, Damian Charles 195, 197, 203
Donlon, Derek Paul 199, 203
Donlon, Gerard 7, 18, 20-22, 40, 47
Donlon, Jack 7, 17, 18, 21, 39, 47, 211, 212
Donlon, Jason Douglas 197, 198, 203
Donlon, Justin Luis 201, 204, 207;
    fiancée, Lacey 204
Donlon, Justine 204
Donlon, Linda Lee 62-67, 184, 194, 203
Donlon, Marion Howard 1, 7, 11, 12, 15, 16, 18-20, 25, 28, 29, 31, 33, 35, 37, 39, 40, 57, 58, 175, 177, 195, 202
Donlon, Mary Bernadette 7, 15, 18, 20
Donlon, Michael 7, 21, 184
Donlon, Mrs. Derek (Melanie) 203
Donlon, Mrs. Gerard (Nita) 7, 22
Donlon, Mrs. Jack (Fran) 7, 21
Donlon, Mrs. Jason (Lori) 203
Donlon, Mrs. Michael (Frances) 7, 21, 71
Donlon, Norma and Roger 204, 220
Donlon, Norma Irving 179-204, 209-216, 219-221

Donlon, Paul 7, 18, 20, 21, 30, 40, 54, 58, 75, 174
Donlon, Paul Augustine 7, 8, 12, 15-21, 25-28, 30, 39, 47, 49, 196
Donovan, Col. William J. 73
Dunleavy, Joseph J. 27

E

Eddy, Capt. John 108, 112, 113
Edgar, Bob 41
Eisenhower, President Dwight D. 213
Emporia State University 203
Erickson, Eric 37
Erickson, Nancy 37

F

Father Augustine Donohue 23
Father Edmund Harty 23, 36
Father Vogel 23
Fitzsimons General Hospital 193
Fort Belvoir, Va. 77, 84
Fort Benning, Ga. 64, 82, 179, 181, 200
Fort Bragg, N.C. 13, 72-75, 78, 84, 86, 89, 91, 99, 105, 106, 109, 166, 174, 209
Fort Carson, Co. 193, 195
Fort Chaffee, Ark. 59, 61
Fort Greeley, Ak. 68
Fort Gulick, Panama 201, 206
Fort Holabird, Md. 77
Fort Jackson, S.C. 62-64, 69, 71, 113
Fort Jonathan Wainwright, Ak. 67
Fort Leavenworth, Ks. 195, 202, 207, 209
Fort McPherson, Ga. 69
Fort Riley, Ks. 74
Frederick, Maj. Gen. Robert T. 73

G

Gage, Jim 212
Gilham, Mrs. Grace 41-44
Gregg, Sgt. Thomas L. 6, 87, 88, 91-94, 96, 97, 103, 104, 115, 116, 118, 119, 121, 123, 125, 127-131, 135, 136, 146-149, 156-158, 162-164, 166, 167, 170, 173, 174, 212
Grieves, Col. William 79
Griffin, Capt. Jerry 169
Guevara, Ernesto "Che" 73

H

Hanoi 214, 215
Hayden, Senator Carl 8, 12
Healy, James Patrick Hopkins 44, 47
Hickey, Dr. Gerald C. (Doc) 3, 4, 110, 119-121, 123, 124, 128, 130, 137, 142, 146, 163, 164, 213
Ho Chi Minh 108, 111, 214
Ho Chi Minh City 214
Ho Chi Minh trails 108
Hope, Bob 192
Houston, Mrs. John Lucius 171, 178
Houston, Sgt. John Lucius 3, 14, 87, 90, 104, 124, 125, 130, 144-146, 148, 156, 165, 170, 171, 174
Howard, Ruth (Sister Mary Florence) 11, 175
Huff, Capt. Jerry H. 7
Humphrey, Vice President Hubert H. 176

I

Iannone, Al 36, 212
Irving, John and Ruth 187, 188, 192, 203

J

Johnson, Gen. Harold K. 5, 11, 176
Johnson, President Lyndon B. 5, 8, 11-13, 70, 77, 80, 175, 206

K

Keating, Senator Kenneth B. 8, 12
Keeley, Jack 212
Kelly, Mrs. Katherine 41, 43, 44
Kennedy, President John F. 5, 7, 13, 72, 73, 77, 79, 80, 112

Kennedy, Senator Robert F. 4, 8, 12
Ketchie, Ken 216
Kha Tre 113, 118, 165

L

Lachmann, Mr. 27, 37
Lackland Air Force Base, San
    Antonio, Tx. 47
Lahoud, Joe 31, 50
Laos 77, 107, 108, 111, 114
Le Tse-tung 118, 124-129, 205, 206
Lente, Elinor 177
Letterman General Hospital 199
Lezette, Bob 36
Lich, *Dai-uy* 118, 124-129, 143, 146,
    164
Lu, Ta One 113
Lu, Ta Two 113
Lu, *Trung-uy* 113, 130, 165, 166

M

Malaysia 4, 141, 214
Maloney, Lieut. Col. George A. 105, 166
Mao Tse-tung 73
Mayer, Col. Edward E. 12
McNamara, Secretary Robert S. 1, 3,
    5, 8, 10, 12, 73
Mekong Delta 85, 109, 197, 214
Merrill, Brig. Gen. Frank D. 73
Middleton, Gen. Troy H. 59
Mission in Understanding to Vietnam
    213
Mize, Capt. Ola Lee 178
Moon, Maj. Walter 77
Moore, Maj. Gen. Joe 172
Mu Nam 113
Mui 172, 173

N

Nam Dong 1-6, 8, 9, 86, 95, 106-109,
    113, 115, 116, 120, 121, 123, 129,
    132-134, 145, 153, 156, 164, 166-
    170, 172, 174, 176, 178, 179, 193,
    205, 206, 212, 214, 216-218

Nam Dong cemetery 217
Nance, Maj. Edwin T. 105, 114, 166, 170
National Education Association 177
Naughton, Col. Frank 68
Newman, Maj. Gen. Aubrey S. 207
Nga Hai 113
Ngo Dinh Diem 111
Nguyen Van Thu 217
Nha Trang 169, 171, 174
Nhi, Trung 110
Nixon, President Richard M. 50

O

Okinawa, Japan 74, 85, 86, 105, 198
Olejniczak, Capt. Julian M. 5, 8, 82,
    90-92, 97, 101, 104, 114, 116, 120,
    121, 123-125, 130, 141, 142, 149-
    152, 154, 156, 163, 167, 169, 171,
    174, 186, 200, 212

P

People-to-People International 213
Phan Rang 111
Phan Ri 111
Pleiku 118
Pope Air Force Base, N.C. 105

Q

Qua Hop 113
Quang Nam 105, 109, 173
Quang Tin 105
Quang Tri 105

R

Rau, Ta 106, 113, 119-121
Reznick, Representative Joseph Y. 12
Rogers, Warren 176
Ruddy, Sgt. Maj. Francis J. 79

S

Saigon 9, 105, 108, 174, 198
Saint Die 20
Samson Air Force Base, Lake Geneva,
    N. Y. 48, 49, 56

Schofield Barracks, Hawaii 178
Seymour-Johnson Air Force Base, Goldsboro, N. C. 174
Shinno, Douglas 211
Silverman, Doc 54, 55
Sinnott, Joe 122
Sister Mary Aloysius 18
Sister Mary Anne 18
Sister Mary Anne Delores 34
Sister Mary Miriam 18, 23
Sister Mary Rose Regina 11, 18
Spruill, Capt. James Polk 109, 117
Stewart Field, Newburgh, N. Y. 49, 51
Stilwell, Maj. Gen. Richard G. 172
Sweeney, Lenny 37, 39
Sylvester, Secretary Arthur 12

T

Ta Co 109, 173
Ta Trach River 113, 116
Tan Son Nhut Airport 105
Taylor, Ambassador Maxwell D. 9, 172
Team A-726 7, 8, 81–94, 104, 118, 173, 175, 212, 214
Terrin, Sgt. Terrence D. 7-9, 87-89, 91, 96, 97, 104, 116, 118-120, 124, 125, 131, 135, 145, 146, 148, 154, 156, 162, 163, 165, 167, 169, 171, 174, 175, 213
Thailand 85, 197, 199, 200, 214
Thornton, George 29, 33
Thua Thien 105, 107
Tripler, Hawaii 198
Truong Chinh 73
Truong Tra 113
Trung Trac 110
Tuan, George 137

U

U.S. Military Academy 49, 56
U.S. Naval Academy 47
Udorn, Thailand 197
ULU Pandan Military Cemetery 214

United States Army Command and General Staff College 195, 202, 207

V

Vance, Deputy Secretary Cyrus R. 12
Viet Minh 107, 110
Vietnam Veterans Memorial 219
Vo Nguyen Giap 73, 110

W

Walter Reed Medical Center 199
Ware, Brig. Gen. Keith 190
Wells, Dr. Kenneth 176
Westerman, Ted 216
Westmoreland, Gen. William C. 172, 218
Westmoreland Scholar Foundation 219
Wharton, Representative J. Ernest 50
Wheeler, Brig. Gen. Lester L. 12, 67-70, 207
Wheeler, Gen. Earle G. 4, 12
Wheeler, Mrs. Lester L. 12, 68-70
White, Doc 27
White House 1, 7, 8, 12, 22, 50, 70, 79, 175, 194, 206
Whitsell, Staff Sgt. Raymond B. 6, 8, 83, 84, 87-89, 97-104, 114, 116, 130, 140, 154-156, 160-162, 170, 173-175, 212
Woods, Staff Sgt. Merwin D. 6, 8, 84, 86, 88, 92, 93, 100, 102, 104, 116, 121, 124, 128-130, 139, 142, 143, 154, 155, 159-161, 163-166, 170, 171, 175, 212

Y

Yarborough, Maj. Gen. William P. 12, 77, 78
Youngblood, Rufus 13

227